CONTENTS

KV-575-700

±17348859
ML

The Textile Institute

WITH THE
CO-OPERATION AND
ASSISTANCE OF

TESSILE DI COMO

UNDER THE PATRONAGE OF   AND WITH THE COLLABORATION OF

Federtessile   CITTA degli STUDI di BIELLA

The Textile Institute,
International Headquarters,
10 Blackfriars Street,
Manchester, M3 5DR,
England.

ISBN   0 900739 98 3

Foreword

P.C. Byrom OBE, BA, CText FTI, FRSA

In 1985, in a foreword to 'Jubilee', the Textile Institute 75th
Anniversary Souvenir Publication, H.R.H. the Prince Philip, Duke
of Edinburgh, Honorary Fellow of the Institute, wrote:

> 'There is much to celebrate but I hope that members will
> also reflect that the next 25 years will decide how much there
> will be to celebrate when the Institute reaches its centenary.'

In September, 1984, in his opening address to the Textile
Institute Conference on Textile Design Strategies at the Royal
Society of Arts, Dr John McPhee, Managing Director of the International Wool Secretariat and at that date President of the Textile Institute, said:

> 'In satisfying markets of desire, rather than need, and in
> the age of competition, design must be paramount. Top design-
> ers, with their intuitive understanding of consumers, are the
> key to business success, since there is no "objective" way of
> monitoring and satisfying changes in consumer preferences that
> can compare in timeliness and cost with their subjective in-
> tuition.

> In textiles, there is no doubt that design is the one con-
> stant that always contributes to successful trading, even for
> plain fabrics, where weave and colour alone determine the look
> of the collection. What counts is that a design concept is
> applied to a manufacturer's full range to produce a collection
> wholly attuned to buyers' needs. This feature is the one which
> separates truly successful firms from the rest.'

I believe that in Dr McPhee's statement lies the response the
Institute must make to Prince Philip's challenge.

The first step had already been taken. In March, 1984, a Working Party on Design had been convened with terms of reference
(inter alia) to:

> 'consider ways of increasing the attention paid by the
> Textile Institute to design matters in general and to increase
> the number of people with design interests or background par-
> ticipating in the Textile Institute's activities ...'

One practical outcome of this working party's deliberations
was the establishment, in September 1985, of a Design and Product-
Marketing Group, with a committee drawn from practitioners in
design and marketing, and including several who were not yet

members of the Institute.

In an explanatory letter to the new committee, the General Secretary wrote:

'... The Textile Institute is a pan-textile organisation encompassing all occupations that contribute in any way to the manufacture, use, or understanding of textiles or textile products throughout the world ... (its) Sections deal with the geographical part of the matrix; the Groups deal with the sectoral/occupational axis. Up to now most of the Groups have focussed on processes, products, or areas of knowledge.'

I suggest that, in setting up a group to concentrate on design and product marketing, the Institute has taken a very significant step. Throughout its previous 75 years, the Institute's successful concentration on technical and material matters has placed it in a unique position in the world of textiles. If the move towards design is equally successful in recruiting into active membership designers, selectors, and marketeers at all levels, the Textile Institute can become the forum which, for the first time, identifies the opportunities existing worldwide in harnessing contemporary design to modern technology.

Typically, throughout the fabric-producing sectors, one hears complaints from the marketeers that they cannot find the choice they seek in fashion fabrics at the moment. Simultaneously, designers are complaining that technologists do not understand what is the effect they are striving for in a new design or fabric development. Meanwhile, the scientists, technologists, and machine builders, amongst whom the Textile Institute is so strongly represented, are certain that the designers and marketeers are not exploiting fully the potential for economic variety inherent in the latest fibres, yarns, finishes, and fabric-producing machinery. An enlarged Textile Institute, with a substantial design/ design-management/product-marketing membership, would have a real opportunity to achieve the release of the wealth-creating energies at present entrapped within these frustrations.

Further opportunities exist within textile education, where the Institute has established a respected professional position throughout the world. For example, in Britain, there is considerable concern that the industry has failed to benefit sufficiently from the world-class creative talent emerging from the U.K. Textile Design Colleges each year. Criticisms are also levelled at the Colleges, that too much emphasis is placed on personal creative development and that their graduates do not understand the latest technology, so that the patterning capability of modern machinery and the new opportunities available in dyeing, printing, and finishing are not fully exploited. Similar criticisms are heard of Textile Design education in the U.S.A. Solutions proposed from recurrent industry/education conferences and working parties inevitably point to the need for more work experience, through sandwich courses, 'years-out', and the like, and for textile courses to be modified accordingly. The Institute, through its members, has an obvious role to play in making opportunities for industrial experience available to the next generation of textile designers.

The Annual World Conference at Como on 4th-8th May, 1987, was the first opportunity for the membership at large to contribute to, and learn from, this important debate in which the Institute has assumed a significant role. Every manager and member of any unit working in textiles has something significant to learn from the authoritative descriptions of how the market influences the product, contained in the papers presented here. Learning by analogy from one sector to another can be equally productive for the fashion-fabric producer as for the manufacturer of machinery or the fabric finisher. How the Institute membership throughout the world responds to the opportunity presented by the urgent need for textile designers and technologists to develop a free-flowing communication in the context of the marketplace will, in my view, determine whether or not there will be 'much to celebrate' when the T.I. centenary arrives in 2010.

Dispersion Retailing: A Global Export Strategy

M.E. Barry, C.L. Warfield, and R.L. Galbraith

Abstract

Dispersion retailing is a new global export strategy, which features market segmentation on a global scale. In this new global form of retailing, manufacturers go directly to the customers.

The world leaders in this phenomenon, i.e., Bennetton (Italy – women's, children's, and men's apparel), IKEA (Sweden – home furnishings), i x i = z (Japan – men's apparel), Laura Ashley (UK – both home furnishings and apparel), and their counterparts worldwide, appeal to a very carefully targeted market. The customer knows what the store stands for, the quality, the look and what kind of an atmosphere this merchandise will create. This specialized form of target marketing is perfected in the host country, and then duplicated in multiple sites around the world.

Successful target marketing must be based on accurate predictions of fashion trends and consumer wants (not needs) coupled with perceived value for the price paid. That perceived value may be both actual value in terms of design, construction, fabric quality, comfort, or any combination of these or psychological values in terms of status symbols or product aesthetics.

What are the implications of this global export strategy? Is a revolution occurring? Is dispersion retailing the wave of the future?

1. INTRODUCTION

Dispersion retailing is marketing by the manufacturer to a target customer based on consumer research and global fashion analysis. Three examples will be discussed to illustrate this type of retailing, a new global export strategy.

The three examples are (i) the Japanese-based firm i x i = z, the dispersion-retailing operation of the largest Japanese men's-apparel manufacturer, D'Urban; (ii) IKEA, the Swedish furniture manufacturer; and (iii) Bennetton, the Italian sportswear manufacturer. Each of these firms has very carefully selected its specific customer.

i x i = z's customer is a young man who is in his early twenties in Japan/Asia and in his thirties in the U.S.A. IKEA's target

1

is the person, male or female, who is furnishing his/her first dwelling place. Bennetton, with its seven divisions, sells to female customers throughout the life cycle and to some male customers. However, each Bennetton division has a specific type of customer as its target.

In each of these three examples of dispersion retailing, the company manufactures the merchandise, and then sells it at retail in several countries.

Indeed, they all sell what they manufacture to consumers on at least two, if not more, continents. These multi-country distribution channels provide point-of-sale, climatic, geographical, and lifestyle information that, through the use of computers, can be programmed to pick up trends quickly.

2. THEORETICAL MODEL

From an analysis of the operations of the above companies, plus those of additional examples such as Laura Ashley, Stefanel, Jaeger, and Conran's, a theoretical model for dispersion retailing has been developed (Fig. 1).

2.1 Manufacturer/Retailer

Dispersion retailing starts with a manufacturer (e.g. apparel or home furnishings) who has vertically integrated, or at least partially so, to become a retailer. The companies cited as examples did not start as retailers, nor did they export their goods initially. Rather, they tried distributing their products through established retailing channels in the home country. When this did not meet their expectations, the companies opened or franchised their own retail stores in their home countries. These retail operations were often accompanied by a catalogue division. When these manufacturer/retailers 'got it right' in terms of a retail format and had saturated their own country with their products, they started export sales to other countries with significant consumer markets. This exportation of merchandise through sales in company-owned or franchised retail operations enabled the dispersion retailers to maximize their respective comparative advantage. In addition, because the manufacturer and retailer were one, a middle step in the distribution chain was eliminated, thus providing a higher potential profit for the firm.

2.2 Customer Selection

One of the keys to the success of these companies is their careful selection of the customer they wish to serve as dispersion retailers. In the three examples used, i x i = z, IKEA, and Bennetton, it is the upscale young customer who is targeted. This customer is usually college-bound or university-educated and just entering the work place in business, industry, government, or education, where upward mobility appears assured. The strategy is long range in that this customer can be followed into other stages in the life cycle.

Analysis of the available demographic and psychographic data for the specified segment of the population in various countries aids the companies in selecting store sites and layout. Among the characteristics studied are income level, lifestyle, family size, stage of the family life cycle, housing status, career needs, location of residence, transportation patterns, status symbols, and taste level. Such customer profiles also contribute to decisions on merchandise design and quality/price ratios.

2.3 Merchandise Decisions

The firms engaged in dispersion retailing generally have a narrower, but deeper, merchandise line than do department stores or even speciality stores. This merchandise line is carefully planned to meet the lifestyle needs (physical, emotional, psychological, economic) of the target customer. In most cases the firm will choose to focus or specialize on line, colour, or design features of the merchandise. The successful firm will promote the merchandise in such a way that the merchandise line is clearly and consistently identified in the customer's mind. In this way, the customer can determine what types of merchandise he or she wants to purchase and choose the store that offers that merchandise.

In addition to the target-customer data previously mentioned, the dispersion-retailing companies utilize analyses of several other types of data. Global analysis, in the aggregate and by country, of sales of textile and apparel production provide fibre, yarn, fabric, dyeing, and finishing, as well as styling, trends. By using trend analysis and sophisticated computer programming, the global production data can be used to predict sales in various countries. This information, when fed into the manufacturer's computer, is utilized by the planning group to make design, production, and marketing decisions.

In addition, fashion and societal trends, cultural, historical, and economic trends are used. Interaction between these and the aforementioned raw-materials production data provide information that the manufacturer can use to determine the colour/line/design features of the product based on a quality/price ratio that appeals to the needs and wants of the target customer. A necessary prerequisite, however, is a thorough understanding of machinery and the production process so that these ideas can be translated into a tangible product.

Point-of-sale information fed into the check-out terminal at the time of customer purchase is almost instantaneously transmitted to the manufacturer. This information, in turn, is used to help the manufacturer predict company sales in specific countries. These predictions are based on the selling trends in stores that have been found to be style leaders or good prognosticators of merchandise that will later be accepted on a widespread basis. Lag times of adoption of fashion concepts from country to country can also be predicted, thereby giving direction to the production component of the company.

2.4 Merchandise Production

The products and lead times the manufacturing division needs from

the suppliers are dependent on the dispersion retailers' decisions about the colour, line, and design features which have been
predicted to meet the target customer's needs and desires. Because,
in successful fashion-retail operations the pipeline response time
is short, the aggregate-data manipulation and interpretation described previously are done by the manufacturer. In this way, control of the quality/price/volume ratio can more easily be effected,
which often means a better product at a lower price for the consumer. There is a high degree of co-operation and interchange of
product information between the manufacturer and the suppliers,
thus permitting a much quicker response time.

The manufacturer maintains strict quality control of his own
production and also demands an equivalent level of quality in all
supplies used in production. This, in turn, permits strict quality-
control standards to be implemented and adhered to in the merchandising operation as well. In many cases, these dispersion-retailing firms have grown so large that they no longer manufacture all
of their own merchandise, but employ contractors for a portion of
it. These contractors are then held to the same quality-control
standards of the manufacturer/retailer.

2.5 Retailing the Merchandise

The retail stores may be owned by the manufacturer or franchised.
In either case, site selections have been based on careful and
extensive analysis of psychographic and demographic data about
the targeted consumer. The store itself has a location, site design, or lighting concept that is easily identifiable with other
retail stores of the firm within the city, county, country, or
continent. Often merchandise, with few props, forms its own display. Background colours are muted; lighting is indirect and clear.
Fixtures are designed to hold merchandise in such a way that it
looks clean and cared for. Window displays convey a message consistent with the merchandise and the store interior - i.e., clear,
uncluttered, and fashion-forward.

The manufacturing division communicates to franchise owners or
managers of dispersion-retail stores the product information concerning the quality, care, and co-ordination of merchandise. The
subsequent communication of this information from the sales personnel to the customer is stressed as an important component of
the firm's competitive advantage. These quality features and care
requirements were chosen to reflect the target customer's needs
and desires. Often colours of the products in the merchandise line
have been selected so that the value, chroma, and hue of various
items can be combined and the items used together. With a single
theme, and narrow, but deep, merchandise selection, the projection
of a store image is not as confused as it can be when products of
several manufacturers are carried in one store. Integration, co-
ordination and congruity are present.

2.5.1 Service

Paramount in the strategies of these dispersion retailers is the
development of a corporate culture of 'service to the customer'.
Many people today decry the lack of service. This lack of service

and the inability of traditional retail formats to meet consumer needs are often cited as reasons for the economic plight of many traditional retailers.

For the dispersion retailer, there is an intense focus on the customer as the key element in producing a satisfactory bottom line. These retailers, as well as their manufacturing counterparts, engage in an ongoing study of the needs, wants, and perceived-value relationships for the targeted customer. This not only involves the formal market research utilizing demographic and psychographic data, but it also involves constant searching for new ideas, new excitement, new adaptations, to an existing look. It means being aware of what is happening culturally, politically, economically, and socially all over the world. Then these developments must be translated into a merchandising mix that is not only fashion forward, but functional for the lifestyle of the target customer, wherever he or she lives, works, and travels.

Because of the need to be aware of the worldwide picture and how development in various parts of the world affect consumers, placement of stores in a variety of cities and countries around the world provides a distinct marketing and production advantage. Through a sophisticated company-wide computer network, fashion trends can be identified early in the cycle, with resultant information communicated immediately to the production operation. This helps to ensure sufficient quantities of the desired merchandise reaching the stores when the customer in any particular part of the world becomes aware of and perceives the need for or desire to purchase the item.

In an industry where few persons in consuming nations truly buy products because of need, uniqueness and product differentiation determine success. The product must say to the customer: 'Buy me. I'll help you show your public another phase of your personality'.

Fashion status is a distinguishing characteristic of dispersion retailing. It is conveyed to the customers through products that are readily identifiable. Through wearing, using, or furnishing one's home with these products, the user is saying 'I know what's happening'. Awareness, frugalness, value for money, taste, and currentness are conveyed. The wearer or user feels his or her personal image is enhanced through the product; value is perceived. No intrusion is felt, only added fulfilment. Shopping at these global retail stores is the 'in thing' to do. A certain status is conveyed upon the customer because fashion-conscious consumers recognize the fashion-forward merchandise of the dispersion retailer.

2.5.2 *Convenience*

Dispersion retailers recognize the need to meet the customer's schedule and lifestyles. Merchandise depth is maximized to help avoid the stock-out problem with its resultant loss of sales. Easy co-ordination of merchandise is not an accident but part of the plan. In fact, merchandise displays are planned and sales personnel are trained to maximize the sale of multiple pieces for a co-orginated package. Though the merchandise lines are rather narrow, these dispersion retailers are generally located in shopping malls

5

or other high-density retail areas. This close proximity to other
retailers not only helps meet customer needs, i.e., one store for
one type of merchandise, another store for other merchandise, but
it also provides easier access to 'monitor the competition'.

Other components of the convenience factor include the store
location, shopping hours, and services offered. Shopping hours
are targeted to the employed singles or dual-career couples. Locations in high traffic areas, e.g., near train or subway stations,
main stopping thoroughfares, or upscale shopping malls, assure a
sufficient flow of people with the desired target-customer characteristics. Service features, such as i x i = z's 'Waters of the
World Bar' in California and IKEA's child-care provisions for customers, are not only distinctive, but effective in recruiting customers.

2.5.3 Store Personnel

Recruitment of personnel is a key to the success or failure of any
operation. This most definitely is the case for dispersion retailers. Their personnel not only must excel in sales, but they must
also be well-versed on the corporate philosophy, product lines,
product information, and product co-ordination. They must be at-
tuned to customer desires and be innovative and tastefully aggressive in helping the customer to fulfil these desires - with merchandise from the dispersion-retail store, of course. The store
personnel must also be attentive in observing and communicating
back to corporate headquarters repeat customer patterns and requests for or interest in merchandise not currently available in
the stores. The ability to communicate this potential or actual
demand to the corporate manufacturing/merchandising level on a
real-time basis provides another component of the dispersion retailer's competitive advantage.

2.6 Long-range Strategy

Because most of these dispersion retailers are privately owned,
they can (and often do) develop long-range marketing strategies,
even though this may be at the sacrifice of present earnings.
These strategies are based on the retailing adage of providing the
right merchandise, at the right time, at the right price, in the
right quantity, sold in the right way. The manufacturing and retail
components are both involved in making these strategic decisions.

An example of the long-range strategy is the firm i x i = z.
Its dispersion-retailing strategy is conceptually the most advanced.
The firm believes that good taste has been lost. Therefore, its
strategy is to make the young, upwardly mobile male want products
that have a design sense; for the most part, such products are not
now present on the general market. Theirs is a long-range education
job. It is working well in Japan and other parts of Asia. Although
the firm has a store in New York City, its U.S. strength is in the
Southwest and on the West Coast. It is also doing well in Canada.
The company expects its stretegy to pay maximum dividends in the
1990s and beyond the year 2000.

3. EXAMPLES

The three dispersion retailers referred to earlier in this paper, i.e. i x i = z, Bennetton, and IKEA, will be described in more detail in the following sections. In addition, other examples of dispersion retailing will be briefly discussed.

3.1 Bennetton

Bennetton, with nearly 4000 outlets in 57 countries, is the most visible and best-known dispersion retailer. In fact, in September of 1985, Bennetton became the first Western manufacturer to open a shop in Czechoslovakia since the inauguration of the Communist regime, in 1948 (1). In addition, the proposed opening of 50 stores in the U.S.S.R. was announced in late 1986. There are Bennetton stores in Peru, Budapest, Hong Kong, Taiwan, Korea, Japan, Belgrade, and throughout Australia, in addition to Europe and the U.S. Its headquarters are located in Treviso, Italy.

3.1.1 Manufacturing Operations

Bennetton, which has its own apparel factories, utilizes the skills of the local agricultural-based population for production in the home and village. These persons work for less because they have none of the expenses of child care, work clothing, commuting costs, and food away-from-home. Supervisory and maintenance costs are at a minimum. Time and energy are maximized.

Raw wool is purchased in Australia and New Zealand. In fact, Bennetton is the world's largest consumer of virgin wool. The wool is then spun to the Bennetton specifications, techniques learned in Scotland being used to soften the wool. Wherever possible, assembled garments, rather than yarns or fabrics, are dyed. In this way, the garment's colour can be applied much more closely to the shipping date, thus making the predictions of demand for colour much more congruent with actual sales. The use of computerized operations throughout the production process leads to efficiency and better quality at lower prices and allows 'production to respond quickly to public demand' (2).

The Bennetton group is now a complex of manufacturing companies. It controls Fiorucci Inc.; the Scottish cashmere company Hogg of Hawick; and the Italian shoe company Calzaturificio de Varese. Sales in 1985 totalled $437 million (3).

3.1.2 Retail Operations

Bennetton, with its seven divisions, is able to adapt to many lifestyles. Fiorucci is very far out. Design extravagance, hard-rock, and extremely fashion-forward customers are characteristic of this group. Sisley carries higher-priced sportswear, selling more cashmere sweaters than any other retailer worldwide. The daughter who shops at the traditional Bennetton often has a mother at home dressed in Sisley, while the younger teenage sister finds Tomato and/or Jeans West a place to obtain her clothing. More moderately priced adult-women's sportswear can be found at the Merceria

chains. The 012 store provides Bennetton clothing for the first
years of a girl's life. In addition, there is also a men's-wear
line. These Bennetton divisions all feed point-of-sale information
immediately into the manufacturer from stores all over the world;
this provides life-cycle data that can enhance production decisions
and planning.

Bennetton believes that the frequency with which consumers see
the green-and-white store front is directly related to its market
penetration. For example, there are eight Bennetton stores on
Fifth Avenue in New York City, plus stores on Madison and Third
Avenues. There are, of course, numerous other Bennetton stores
throughout the New York metropolitan area. A 'profitable sense of
competition' is thus established. The customer sees the same product displayed in different ways in varying colour combinations in
stores throughout the city and around the world.

Bennetton's focus has been colour. The 'United Colours of Bennetton' are used in its catalogue and advertisements worldwide as a
marketing tool, but the meaning goes deeper. 'We are definitely
interested in peace and a kind of universalism. Our clothes are
appealing in very different countries and people who consume the
same product have one more way of understanding each other', said
Luciano Bennetton (4).

Bennetton's store layout is uncluttered. Rigid policies must be
followed, e.g., sweaters are not to be taken off the rack without a
salesperson's help. The merchandise is the display, with floor-to-
ceiling fixtures holding the merchandise. This highlights the tremendous colour selection. Folding, rather than hanging, sweaters
gives the consumer the feeling that product knowledge is the basis
of the store. When sweaters are hung, as in most stores, stretching
occurs. Salespersons, as well as customers, can see it. Stores
generally hang sweaters to make their lives easier, but it is harm-
ful to the merchandise. Again, the subtle cues are not lost on the
consumer.

Bennetton places its mannequins very close to the glass pane of
the window. It wants these 'pups' to entice the customer into the
store, but also to look like someone one would see on the street.
Perfume has even been added to appeal to another sense to attract
the customer and to achieve instant recognition.

The Bennetton advertisements strive to present real-life people
in real-life situations. The appeal is to the basic emotions,
rather than a glorified advertising campaign. Life, love, and the
pursuit of happiness are stressed. Amusing, interesting, just a
bit new is the idea. The advertisements make one feel excited, but
comfortable. One can see oneself in the advertisement. It's not
perfect, but believable.

3.2 i x i = z

While Bennetton's primary focus has been on colour, i x i = z has
chosen to excel in design. Its long-range strategy for the 1980s
involves an attempt to formulate a design/function interchange in
its products. The idea of good taste, ease of use, and comfort is
stressed. The firm's management believes that good taste has been

lost. Some persons have never been exposed to it, whereas others have changed their tastes because of rebellion against parents, society, or institutions.

Products that i x i = z does not make itself are contracted out to others, but the i x i = z label is used. i x i = z maintains strict control over the products from these contractors to ensure that the firm's standards of design for function are maintained. An example of this is its writing instrument. Grooves close to where the hand grasps the pen facilitate comfort of hand and arm muscles when writing. This concept of design for function is carried throughout all of the company's products.

i x i = z's product line stresses design. To emphasize the design, a monochromatic colour palette of black, the absence of colour, and white, the reflection of all colour, is used. Wood, chrome, and glass keep colour to a minimum. Clean, clear design gives the product its setting. Rather than 'playing it safe' with classical, traditional merchandising, innovative design concepts are highlighted.

Mr Watanabe, one of the directors of D'Urban, Japan's largest menswear manufacturer, also heads i x i = z. He travels the world, but spends a great deal of time in Italy. The fertile belt of design, workmanship, and individual talent in Northern Italy breathes creativity and craftsmanship. Combining the Italian design resources with the talents in Japan provides the resources to make i x i = z a firm that bears watching as a harbinger of things to come. Quality knows no exceptions; it cannot and will not be compromised.

3.3 IKEA

IKEA uses line and value for the price to distinguish its product. Compared with most other dispersion retailers, IKEA has a very extensive product line of furniture and accessories for the home. However, all of the lines of the furniture and accessories are straight, clean, and functional. The furniture can be stacked, built, combined, and used, both now and at a later time in life, when upward mobility generates greater economic resources. Assembly is done by the purchaser, and thus cost is lower. Transportation costs can be saved, and store costs are less, since RTA (ready-to-assemble) furniture takes less space in shipping and warehousing. The consumer's costs are further lowered because most purchases can be taken home in the customer's car, rather than being delivered in a company truck.

Clean lines provide a perfect setting for the textiles used within the model rooms in the IKEA showroom. The design and colour of the fabrics blend with and complement the stark line of the furniture. Here individual tastes and preferences can be indulged. Although the lines of the furniture are clean and straight, the textiles, through the use of colour and design, help to prevent the institutional or stark appearance that might otherwise be conveyed.

Much of IKEA's furniture is produced in Eastern Europe. Craftsmen are still available there, and prices are low for good workmanship. Because of the tremendous volume generated by IKEA stores throughout Europe and now the U.S.A., the governments of COMECON countries are very willing to adapt policies for IKEA that will provide employment and revenue for people of the COMECON nations.

As mentioned earlier, child-care facilities are provided on the premises of the IKEA retail establishments. Eating facilities are also provided, in an attempt to make it easy for the customer to shop in a leasurely fashion, thereby spending both time and money in the store. A catalogue is available, which helps to direct the shopper to the desired merchandise. Because in-store demand has been so great in the U.S. stores, catalogue orders have not been possible to date.

3.4 Other Dispersion Retailers

The oldest firm practising dispersion retailing is Jaeger. Its clothing was originally designed to meet the English country gentlewoman's needs. Eventually, this expanded into career needs, and the firm has been a going concern for over a hundred years. It is now operating on several continents. Its styling was and is, however, not as narrowly targeted as it is for many dispersion retailers.

Another firm from the British Isles is Laura Ashley, which prospered and grew during the 1960s and 1970s. With the advent of the Women's Liberation movement at that time, her floral fabrics provided traditional comfort and emotional support. Today, one can furnish one's house, be married in, clothe both self and children in, and even purchase domestic linens with Laura Ashley designs. A distinctive style has been created. Company stores are established worldwide. Individual design, line, and colour variations are used to expand the Laura Ashley style.

Storehouse, a British firm run by Sir Terrance Conran, is another example of dispersion retailing. Conran's Habitat store popularized the IKEA concept, but with a far smaller focus. Conran's product range, size of store, and merchandise mix do enable the first home to be furnished, but not so completely as from what IKEA provides.

Storehouse also includes Mothercare, which operates stores in many countries. Global market coverage is sought, but targeting is not done as completely or specifically as is true for most dispersion retailers. The Mothercare products are well designed, but their breadth precludes easy selection. Everyone can buy there in person or through their catalogue - labour or management, rich or poor. Taste levels and target markets have not been firmly established. Some of the confusion of the traditional speciality store and department stores is therefore present.

One of Bennetton's closest competitors in Europe and the United States is Stefanel, whose corporate headquarters are very close to Bennetton's outside Venice. Its catalogue, printed in Italian, French, German and English, states 'STEFANEL: FASHION THAT SPRINGS FROM QUALITY'. Stefanel has 600 shops in countries such as Italy, Austria, Switzerland, France, Germany, Spain, Belgium, the United Kingdom, and the United States. It features clothing and accessories

for fashion-forward men and women. Quality is emphasized; colour
and design are vibrant and distinctive.

4. IMPLICATIONS

On a worldwide basis, dispersion retailing appears to be a growing
trend. France has hundreds of CAROL shops worldwide. Mexico has
the Aca Joe Shops. Hennes of Sweden is all over Europe. The Cali-
fornia-based Esprit operates in Asia, Australia, Europe, and the
U.S.A. Traditionally, the company has sold to other retailers but
is rapidly in the process of adding its own stores, which are
proving very successful.

Companies such as Ralph Lauren Hermes, Hannae Mori, Gucci,
Pucci, Valentino, Celine, Mark Cross, and the newer designer-based
companies have always been worldwide. Their clientele travel the
world, unlimited by geographical boundaries or money. Frequently,
the women travelling with busy husbands have very little to do.
Shopping is a major task. The wives have corporate duties like
those of their husbands, and they must dress the part. The women
have had a role as educators, facilitators, and role models for
younger executives' wives. These name stores have eased homesick-
ness, size, and taste problems.

Today, one travels through a shopping mall in Boston and sees
Canadian 'dispersion retailers'. Spanish-based firms are seen in
Miami, Oriental ones on the West Coast of the United States.
Throughout Asia, Australia, and Europe, one sees the ever-increas-
ing participants in this new form of retailing/manufacturing.

Close examination of profit reports of such large American manufacturers as the V-F Corporation, West Point Pepperell, the Russell
Corporation, Oxford Manufacturing, and many others shows store expansion. To our knowledge, at this point, none have stores outside
the U.S.A. These company stores, which often started as factory
outlets, now utilize sophisticated merchandising techniques and
present fashion-forward merchandise at reduced prices to the consumer.

As their stores become more successful, higher-priced, more
fashion-forward merchandise takes the place of the original
'seconds, close-outs, or overruns'. These manufacturers are finding retailing both profitable and a good source of consumer reactions. Although not yet 'dispersion retailers', the time may come
when they expand their retail operations to other countries.

Will dispersion retailing grow? Yes. Has it peaked? No. What
percentage of the market might it take? A conservative educated
guess would be between 10 and 20%, which is in and of itself a
lot of money.

REFERENCES

(1) 'Profiles: Bring Everywhere Andrea Lee', New Yorker, 1986,
    10 Nov., 54.

(2) 'Profiles: Bring Everywhere Andrea Lee', *New Yorker*, 1986,
    10 Nov., 58.

(3) 'Profiles: Bring Everywhere Andrea Lee', *New Yorker*, 1986,
    10 Nov., 54.

(4) 'Profiles: Bring Everywhere Andrea Lee', *New Yorker*, 1986,
    10 Nov., 64.

Consumer Affairs Department,
School of Human Sciences,
Auburn University,
Auburn,
Ala.,
U.S.A.

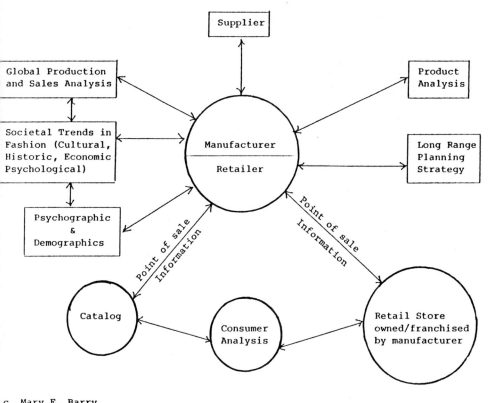

Fig. 1 Dispersion retailing: a theoretical model

Quality and Innovation

Alessandro Bertolotti

1. QUALITY

For many years, quality was considered as something produced internally in an organization. However, in recent times, there has
been a conviction that product and corporate quality is largely
influenced by external factors.

Many governments are now convinced that a quality system at a
rational level can contribute in a relevant manner to achieving
market share, corporate competitivity, a national image, and, not
least, growth in employment. As a consequence of such convictions,
campaigns have been launched to differentiate, sustain, and stipu-
late quality in one's country, including an awareness of the problems connected with it.

What is the attitude adopted towards quality by the major
European enterprises? In order to give an impression of the situ-
ation, reference may be made to an annual survey conducted by
INSEAD, based on a sample of 500 enterprises.

In the years 1983-1985, 85% of the companies surveyed considered the first factor needed to achieve success to be the ability
to offer a 'consistent and reliable' quality. The 1986 survey
demonstrated a dramatic change, and, in the first place, the 'educational' factor was considered, which goes horizontally all the
way through the organization so as to attain a 'total quality
system'. The relevance of such a change is substantial, because,
from a philosophy of the intrinsic value of a product, one passes
to a concept of service. One evolves from an approach of 'quality
control' to that of 'quality assurance', defined as the fine-
tuning of an integrated system focussed on prevention of problems
and oriented to an ideal-use concept.

There is a growing acceptance of considering quality as a
general objective of the whole organization and not as an additional cost burden. Even though identifiable costs of attaining
quality are not widely utilized, it is estimated that costs pertaining to 'non-quality' are high and in certain cases equivalent
to the profit before taxes achieved by the enterprise concerned.
Such considerations bring us to the following conclusions: it is
insufficient to face the problems related to quality by mobili-
zing single or isolated specializations, since it is inadequate
to support a quality policy with good intentions (no one is
against quality!).

15

One is confronted with a series of cultural and organizational problems, and it requires a cultural leap, since the philosophy expressed in our considerations is against an operating style of centralization and verticalization, in that it involves the total organizational structure.

In an industrial atmosphere, quality is synonymous with 'adequacy for use'. This definition underlines a co-ordinated effort in order to realize products and services adequate to the necessities of the end-users. When one associates with the word quality the definition 'adequacy for use', the objectives are concentrated on the end-users, which means human beings, without neglecting the product or service, but avoiding errors committed in the past, which identify quality as relating to a product; this coincidence in unacceptable.

When one thinks of quality, one contemplates achieving the best results with the resources that are available. Quality is a consequence of human efforts and depends on people's attitude towards quality. Analysing production activity with poor quality results, one realizes that the individuals responsible operated according to what they felt was required. Without a precise philosophy and transparency of principles, the results are, almost without exception, negative.

Today's world needs the establishment of an over-all 'quality plan' in order to realize a quality standard that, in Ruskin's words: '... is never an accident. It is always the result of an intelligent effort. It must be the consequence of the determination of accomplishing superior objectives.'

Quality is excellence, excellence in the determination of the strategy, planning, and operations and in the choice of human resources that are predisposed to accept such processes.

It may seem strange that, in a textile context, quality in the textile sector has not been mentioned: this was intentional! The concepts expressed here have a universal value, and in our organization we make efforts to apply them. The difficulties encountered in implementation are not of a technical but of a cultural nature. Culture equals people; people equal management. We do need a new model for management.

We are still trying sometimes to run our industry on the basis of an outdated method of operation, breaking down jobs into their smallest and simplest elements, analysing each element for efficiency improvements, and then training people to do just one or a very few of these elements. This became the ideal of efficiency, and the work-study engineer was king!! After World War II, the Japanese started to pioneer and develop a different model, which was accelerated during the oil crisis of the 1970s.

What is the key to this new approach? There are several such keys, but they all use quality as a strategy. This may be an oversimplification, but, by using it, we can compare some elements of the traditional and of the new model.

(1) The old model is based on specialization; the new model encourages multiple skills, in the belief that speciali-

16

zation is inefficient.

(2) The old model puts the system first; the new one puts people first.

(3) The old model believes that high quality equals cost; the new model believes that high quality equates with the lowest over-all cost.

(4) The old model is based on long production runs for low cost; the new one is based on short runs and rapid customer response.

(5) The old model uses inventory as a safety factor; the new model believes inventory should be zero.

(6) In the old model, the acceptable quality level was based on realistic standards; in the new model, the only acceptable level is zero defects, or total conformance to requirements.

(7) The old model puts cost first; the new model puts customer service and value first.

It will be hard to achieve this progress if we persist in trying to adjust or fine-tune the old model to meet today's needs and tomorrow's challenges. We have to do it fast, because time is not on our side.

2. INNOVATION

During the 1970s, there was a widespread belief that there was an evident contraposition, fundamentlaly based on the nature and technological content of products, between sectors defined as traditional or mature (or both) and sectors considered innovative. Backed by events at the time, this distinction ended by assuming the importance of a valuable judgement and finally a political prescription.

Consequently, one often hears that the new international division of work would have been defined in relation to this distinction and that the economic policy would therefore have had to consciously and coherently introduce a rational stand on this or that side of the line in countries endowed with a manufacturing structure founded on the possession of advanced technologies or those that produced traditional goods on a large scale. For industrialized countries, the alternative, as far as development was concerned, was thus an *advanced* or *backward* option, which would have exposed them to too much competition with emerging countries with low labour costs.

The choice of *positive* adjustment, as one said at the time, seemed to be *inevitable* for industrialized countries. In fact, experience in later years has shown how the phenomenon of innovation has taken on complex characteristics and radically invested the productive processes of mature sectors. It can be clearly seen how rarely sectors characterized by innovative products have developed ways of production as advanced as those of traditional

17

manufacturers and, on the contrary, how they are sometimes based on virtually artisan processes. On the other hand, products with traditional technology have often been the object of complex perfecting, which, albeit in an increasing way and by means of a long and slow process of refining, has led to important revisions in the conception of products based on the sophisticated knowledge of traditional technology. If innovation is presented as a complex pervasive phenomenon in this light, one must, however, stress its highly dynamic nature and decisive weight in defining the competitiveness of production.

Innovation could therefore not avoid assuming an absolutely central role in an effort for adjustment. We thus ask ourselves a question of fundamental importance: how can the innovation of a single element become an effort for the general modernization of a country? How can the restructuring of the individual company become an over-all adjustment of a productive system?

In this regard, one must consider the fact that, beyond the innovative dynamics of single productive compartments, restructuring phenomena in recent years have led to the emerging strategic opportunity that is brought about by the integration between the various innovative paths linking up with sectors that are distinct from one another (both traditional and innovative) and the development of relative technological and productive synergies.

Even in a mature sector like textiles, the future is full of innovative opportunities, and they will be different from those of the past. *To innovate* means doing things in a different way. Innovation is certainly a mental form that is neither learned nor acquired but can be developed in a suitable environment. Innovation is said to find favourable development conditions in small and flexible units.

It is therefore surprising how some large corporations were capable of maintaining the innovative *pace* through decades. What are the rules for this success?

(i) Hire people who have already proved to be creative.

(ii) Treat different people differently.

(iii) Master and do not set rules.

(iv) Think of the unthinkable.

Legler Industria Tessile SpA,
Bergamo,
Italy.

18

Textile-Design Education: It's Contribution to Product Design and Marketing

M.S. Burnip and T.J. Moscovitch

1. INTRODUCTION

The synopsis for this paper when originally submitted bore the sub-title 'Pushing the tank up the (correct) hill – with apologies to Fiona MacCarthy'. Those who have read her address on the British tradition in design (1) will know that in turn she quoted from Sir Gordon Russell's book (2). Both of these designers were concerned with furthering through another chartered body, the Royal Society for Arts (or, to give it its correct title, the Royal Society for the Encouragement of Arts, Manufacturers, and Commerce), the purposes of design.

The connection was deliberate, since the Royal Society for Arts has attempted to do for all aspects of design, and those concerned with its development, what the Textile Institute has attempted to do for textile design, manufacture, and commerce.

The development of industrial techniques for mass production dramatically changed the relationship between the designers and the makers of products (3). There have been those in industry and education, in design and manufacture, in business and commerce who have seen no reason to be concerned by this. There are those, including many Textile Institute members and others, who strive to ensure that the connections between design and manufacture and between the product and the marketplace provide the focus for activity in textiles. The processes of textile education have a contribution to make to this focussing; whether their purpose is lighting the lamp, providing the illumination, or identifying the object on which to focus may emerge from this paper. The processes of education, important as they are, are likely to be less important than the human product they turn out. This paper attempts to describe some of those processes and examine the potential of some of those products.

2. THE DEVELOPMENT OF DESIGN EDUCATION IN BRITAIN

Whereas this commentary is essentially concerned with Britain, parallels exist in all industrial countries, some of which are the subject of other papers at this Conference.

Between 1836 and 1864, more than 90 Schools of Art and Design were established in Great Britain, as a result mainly of the evidence presented to the 1835 Commons Select Committee on Art and

Manufacture. The Committee was set up by the Government because of growing concern over the superiority of foreign manufacturers in design over our own.

It may then seem rather remarkable that 150 years later the Government in the United Kingdom is focussing upon this selfsame topic with its various initiatives (4) in promoting design as a crucial ingredient of today's industrial success.

A fundamental issue indicated by the 1835 Select Committee was that the country's Art Schools concentrated on the 'gratuitous dissemination of that kind of knowledge which never was, nor by possibilities ever could be, of the smallest practical utility to men devoted to productive industry'. This statement was made by Charles Topliss, Vice-President of the London Mechanics' Institute, who indicated that the development of Mechanics' Institutes throughout the country was evidence that there was a genuine need for people to meet the needs of manufacturing industry. The Mechanics' Institutes eventually became the Colleges of Technology with the emphasis on vocational and part-time education. A hundred years later, in 1937, Britain still compared poorly with, for example, Germany. In that year, Britain had just 20 000 students in part-time further education, whereas Germany had over one and three-quarter million. In full-time vocational and technical training, Germany had more than twice as many young people as Britain involved, and, whereas in German industries there were 100% in job vocational training, in Britain the figure was about 10% (5).

Returning to the development of the Schools of Art and Design, it is important to stress that these were set up, not by an educational body, but by the Board of Trade. 'To us, a manufacturing nation, the connection between art and manufacture is most important ....'

There were three key themes central to the philosophy of the schools: drawing, ornament/decoration, and workshop training. It is interesting, with the current debates about core curricula for schools and industry-driven initiatives for City Colleges in Britain at present, to note that there were similar issues then.

The separate, but parallel, developments of Schools of Art and Mechanics' Institutes were inevitably not going to create an integrated approach to design and manufacture. By the middle of the century, art (as opposed to design) seems to have won, but, as Nuttgens (6) recently stated, 'The problem with all of them (Art Schools) was the same - the national inclination to escape from the harsh realities of industry and commerce into the delightful world of art for art's sake'.

William Morris and the advent of the Arts and Craft Movement at the end of the nineteenth century formed a turning point in the evolution of design, which eventually was to lead to the most important development in design education in Europe, the Bauhaus.

Walter Gropius and his colleagues attempted to reach a fully articulated philosophy of design, preaching the fundamental unity - underlying all branches of design and the importance of a rational and systematic analysis of the problem. The Bauhaus brought

20

together in one educational institution designers of all artefacts
from knives and forks to buildings and groups of buildings. Industrial design was thus seen as the same discipline of the mind (7).
The School's view that it is far harder to design a first-rate
teapot than to paint a second-rate picture was unarguably right.
The philosophy of the Bauhaus, according to Hughes (8), did more
to dignify the work of designers than any other cultural strategy
of the last half-century. There were in the Bauhaus strong links
with industry with students encouraged to design, especially in
the metalshops,in terms of mass production.

It has recently been suggested that in the 1830s Great Britain
chose the French (drawing-based) rather than the Bavarian (engi-
neering-based) system for teaching its designers (9). This concurs
with the witness statement 150 years earlier to the Select Committee from Baron von Klenze, Architect and Privy Councillor to
the King of Bavaria, who in August, 1836, stated how important
design was in ordinary schools in Bavaria. He also maintained
that the Gewerbe Institute in Berlin 'an institution for the manufactures as well as the arts, that is, where the artists and manufacturers are united to form manufacturing artists' was the best
institution of its kind on the Continent.

In Britain, the development of Bauhaus ideology and principles
was very erratic. In the first instance, there was the Design and
Industries Association, formed in 1915 with the harmonization of
design and manufacturing efficiency and acceptance of the machine
in its proper place as a device to be guided and controlled, not
merely boycotted, as one of its aims.

A later, more far-reaching, event was the setting up of the
Council of Industrial Design by the Government in 1944 'to promote by all practicable means the improvement of design in the
products of British industry'. One of its important early acts
was to organize the 1951 Festival of Britain. The Design Centre
in London opened in 1956. Today, this Centre has become the Design Council.

The Design Council is involved in a variety of Government
initiatives to promote design. One is its 'Investment in Design',
a funded consultancy scheme: 'For years the Design Council has
been encouraging British industry to become more competitive by
improving the design of its products .... The aims of the (Funded Consultancy) scheme are simple: in the short term to help
British companies get well-designed products on the market quickly;
in the longer term to persuade companies, through their own practical experience, that investment in design pays off - in fuller
order books and healthier profits'.

The Design Council - a charity with a Royal Charter, but funded by the Department of Trade and Industry - has flourished
since the Prime Minister 'discovered' design in 1982 (10) and
has promoted through its services, exhibitions, and publications
the causes of industrial design (11), including the training of
designers, the provision of marketing assistance, and the encouragement of sales of British goods.

The Art and Design educational system in Britain meanwhile has
developed from college and regional awards, first to National

21

Diplomas in Design (NDD), than to the Diploma in Art and Design under the National Council for Diplomas in Art and Design, and subsequently, after the merging of NCDAD with the Council for National Academic Awards (CNAA), to the award of degrees, either through the CNAA or, to a more limited extent, through the universities. Diplomas and Higher Diplomas in Design are now the remit of the Business and Technician Education Council (BTEC). Before these things were to happen, however, two major reports from Coldstream and Summerson (12,13) had changed the view that fine art contained the fundamental skills and disciplines that underline and sustain any form of specialization. 'Design', as Nuttgens has stated, 'was now belatedly recognized as an academic pursuit in its own right' (6).

Both CNAA and BTEC have contributed to the debates about design education (14-16), though not necessarily acting as more than catalysts to enhance reactions that were already proceeding. Nevertheless, some impressive developments have taken place in making a variety of courses more relevant. Two aspects of this form the subject of other papers (17,18) at this Conference.

A further re-examination of Art and Design education, at least in the public sector where the major part of it is found, has taken place recently in Britain, under the aegis of the National Advisory Body (NAB). Its report (19) indicates quite clearly that it remains of the utmost urgency that design education and industry integrate more closely, an endorsement of the White Paper 'Working together: Education and Training' (20), which identified design, making, and selling as the key to economic survival and success. The Royal College of Art, itself set up 150 years ago to provide Britain, including its industry, with leaders in art and design, has undergone similar self-analysis and change. Its Rector (21) recounted that every student to whom the DES Permanent Secretary spoke at a design show in the mid-1980s was going to work abroad: small wonder that he later (22) conceded 'we are aware that, for a postgraduate institution of university status in the second half of this century, to develop rapidly is not an option, it is necessary in order to survive. So great is the pace of industrial and technical advance in the disciplines we offer that, if we are to regain our position in the van of advanced knowledge and our reputation for innovation and for experimentation in art and design, we cannot rest for one moment!'.

3. MANUFACTURE IN BRITAIN

Britain was the first industrialized nation, developing from an agrarian economy, but with wool cloth as the chief manufacture (23), through trade following voyages of exploration, so that, by the late eighteenth and early nineteenth centuries, rapid growth had enabled wealth, based upon coal-mining and the manufacture of iron and steel, heavy machinery, and textiles, to enhance its position.

The textile industry in all its forms, but mainly based now upon cotton, dominated U.K. manufacturing and employment. The subsequent decline of the manufacturing base of Britain is both well known and commented upon (24,25), but not necessarily understood.

More careful analysis has been devoted to understanding and explaining the causes of the decline of textile manufacture, not only in Britain (26,27) but in other developed countries as well (28,29). Nevertheless, the scale of the U.K. textile and clothing industry is more substantial than most people in Britain believe, and some brief statistics (30) may help to put it into perspective.

The U.K. textile and clothing industry employs 10% of the work force in manufacturing industry (31) (Table I). The industry uses some 510 million kg of fibre per annum, of which some 70% is man-made (Table II), and produces some 360 million kg of yarn, of which 60% is man-made (Table III). From this yarn, some 1200 million m^2 of fabric and 140 million m^2 of carpet are produced (Tables IV and V). Imports of fabric are highest (c.75%) in cotton and man-made-fibre fabrics, 50% in wool fabrics, less than 20% in knitted fabrics, and just under 40% in carpets (Table VII).

The clothing industry has total sales of £4.3 billion, a home market now exceeding £5 billion, and some 30% of imports. These imports are highest by percentage in women's outerwear (44%) and highest by value (over £400 million) in women's dresses (Table VIII). Taken together with the sales (Table IX) of the U.K. textile industry, which exceed £9 billion, with imports of around 41%, the U.K. textile and clothing industry represents sales of over £12 billion and exports of over £3 billion (Table X).

With imports of less than 40%, the U.K. textile and clothing markets represent home markets of over £14 billion (Table X). The final points of importance are that, whereas producer prices for home sales from 1980 had risen by 44% to the end of the third quarter of 1986 for manufacturing as a whole (latest available figures), for textiles the rise had been only 34% and for clothing less than 30%. Nevertheless, the consumer price rises over the corresponding period in Britain were 14% for all manufactured goods since 1980, a mere 0.6% for household textiles and soft furnishings, but 33% for clothing items.

This analysis is included to demonstrate that, through 'the wholly understandable and correct trend whereby (cotton) processing has materially diminished in the non-growing areas and the whole of the growth in the total volume has effectively been absorbed by the producer countries (32), Britain is now a major market for both textiles and clothing'. Nevertheless, Britain too, with more than half a million employed, has one of the major textile and clothing industries of Europe (33) and is a major producer in her own right, whose total product value is far larger (34) than a number of better-understood and more glamorous industries.

This is the reason why the skills of design and marketing need to be employed effectively and efficiently in support of the U.K. industry. This in turn is why textile education has such a key role in securing the present and long-term future for these industries.

23

Table I

The UK Textile and Clothing Industry: Employment

Sector (thousands)	1984	1985	1986
All manufacturing industry	5563	5533	5262
Textiles, footwear, and clothing	553	549	573
Percentage of all manufacturing	9.9	9.9	10.9

Table II

UK Textile Industry: Fibre Consumption

Sector (Mn kg)	1985	1986
Man-made fibres	339.5	349.0
Cotton	45.9	47.3
Wool and hair	95.0	98.3
Jute	13.6	15.3
Total	504.0	509.9
Percentage man-made fibre	69.3	68.4

Table III
UK Textile Industry: Yarn Production

Sector (Mn kg)		1985	1986
Man-made continuous-filament		99.2	101.4
of which textured		30.6	30.9
Cotton system:	cotton	47.5	47.7
	mmf*	50.0	50.7
Worsted system:	wool	24.3	25.0
(inc. semi-worsted)	mmf*	43.0	49.0
Woollen system:	wool	52.8	61.4
	mmf*	8.6	10.8
Jute system		13.6	15.3
Total		339.0	361.3
Percentage man-made fibre		59.2	58.6

* Man-made fibre.

Table IV
UK Textile Industry: Fabric Production

Sector (Mn m^2)		1985	1986
Woven fabrics		803	823
of which:	cotton	315	312
	tyre-cord	22	23
	continuous-filament	210	221
	spun mmf*	165	174
	worsted > 50% wool	35	34
	< 50% wool	14	13
	woollen > 50% wool	34	39
	< 50% wool	8	7
	linen	19	15
Knitted fabrics		349	356
of which:	weft-knitted	212	217
	warp-knitted	137	139
Total fabrics		1171	1194

* Man-made fibre.

Table V

UK Textile Industry: Carpet Production

Sector (Mn m²)	1985	1986
Woven	20.2	19.7
Tufted	116.4	113.5
Non-woven	3.8	4.0
Total	140.4	137.2

Table VI

UK Textile Industry: Fibre and Yarn Imports

Sector (Mn kg)	1985	1986
Man-made fibre: staple-fibre	107.3	123.0
percentage	55.3	63.4
continuous-filament	142.4	142.4
percentage	91.7	91.8
Spun-man-made-fibre yarn	47.3	59.3
percentage	34.8	37.4
Cotton	57.0	55.0
percentage man-made fibre	56.7	56.0
Woollen and worsted	11.3	11.1
percentage man-made fibre	16.0	13.6
Jute	10.8	5.1
percentage man-made fibre	56.2	33.8

Table VII

UK Textile Industry: Fabric and Carpet Imports

Sector (Mn m^2)	1985	1986
Cotton fabric	637	553
percentage	77	74
Man-made-fibre fabric	684	795
percentage	73	75
Woollen and worsted fabric	27	28
percentage	53	47
Jute fabric (Mn kg)	27	20
percentage	34	26
Knitted fabric (Mn kg)	12	11
percentage	19	17
Carpets	66	71
percentage	35	38

Table VIII

UK Clothing Industry: Sector Imports

Sector (£Mn)	1985	1986
Weatherproof outerwear	110.4	122.2
percentage	34.5	33.4
Men's and boys' outerwear	319.7	334.2
percentage	42.4	42.2
Women's and girls' outerwear	237.7	281.8
percentage	40.1	44.0
Work clothing and jeans (men)	104.5	103.5
percentage	25.9	24.3
Men's shirts and underwear	183.9	188.8
percentage	31.5	31.2
Women's dresses and underwear	409.3	432.6
percentage	23.9	24.7
Other dresses	166.5	165.6
percentage	31.0	30.3
Total Clothing Sales	4138.3	4277.6
Exports	762.5	777.3
Imports	1532.2	1628.5
Home market	4908.0	5128.8
Percentage imports	31.2	31.8

Table IX

UK Textile Industry: Imports

Sector (£Mn)	1985	1986
Total sales	7820.5	7898.0
Exports	2401.5	2350.2
Imports	3772.7	3936.4
Home market	9191.8	9484.2
Percentage imports	41.0	41.5

Table X

UK Textile and Clothing Industry: Imports

Sector (£Mn)	1985	1986
Total sales	11958.8	12175.6
Exports	3164.0	3127.5
Imports	5304.9	5565.2
Home market	14099.8	14613.0
Percentage imports	37.6	38.1

4. TEXTILE-DESIGN EDUCATION IN BRITAIN

Having sketched the development of design education and the size
and state of the current textile and clothing industry, one must
briefly examine the provision of textile education in support of
one of its major industries. A number of studies (35-38) of all
textile education have been followed by others concentrating upon
textile design, including education (39-41).

The realization that textile-design education, already very
extensive compared with that for technology (36), could forge the
links between design and manufacture that were spoken of, but not
realized in quantity, clearly struck a number of different organizations at around the same time. No doubt in response to the increased importance given to design by Government, a spate of reports on textile-design education and its industrial links (or
lack of them) now appeared (42-44). Seminars and conferences, too,
played their part in enhancing links where they already existed
and encouraging them where they did not. If to some, including
those closely involved with the Textile Institute and its educational policies in textile education, including design, there was
an element of *déjà vu*, to others conversion was to come Paul-like,
if not on the road to Damascus, then at least on the way to a
NEDO seminar!

There are 31 institutions of higher education in the United
Kingdom offering 39 degree courses in Textile Design or Fashion
Design. Eleven are in London and the South of England, seven are
in the North of England, one is in Northern Ireland, and five are
in Scotland.

Between them, these institutions turn out some 700 graduates
a year in textile design or fashion design. Three of the courses
are offered in Universities and thirteen at Polytechnics (as well
as two at Scottish Central Institutions, which are similar to the
Polytechnics), while the remaining thirteen are at Colleges of
Art in England and Scotland. The 31 institutions offer a varied
range of courses, as might be expected. Some institutions offer
either Fashion Design or Textile Design, others offer a combination of the two with opportunity to specialize (45).

There are some sixteen degree courses in various forms available for students of Fashion Design. At one time, it might have
been thought they held no interest for the textile (as opposed
to the clothing) industry. This is no longer the case for several
reasons: many textile manufacturers are also clothing manufacturers; the clothing industry takes half of the textile industry's output and is therefore its biggest customer; knitwear is
'claimed' by both fashion- and textile-design courses and is
taught (with differing amounts of emphasis) on both types of
course; both the textile and clothing industries serve the retail
industry, which is interested in both fashion and textile design;
and some of the innovations in course design on fashion courses
are mirrored by or have relevance to textile-design courses.

There are some 24 degree courses in various forms in Textile
Design in the United Kingdom, of which eighteen are in England
and six in Scotland or Northern Ireland. Those in England are
distributed between London and the South (seven), the Midlands

and West (six), and the North (five). Of these, some cover both printed textiles and constructed textiles; some cover one rather than the other. It is difficult to be precise about the exact split, but (say) twelve courses could be regarded as having a major specialization in printed textile design and sixteen courses in constructed textile design - some obviously making a major contribution in both areas.

At a level below that of degree is the Business and Technician Education Council, whose role is to advance the quality and availability of work-related education for those in or preparing for employment, and whose aim is that students on BTEC courses should develop the necessary competence in their careers in their own, employers', and the national interest (46).

BTEC has two levels of course: Ordinary National Diplomas and Certificates, and Higher National Diplomas and Certificates, both of which normally take two years of study. At the HND level, there are eleven courses in Fashion and Textiles, all of which embody industrial experience and collaborative projects with industry. The two-year duration is intended to concentrate quite clearly and rationally on the demands of the specific design vocation. 'Work-related education for those in, or preparing for, employment' is the cornerstone of the BTEC philosophy. In particular, BTEC has focussed importantly on aspects of design education that may have been lacking and the need for skills in design that could be put to use in industry, these including knowledge and experience of marketing and business and the value of computing. It is unfortunate for a new validating body that it began with such fixed perceptions of the purposes of textile design and of its execution.

The professional bodies, it could be argued, have more collective experience than most in meeting industrial needs, since most of their members are likely to be practitioners rather than educators. The Textile Institute, in design as in technology, has proceeded by both recognizing courses for exemption from its professional qualifications and by validating courses operated on its behalf. Thus a number of honours-degree courses (such is the level required) in Textile Design give exemption from the Institute's Associateship examinations in Textile Design, these having been adjudged to involve the integrated study of design, management, and manufacture in such a manner that creative design is enhanced. In addition, one U.K. centre provides a course for graduates or HND diplomates to meet the Textile Institute's Associateship requirements in design.

5. MODELS OF ASSOCIATION IN TEXTILE-DESIGN EDUCATION

One method of integrating the textile-education course with industry is to provide an industrial involvement in its design, in its operation, in its teaching, and in its examining.

There are eight Textile or Fashion degree courses providing industrial experience as part of the course. By this is meant that it is a condition of the award of the degree as a sandwich degree that the appropriate amount of industrial training is satisfactorily completed. The satisfaction has to be to the requirements of the agreed programme, by the host industrial company in conjunction with the college.

The nature of the arrangements varies; for example, courses include both thin sandwich courses, with industrial placements in two or more years of the course, and thick sandwich courses with all the industrial training in one year (usually the third) of the course.

Of the eight sandwich courses, four are in Fashion Design at Lancashire Polytechnic (24 weeks thick); Newcastle Polytechnic (Fashion Option 24 weeks thin, Fashion Marketing Option 48 weeks thick); North-east London Polytechnic (24 weeks thin); and the London Institute at St Martin's College (from 12 weeks to 48 weeks thin). The sandwich degree courses in Textile Design are at: Brighton Polytechnic (36 weeks thick); Huddersfield Polytechnic (48 weeks thick); Kidderminster College through Wolverhampton Polytechnic (36 weeks thin); and Trent Polytechnic (24 weeks thin).

Running such courses is worth while because of their value and the reality brought to the formal taught component. Those running them are grateful to industry for the enthusiasm and support it provides by way of industrial placements. The number of placements involved, even when spread across the textile, clothing, and retail industries, is considerable. Whereas in some cases grants are available, these are insufficient and the grant covers less than a third of the cost of the placement. The training organizations, employer organizations, and DECO EDC's who have provided support in discussions and arguments with funding bodies over the number of grants are deserving of our thanks.

Any expansion of the sandwich-course principle too must recognize the problems of providing sufficient industrial-training places of appropriate quality. The development of post-education schemes, such as Designers into Industry or work-experience schemes, usually unpaid, such as exist on many BTEC courses, may, however, make the procurement of sandwich placements more difficult.

6. TECHNOLOGY AND BUSINESS

To make the most of the industrial-experience component, and because largely industrial design is also about mass-production, a knowledge of technology is an important and vital supporting component of a designer's training. Huddersfield Polytechnic is a passionate advocate of designers understanding the technology of manufacture for their designs, not just in a studio environment but also in a shop-floor sense. All textile-design courses at Huddersfield embody this principle; thus, it is part of the make-up of our BTEC HND Textile Design Course and the honours-degree course in Textile Design, and it forms the basis of the post-experience design course for the Textile Institute's Associate-ship that we run, as well as being part of much of the post-graduate research we conduct in textile design.

It is interesting to note that it is from the creative use of technology applied to design studies that two new elements of textile design, those of yarn design and nonwoven-fabric design,

have been developed and incorporated in all textile design at
Huddersfield (47-49). These emerging textile-design disciplines
have, like the other results (50,51) of design-led research,
emerged from market-led problems. The impact of yarn design upon
the future competitiveness of the U.K. textile industry is understood (52,53) and growing: that of nonwoven-fabric design will
take longer.

Huddersfield, like few other major centres, is fortunate to
have degrees in Textile Marketing and Textile Technology to provide and justify the infrastructure of equipment and support
staff necessary. That others have found this helpful, though, can
be judged by the success of our short-course design programmes,
which permit other colleges to visit and use our facilities and
understand something of the creative use of technology for design.

Fitness for purpose in design does not happen, nor can it, any
more than aesthetic design, be added at the end, or as an after-
thought. A knowledge of products, their behaviour, and that of
their constituents must therefore be seen to be an important component of the designer's range of skills and experience. This
approach is shared, in various ways, by courses involving industrial training, certainly in textile design, and by some other
courses, mainly in traditional textile-producing areas. Lest the
current fashion in education to embrace technology (primarily because the DTI is putting the funds there) (59) causes all design
courses to lose their identity and individuality, it is important
to recognize that the models here being described are but one
attempt to contribute to product design and marketing.

Product design, specification, and evaluation are equally important, especially if articles for mass-production are being
considered (54,44), and their needs should be recognized on textile-design courses if both import substitution (56,57) and export stimulation (58) are to increase for the U.K. textile and
clothing industry. To achieve a meaningful integration of such
studies within design courses is, however, difficult and can only
be achieved by constant examination of the relevance and market
size of particular textile products.

'Good design is anything that sells', but the most ardent en-
thusiast for ensuring that designers know something of business
would not wish the purpose of design courses to be diverted or
distorted to this extent. Nevertheless, for two cogent reasons,
namely the purposes of any business are to satisfy the customers
and to make money for the shareholders, design students, whether
they found small businesses or join large-scale design-based manufacturers, must realize that the efficient and effective organization of resources, including the design function, is vital to
future profitability.

Whether, therefore, the business studies concentrate on accounts or management' or marketing, the attitudinal effect must
be to make designers aware that their important creative function
also both has a cost and is capable of creating wealth through
the added value it provides to the product.

A great advantage of incorporating the National Council for
Diplomas in Art and Design (NCDAD) within the CNAA system, as

Bob Strand's forthcoming book will no doubt reveal, is that it provided an opportunity for public-sector Textile Design degrees to draw upon the expertise that resided in the other committees, such as Business Studies, of the CNAA. Likewise, in Polytechnics in particular, the opportunity for interdisciplinary contributions to design courses was a strong element in assisting many, including Huddersfield Polytechnic, to ensure that all designers had a knowledge of marketing and the economic structure of the textile industry.

Discussion papers recently (59,60) on business awareness and in management and marketing studies have stressed that professional and business studies for designers should include personal skills of financial literacy, management of time, self-presentation and communication in relation to professional practice, and public and private industry or commerce. Since it is correct to educate managers about design, as another Conference paper will show, then equally those who are to be designers should know something of management. Whether, in truth, design management as a subject actually exists is perhaps a debatable point: what is not is the concept that the design function, as part of a team effort that must relate also to production, marketing, and sales, requires co-ordinating and that designers as part of a team require managing.

7. INTEGRATION AND DESIGN SPONSORSHIP

The topics highlighted as desirable features of textile-design courses at any level, namely, industrial experience, technology of manufacture, business, and management understanding, have four important drawbacks. They are very demanding in time; it cannot be assumed that the importance and relevance of each is clearly perceived, and hence they need integration; they must not be allowed to become an excuse for the blunting of the creative activity of the student; and they demand a very high-calibre and committed student, whose selection requires more care and a wider understanding of desirable attributes than just a good portfolio.

It would be unfair and presumptious to suggest we have found answers to all these points, but, by running a linked series of three textile-design courses at HND, professional and post-experience, and degree level, it is possible to cater for students' needs and attributes, while attmepting to provide design studies in the context of industrial experience, technology, and marketing.

A key vehicle for both integration and relevance is the sponsored project, which, if appropriately and sensitively developed, provides the means and stimulus for focussing students' attention on the importance of all topics that support good design. By inviting industry severally to sponsor projects, assist in writing the brief, provide 'crits' for the project work, teach on courses, and help in the assessment, the relevance and perspective of design studies is enhanced. Textile-design project briefs invariably include manufacture, product performance, or evaluation and require group or individual planning, all of which contributes to the creation of the textile design.

Interestingly, adjacent disciplines are gradually awakening to this integrated approach; engineering and product design are important examples. Cyril Laning at Imperial College warns that 'so long as the split continues, Art and Design Schools will go on being fashion houses, and Universities will continue to be houses of science'. He indicates that the best prospect lies with the Polytechnics 'getting their act together and presenting courses that are truly redesigned for the engineer-artist in the modern world' (61). How fascinating to see this identical philosophy actually being carried out 150 years earlier at the Gewerbe Institute in Berlin, 'where the arts and manufactures are united to form manufacturing artists'!!

8. CONCLUSIONS

World fibre consumption is some 30 million tonnes per annum – a *per-capita* consumption of more than 6.5 kg. Exports of textiles and clothing alone total more than $100 billion, representing, with home production, employment for substantial numbers throughout the world. The textile and clothing industries in Europe provide for one in ten of the persons employed in the EEC. Especially in developed countries do the demands of the market grow insistently more complex and sophisticated, and thus product design and marketing play an increasing role in the successful manufacture of textile and clothing products.

The United Kingdom, with the largest textile and clothing employment in Europe and a home market worth over £12 billion per annum, must ensure that both its industry and its markets remain healthy and competitive. A key feature in the competitiveness of its textile and clothing industry is a continued supply of well-educated, trained, and motivated young people, including textile designers whose creative abilities have been whetted by the understanding of the importance of technology and business in their education.

Some of the ways in which textile education has contributed to the design and marketing of its products are described in this paper. In particular, the ways in which Huddersfield Polytechnic has developed different types of design course, each including industrial, technological, and marketing contributions to the textile-design process, have been described.

It is fitting to note that the Textile Institute, through the requirements for its Associateship in Design and as the body that nationally and internationally sets the standards for professional competence in manufacturing textiles, should be one of the educational contributors to product design and marketing.

REFERENCES

(1) Fiona MacCarthy. Pushing the Tank Uphill, Royal Society of Arts, London, October, 1981.

(2) Fiona MacCarthy. Royal Designers on Design, Design Council, London, 1986.

(3) His Royal Highness the Duke of Edinburgh. Royal Designers on Design, Design Council, London, 1986.

(4) Hugh Pearman. *Design Magazine*, 1987, March, No. 459.

(5) Corelli Barnet. 'The Audit of War', Macmillan, London, 1986.

(6) Steve Braidwood. *Design Magazine*, 1986, September, No. 453.

(7) Patrick Nuttgens in: Report to the Design Council on the Design of British Consumer Goods, Design Council, London, July, 1983.

(8) Robert Hughes in: 'The Shock of the New', BBC Publications, London, 1980.

(9) Steve Braidwood. *Design Magazine*, 1986, September, No. 453.

(10) Paul Burall. 'The Arts, Crafts, and Design Councils and the Contemporary Visual Arts', Crafts Council, 1985.

(11) 'The Design Council, What We Are, What We Do, Why We Do It', Design Council, June, 1984.

(12) Ministry of Education. The National Advisory Council on Art Education, HMSO, London, 1960.

(13) Joint Committee. The Structure of Art and Design Education in Further Education Sector, HMSO, London, 1970.

(14) Council for National Academic Awards. Supervised Work Experience: A Case Study on Sandwich Degrees in Design, CNAA, London, 1985.

(15) Business and Technician Education Council. The Design Needs of Industry, BTEC, London, September, 1985.

(16) Sandy McLachan. 'Design By Experience', BTEC, London, February, 1985.

(17) Peter Byrom. 'Young Designers into the Textile Industry The British Experience - Case Studies from a Pilot Year', in: Textile Institute Annual Conference, Como, 1987.

(18) Louis van Praag. 'The Management of Design' in: Textile Institute Annual Conference, Como, 1987.

(19) National Advisory Body. 'A Wider Vision', NAB, London, January, 1987.

(20) Department of Education and Science. 'Working together: Education and Training', HMSO, London, 1985.

(21) Jocelyn Stevens in: 'Directors on Design', SIAD Design Management Seminars, 1985 (edited by Beryl McAlhone), Design Council, London, 1985.

(22) Jocelyn Stevens. *J. Royal Soc. Arts*, 1986, March.

(23) Central Office for Information. 'Britain: An Official Hand-book', HMSO, London, 1985.

(24) Committee of Enquiry into the Engineering Profession. 'Engineering Our Future', HMSO, London, 1980.

(25) Amin Rajan and Richard Pearson (Editors).'U.K. Occupation and Employment Trends to 1990', Butterworths, London, 1986.

(26) Philip W. Smith. 'Textile Industries in Developed Countries' (the 1974 Mather Lecture), *Text. Inst. Industr.*, 1974, 12, 264.

(27) N. Brian Smith. 'World Trade in Textiles' (the 1981 Mather Lecture), *Text. Inst. Industr.*, 1981, 19, 143.

(28) Diane Tussie. 'The Less Developed Countries and the World Trading System', Pinter, London, 1987.

(29) Vincent Gable and Betsy Baker. 'World Textile Trade and Production Trends' (Report 152), Economist Intelligence Unit, London, 1983.

(30) British Textile Confederation. 'A Plan for Action', London, March, 1983.

(31) Department of Trade and Industry. Bulletin of Textile and Clothing Statistics, London, March, 1987.

(32) Philip W. Smith. 'Textile Industries in Developed Countries' (the 1974 Mather Lecture), *Text. Inst. Industr.*, 1974, 12, 264.

(33) EEC Commission. Official Journal of the European Communities, C290, November, 1986.

(34) British Textile Confederation. 'A Plan for Action', London, March, 1983.

(35) Raymond Harwood. 'A Survey of Textile and Related Education in Britain', the Livery Companies Textile and Colouration Craft Association, London, 1985.

(36) Malcolm Burnip. 'The Current Position and Development of Textile Education in the United Kingdom', *Text. Inst. Industr.*, 1980, 18, 132, 158.

(37) John Hearle. 'U.K. Textile Education is in Danger', *Text. Horiz.*, 1982, 2, No. 8, 34.

(38) Malcolm Burnip and Kenneth Durrands. 'Education for the Textile Industries in the United Kingdom', December, 1982.

(39) Alexandra Buxton. Textile Design: Education and Industry, Royal College of Art, June, 1985.

(40) National Economic Development Council, Design Working Party. Education Recommendations, Appendix 3, NEDO, London, June, 1986.

(41) Christopher Hogg in: 'Directors on Design' (SIAD Design Management Seminars 1985) (edited by Beryl McAlthone), Design Council, London, 1985.

(42) Cotton and Allied Textiles EDC. 'Designing for Success', Chapter 5, NEDO, London, October, 1984.

(43) Confederation of British Wool Textiles, Textile Design Education, 1986.

(44) **Alexandra Buxton. Textile Design: Education and Industry, Royal College of Art, June, 1985.**

(45) Malcolm Burnip. 'More CNAA Degrees in Textile Design and Fashion', NEDO Conference, Manchester, January, 1987.

(46) Neal Raine. 'Design by Experience', Business and Technician Education Council, London, February, 1985.

(47) Malcolm Burnip and Janet Castle-Mallory. 'Yarn Design – What Implications it has for the Knitter' in: 27th Congress of the International Federation of Knitting Technologists, Leicester, October, 1983.

(48) Malcolm Burnip and Linda Grady in 'Designing for the Market', UMIST, Manchester, June, 1986.

(49) Malcolm Burnip and Graham Marsden. 'Faktoren, die die Herstellung von gemusterern Nadelvliesstoffen beeinflussen', *Melliand Textilber.*, 1978, <u>59</u>, 542.

(50) Stephen Knox, Karen Priestner, and Y. Overington in 'Designing for the Market', UMIST, Manchester, June, 1986.

(51) Council for National Academic Awards. Research in Art and Design, Middlesex Polytechnic, May, 1984.

(52) J.R. Tindall in: 'Designing for the Market', UMIST, Manchester, June, 1986.

(53) Christopher England in: 'Designing for the Market', UMIST, Manchester, June, 1986.

(54) Ludwig Gan in: 'Quality, Design and the Purchaser', The Textile Institute, Manchester, 1983.

(55) Freddie Strasser in: 'The Fabric Revolution', The Textile Institute, Manchester, 1981.

(56) L.A. Merier. 'Survey of Furnishing, Fabrics and Household Textiles: Better Made in Britain', NEDO, London, 1986.

(57) Cotton and Allied Textiles Economic Development Committee. 'Partnership for Profit', NEDO, London, September, 1986.

(58) Joint Textile Committee. 'Lifting the Barriers to Trade, NEDO, London, June, 1986.

(59) Giles Shaw. Parliamentary Answer, Hansard, March, 1987.

(60) Council for National Academic Awards. 'Management, Promotion and Marketing Studies in Art and Design Degree Courses', CNAA, London, March, 1986.

(61) Council for National Academic Awards. 'Professional and Business Awareness in Art and Design Degree Courses', CNAA, London, October, 1986.

(62) Christopher Lorenz. 'Europe Tries to Heal its Design Schism', *Financial Times*, 1986, 14 November.

Department of Textile Industries,
Huddersfield Polytechnic,
Huddersfield,
West Yorkshire,
England.

Young Designers into the Textile Industry

The British Experience - Case Studies from a Pilot Year

P.C. Byrom and G.E. Byrom

Abstract

This paper concentrates on the difficult period of adaptation necessary for a young designer coming out of college and going into a career in the textile industry.

A brief historical survey of the British experience is included to demonstrate how much attention has been put upon design by government over many years. This survey reveals how the emphasis has changed from, first, the setting up of schools to, second, the development of courses, and latterly to the problem of how the excellent talent emerging from these courses is to be put to work.

The Young Designers into Industry scheme (YDI), sponsored by the British Department of Trade and Industry (DTI) and administered by the Royal Society of Arts (RSA) is explained in some detail as an example of a successful attempt to ease the difficult transition from the creative freedom of the college environment to the more constrained situation in manufacturing industry. The unique elements in this scheme are identified as an indication of the care and attention necessary if there is a serious intention to make a positive contribution in this area.

Finally, some indication is given of the variety of employment being achieved by the graduate designers emerging from textile courses, to illustrate the significant impact such talented young people can have upon the vitality and economic success of the textile industry.

1. HISTORICAL BACKGROUND

1.1 Nineteenth-century Concerns

Self-criticism of British textile design is not a new phenomenon. As long ago as 1835, the British Government was sufficiently concerned to appoint a Select Committee (1) to:

'inquire into the best means of extending a knowledge of the Arts, and of the Principles of Design amongst the People (especially the Manufacturing Population) of the Country; also to inquire into the Constitution, Management and Effects of Institutions connected with the Arts ....'

39

The method of the enquiry included comparing and contrasting
methods of design education and training in Britain with those
of Bavaria, France, and Prussia, Continental competitors where
Design Schools were already established. One recommendation of
the Select Committee was immediately implemented. In 1837, a
School of Design was founded, under the Board of Trade, at Somer-
set House, in London. By 1842, branch schools had followed in Manchester, Birmingham, and Glasgow. After the Great Exhibition of
1851, the Normal Training School of Art, as it had been renamed,
moved to a permanent home on the South Kensington campus, bought
from the proceeds of the Great Exhibition to 'extend the influence of Science and Art upon productive Industry'. In 1896 this
School became the Royal College of Art with the granting of a
Royal Charter, which defined its objects as:

> 'to advance learning, knowledge and professional competence
> particularly in the field of fine arts, in the principles and
> practice of art and design in their relation to industrial and
> commercial processes and social developments and other subjects
> relating thereto through teaching, research, and collaboration
> with industry and commerce.'

These terms of reference, given more than 90 years ago, remain
as challenging to the College today as they were when written.
The inclusion of the relationship of art to social developments
will ensure that they will continue to challenge the College well
into the next century.

1.2 Twentieth-century Actions

Although much wisdom was contained in the terms of reference given
to the Art Colleges established in Britain in the nineteenth century, 'wishing' did not make it so. In a report to the Joint
Standing Committee (Industrial and Educational) of the British
Cotton Industry Research Association, written in the first half
of this century, members observed:

> 'It is sufficient here to say that much of what was written
> in 1836 on the subject of Textile Design might be repeated
> with as much truth today .... There are signs of mutual dis-
> trust between artists and industry, of the aloofness of the
> schools and of the lack of practical value in their work' (2).

In the post-war investment in public education, government's
attention was directed towards the content of courses in design
education. A National Advisory Council on Art Education was set
up to advise the Minister of Education on all aspects of art education. One consequence of this Council's advice was the introduction of a new qualification, the Diploma in Art and Design,
having qualities similar to those of a University first degree,
to be administered by a new National Council. In its first report,
in 1964, this Council stated:

> 'The study of design in the Textiles/Fashion areas need not
> necessarily be related to industrial production. But the ties
> are, in general, so close that some understanding of the pro-
> cess of production and of the fashion industry is a necessary
> part of the designer's educational equipment ...' (3).

The idea of segregation implicit within this 'not necessarily'

was further enhanced by the simultaneous introduction by this
same National Committee of vocational courses, below degree level:

'... directed more specifically towards certain categories of
industrial and professional design practice' and '... having
a substantial specialized technological content ...' (4).

In 1985, there were five Colleges and Art Schools in the U.K.
offering these vocational courses in textiles, validated by the
Business and Technician Education Council, and 20 establishments
offered full-time or sandwich degree courses in Textile Design,
validated by the Council for National Academic Awards (CNAA).
Some 517 students gained a CNAA degree in Textile Design in this
year, and some 218 gained a BTEC Diploma (5).

Significantly, the CNAA continues to recognize the value of
both 'art'- and 'industry'-orientated courses, avowing in its
'Principle 3':

'The Council has found a wide range of specific objectives
appropriate for programmes of studies leading to its awards
and this range is being continually extended. Thus, some programmes will seek to prepare students for a particular profession or vocation; some will seek to develop a student's
artistic development; some will seek a breadth of subject
coverage, while others will encourage specialization and yet
others will transcend traditional boundaries of knowledge'(6).

With this wealth of variety in objectives and indeed in at-
tainment by the U.K. textile-design educational establishments,
it is no wonder that the industry has a very varied view on what
the product of the educational system is. Understanding what the
educators' aims are in each establishment, and in departments
within establishments, can remove many of the prejudices that at
present hinder the entry of the available talent into those positions in industry where they can have an early beneficial effect.

One experienced industrialist, working with the Young Designers
into Industry selection panel, observed:

'When I look at the work of young designers in the colleges,
I am looking for those with exciting new ideas, which can then
be interpreted into our own fabrics. When I hear competitors
complaining that the colleges do not teach students to put
their designs onto production machinery, I know they are missing the main benefit to be had from young designers. We have
plenty of people in our mill who know how to put designs onto
our machines.'

Anyone who is seriously seeking a better understanding of the
complex issues involved here is strongly recommended to study the
report 'Textile Design: Education and Industry', produced by
Alexandra Buxton while she was part-time research fellow in the
School of Textile Design at the Royal College of Art, 1982-1984
(7).

2. INDUSTRY'S CONCERN

Throughout the above evolution of British design education, there has been a parallel dialogue between the textile industry and the Colleges. More recently, an awareness has emerged that there is more to be gained from an examination and implementation of the best practice, worldwide, of employing design talent in textiles than from recurrent restructuring of Design Colleges and courses. Concrete evidence of this awareness exists in studies of the training and early employment of young textile designers under-taken by many industry bodies, e.g.:

> the Scottish woollen industry, 1984, which resulted in its Design Development Scheme, funded by the Scottish Develop-ment Agency;
> the Confederation of British Wool Textiles (CBWT), 1984 (8);
> the National Economic Development Office (NEDO), which has provided a forum for much of the textile industry's concern, publishing a series of thoughtful reports prepared by the Cotton and Allied Textiles Economic Development Committee (9-11).

The most recent of these NEDO reports, entitled 'Designing for Success: Approaches to Managing Textile Design', published in 1984 (10), is based on a series of visits to British and Continental textile companies and attempts to identify best practices common to their success. Within the many valuable conclusions and recom-mendations arising from this report, an over-all awareness emerges of the need to integrate the design function more successfully within the other management functions, not only sales and market-ing, but also production, research, and development. Design strat-egy is to be seen as an integral part of the over-all market stance of a company.

The CBWT Report (8) similarly recognizes changing attitudes towards design:

> 'There was virtually unanimous acceptance of the fact that the designer's rôle in wool textiles had changed radically from a purely technical contribution, to a creative part of the total marketing team, fully involved in the development of new ranges through regular contact with customers at mills and trade shows.'

Concurrent with this change in work performed, a change in the profile of the industry's designers is recorded:

> 'The established designers were majority male (17 of 22), 16 were aged 30-45 years, basic education was terminated at an earlier stage than is now customary, only four attended a Foundation Course and more than half (13) learned designing through part-time education or at their place of work. Only four had the ambition to be a textile designer originally. The trainee and new-graduate designers were largely female (39 of 42), 39 were under 30 years old, 39 had taken 'A'- or 'H'-level exams, 36 attended Foundation Course, and 41 had taken full-time design training at college. Less than half (19) had ambitions to be a textile designer when starting their course of further education.'

One further area of action by the industry should be noted. In the post-war years, there have been a number of initiatives by leaders of the British textile industry to stimulate increased use of young designer talent. One of the most professional and sustained of these was launched in the late 1940s by the Cotton Board in Manchester as an annual event to present the work of the best of British textile designers to the industry. This exhibition was the seed from which the Design Council has in recent years developed its excellent annual TEXPRINT exhibition in London. Here the most promising textile graduates from the British Colleges are given the opportunity to show their work to both a national and an international audience of textile, fashion, and retail professionals.

The Design Council's international approach to textile design has also provided the opportunity for young British designers to show their work in appropriate design fairs in both Continental Europe and the U.S.A. These initiatives have been of considerable value to young British designers, and it is perhaps surprising that no significant contra-flow of overseas designers into Britain has yet been observed.

3. GOVERNMENT'S INTERVENTION

Attempts by government to intervene in the reshaping of the British textile industry during the past 35 years have almost invariably been on a grand scale and almost invariably have failed to achieve their long-term objectives or have suffered the ignominy of seeing the intervention cause an opposite effect. Examples are the attempted reorganization of the cotton industry in 1953 and government's role in the merger-mania of the late 1960s, with substantial public funds invested in re-equipping factories that are now closed down. In January, 1982, however, a remarkable new initiative was taken: remarkable for the comparatively low cost and for the potentially high impact. These are some of the recent U.K. government initiatives to support and promote design:

January, 1982:	Prime Minister holds a seminar on Product Design and Market Success; many suggestions for government action to encourage greater use by industry of U.K.'s outstanding design talent.
1982 to date:	Support for Design Scheme; subsidized design consultancy for small and medium-sized firms; managed for the DTI by the Design Council.
1982-1986:	Support for design-management training at the London Business School and through the CNAA.
1983:	Design for Profit-awareness campaign.
November, 1983:	Publication of research on the economic consequences of design.
February, 1984:	London design seminar for financial institutions.
1984-1986:	Touring Exhibition - Support for Design case studies.
May, 1984:	John Butcher, Under-Secretary of State for Industry, published 'Design for

Design - a Framework for Action'.

October, 1984:   Strategy Group report published.

1985:   Launch of Young Designers into Industry
                   scheme with the initial trial year taking
                   place in the textile industry.

An RSA press release dated 11th February, 1985, announced that
the Royal Society of Arts was to administer the Young Designers
into Industry scheme in partnership with design education and industry. Funding was to come jointly from the host companies involved and from the Department of Trade and Industry.

In a press notice from the DTI, dated 12th February, 1985,
under the heading 'John Butcher calls on Industry to use Young
Design Talent' the Under-Secretary of State for Industry said:

'Industry and education have been equally guilty in the past
of dividing the practical and the aesthetic into separate pigeon-holes. Design should be the fusion of the two. Its practitioners have the creativity and the knowledge to apply practical solutions to particular problems and thereby to help industry keep abreast of technological progress and changes in
consumer demand. Design, in other words, is a key instrument
in helping us produce goods and services which will sell.'

4. THE ROYAL SOCIETY OF ARTS

The full title of this society is the Royal Society for the Encouragement of Arts, Manufactures and Commerce (RSA). In a paper
presented on 17th November, 1980, to the Faculty of Royal Designers for Industry, whose headquarters are at the RSA's House in
London, Jean Muir urged the Society to resume its full title and
to redirect the considerable efforts it makes through its annual
Bursaries Competition in Textile Design towards the needs of the
times. She stated her view that

'the training of a designer in this country must be allied to
technical practice and manufacturing knowledge with a background of the commercial formula',

and she continued:

'Comparison with other countries does not hold up in argument, because the situation is different. Why should we com-
plain or boast that many of our good young designers go abroad?
Surely that should point to the fact that we are not training
for the situation as it exists in this country?'

This paper struck a sympathetic chord in the Design Section
at the RSA, who, in April, 1981, circulated a response expressing
interest in exploring views

'relating to the true functions of design and designers, *how
student designers should be prepared for the fulfilment of
their true professional function*, and how the Design Bursaries
Competition could do more to help'.

However, the inevitable caveat was added that the RSA must be assured of the necessary resources to see any additional effort
through to an effective conclusion.

It was March, 1984, before Christopher Lucas, Secretary of the RSA, was able to write to Jean Muir to hold out some hope that funds might become available (from the Department of Trade and Industry, see above) and enlist her support for the proposed scheme, which was to become the YDI.

Although Christopher Lucas is quoted in *Designer*, July/August, 1984, as saying: 'There is no particular reason to choose textile design ...' (for the YDI trial year), it should be apparent from all of the above that there was already in textiles, and in the RSA Design Section, a readiness for this particular experiment.

5. THE YDI SCHEME

This scheme aims to enable industry to make fuller use of Britain's talented young designers by putting attention onto the critical moment when industry and the young designer establish their first contact together. It achieves this aim by selecting, in collaboration with the Design Colleges, those undergraduates demonstrating exceptional promise as industrial designers, and offering them to those companies that have expressed interest for a twelve-month placement, during which the cost of their salaries is shared equally between the host company and the DTI. After a three-month probationary period, the success of each placement is assessed during a monitoring visit from the RSA, together with a member of the Textile Panel. This monitoring is maintained until completion of the placement, when the young designers receive a Certificate of Post-Graduate Industrial Experience issued by the RSA.

5.1 Selection

The selection process is clearly a vital element in the scheme and one which, if successful, offers the greatest potential benefit to employers. It is therefore explained here in some detail, because it is arguably the priceless input freely given to this process by experienced textile practitioners that should most forcefully commend the scheme to industry.

5.1.1 College Selection

The first stage in the selection process takes place in the Design Colleges, where the tutors and heads of department are asked to identify among their textile students — whether concerned with weave, print, knit, or embroidery, etc. — those students who, in their final year of a degree or BTEC HND course, demonstrate an aptitude for the industrial environment. This need not necessarily mean a commitment to a career working in an industrial company. Those designers with a strongly individual creative style, who are perhaps more likely to make their contribution to the success of British textiles as freelance designers, or within the very important design consultancies that this industry is fortunate to have available, are strongly recommended to experience this one YDI year within the industry they will be serving, as an invaluable preliminary to a freelance career.

5.1.2 RSA Portfolio Selection

The second stage of selection takes place at the RSA, where the portfolios of the students recommended by the colleges are examined by the core-group of the Textile Panel and a short list is drawn up for interview. In each of the past two years, more than 130 submissions have been examined to invite perhaps 30 students for interview. In making this initial assessment, the core-group is greatly assisted by the accompanying statements written by the tutors and the students in support of each application. It has always been possible to find work of excellent standard among the submissions, and in the second year of the scheme the number of placements was increased from twelve to eighteen. Nevertheless, a tendency still exists within some Colleges not to put forward their 'best' students for YDI, perhaps because they are still in ignorance of the exciting changes that have taken place in some leading industrial companies' attitudes to designing during recent years. Those Colleges that have supported YDI in years one and two are therefore urged to communicate the success their graduates have enjoyed to those colleges that have not yet encouraged their students to apply for this experience.

5.1.3 RSA Interview

The third stage of selection is the interview, at the RSA, where a panel of leading textile designers, educators, and industrialists is assembled, appropriate to the end-use: weave, print, or knit. The RSA exercises its particular magic to persuade practitioners of the highest professional competence to volunteer for this work. These interviews take place over three days, with the membership of the panel changing according to the end-use. Any students attending one of these interviews, whatever the outcome, have the benefit of something resembling a master-class tutorial on their work and career aspirations.

5.1.4 Host-company Selection

Throughout this selection process, the selectors are aware of the list of companies offering placements and are looking for students with talents and even personalities suitable to the places on offer. As one member of the core-group put it:

'We are looking not only at the work, but the mind behind the work; and then thinking *who* would appreciate *that* mind?'

Obviously, it is not possible to find a young designer who is perfectly suited to each and every one of the companies wishing to take part in the scheme every year, and some company applicants will be disappointed each time, just as many of the student applicants must be. However, it is equally obvious that the more companies that offer themselves as potential hosts, the wider the choice will be for the selectors and the more likely they will be to make successful matches. Initially, the policy agreed with the DTI restricted the selection of host companies to those that employ textile designers in manufacturing plants. With experience, this policy has been modified to permit the placing of graduates in design consultancies, which thus makes the benefit available to the trade at large. This policy is to be further widened in year three, to permit two or three small companies who, severally, cannot provide full-time employment for a designer, to be considered as joint hosts for a YDI graduate working within a design consultancy. Major retail groups that employ textile designers as selectors and product developers will also be eligible.

5.1.5 Host-company Interview

After selection by the RSA Textile Panel, the newly graduated students go for interview by the selected host company. At this stage, there is no commitment either way that the placement will follow. However, if the host company does not accept the graduate offered, it is very unlikely that an alternative will be found at that late date because the place on the scheme is occupied by the graduate, not the host company. The RSA has shown remarkable diligence in finding suitable hosts for any candidates rejected at this stage, but the commitment cannot be open-ended.

5.2 Monitoring

Once in post, the relationship between the newly graduated designer and the host company is that of employee and employer. The DTI contribution to the designer's salary is paid from the RSA to the host company, which is responsible for all normal on-costs. However, the RSA remains in contact with both parties, and three months into the placement will arrange a monitoring visit by a member of the core-group and an RSA staff member. Both the young designer and the responsible executive in the host company will be interviewed separately, and a series of formal questions will be put to both, to ensure that the full potential of the scheme is being realized. It has been established in practice that a monitoring visit, at this stage of the placement, is of great value to all parties, revealing how programmes can be modified to remove frustrations and accelerate the positive contribution a young designer can make.

6. WORK PERFORMED

A recent design conference in Manchester discussed the problems of training and employing textile designers, throughout a full day, without any significant mention of any prospective employment other than print design, despite the fact that the NEDO Report, which was the prime cause of the conference, defined textile design as

'a means of differentiating fabrics by means of printing, surface differences, texture, drape, varying types of finish, coloration, or any combination of the foregoing'.

YDI work experience has proved even more varied. During their first year in industry, 1985-86, YDI graduates have worked in the following areas:

fashion print design for U.K., Japan, U.S.A., and Italy;
floor, ceiling, and wall finishes and design;
co-ordinated textile and ceramic design;
retail merchandising;

47

part-time teaching of textile design;
home-furnishing prints for Marks & Spencer plc (M & S);
story-boards for presentation of fabric ranges to customers;
development of MICRODYNAMICS colour computer for print design;
printed wallpapers and co-ordinating textiles;
market-intelligence reports on trade fairs in U.S.A. and
  Europe;
developing a new knitwear fashion-forecasting service;
textile graphics for range presentations;
market research and forward-fashion presentations for IWS;
technical print production;
creating new upholstery ranges for U.S. contract furnishings;
presentation of new fabric ranges to new customers in U.S.A.;
designing knitted garments for M & S: negotiating with selectors;
presenting established ranges of fancy doubled yarns at overseas fair;
designing and developing new season's ranges of fancy doubled
  yarns;
developing existing woven upholstery fabrics for individual
  customers;
designing a new range of upholstery for the aircraft industry.

This list is fairly typical of the widening role being performed
in industry by the 500 or so graduates trained as textile designers in Britain each year. Increasingly, one finds qualified designers presenting their company's products to customers alongside their marketing colleagues, and simultaneously one observes
an increasing number of buyers or selectors in manufacturing and
retailing with a design background. This trend toward the employment of visually educated people in key positions controlling the
selection of textile products can only be good for the industry
worldwide.

7. COSTS

Total expenditure of public funds on YDI for the whole of the pilot year (which were inevitably inflated by the costs of publi-
cizing a totally new idea) averaged approximately £5700 per
graduate designer, *including* the contribution of 50% of salary.
The tuition cost of training a designer throughout a foundation
year and a three- or four-year degree course is estimated at between £15 000 and £18 000. The tuition cost of a further post-
graduate year is in excess of £4700 p.a. The further charge on
public funds to finance the YDI scheme not only obtains prompt
benefit from the initial investment but also encourages hesitant
manufacturers to make a commitment to improving the design and
development of their product. The DTI has stated throughout that
its funding is available only for the first five years, to set up
the scheme. Thereafter, both the administrative costs and the subsidy for the graduates' salary must be paid by industry, if the
scheme is to continue in its present form. Exploratory discussions
have commenced with representative textile trade organizations to
explore how this may be achieved.

8. CONCLUSION

The Young Designers into Industry scheme has had a successful first year in British textiles. This success is being repeated in the second year, which will be completed in September, 1987. Whereas the authors have no personal knowledge of similar schemes operating in other countries, they believe that there are universal lessons to be learned from this British experience. The principal elements contributing to the success of the YDI scheme are identified as:

(a) an abundance of talented students within the Design Colleges, whose creativity has been developed and focussed by their textile-design education;

(b) the thoughtful selection of undergraduate candidates by their tutors and heads of departments in the Colleges;

(c) careful enquiry at interview by a panel of experienced design practitioners, industrialists, and educators to elicit candidates' strengths and weaknesses;

(d) considerable understanding by the selection panel of the requirements of each placement, in terms not only of work to be performed, but also of personality requirements;

(e) subsidy from central funds for the first year's salary costs;

(f) caring supervision of the young designers by RSA staff, especially in the early days of the placement, to remedy personnel problems at source;

(g) formal monitoring of placements after a three-month settling-in period, to ensure that expectations of all parties are as far as possible realized; and

(h) formal review on completion of the placement, revealing to all parties the positive and negative lessons from each experience.

Attention will now be directed towards planning for the continuation of this valuable scheme once the setting-up period, funded by government, is past.

ACKNOWLEDGEMENTS

Thanks are due to:

the Design Section at the RSA for splendid support in the preparation of this paper, and particularly for the untiring efforts of Jacqui Hayler in pursuing all the YDI designers of year one, and their hosts, until all had written and submitted their reports;

Stephen Knox at UMIST for introducing the authors to the Doctoral Thesis by Dr A. Aggrey, 'The Role of the Designer in the British Textile Industry', which provided the context for much of the historical background.

REFERENCES

(1) British Parliamentary Papers: Report from Select Committee on Arts and Manufactures (Facsimile Reproduction), Irish University Press, 1970.

(2) G. Turnbull. 'A History of the Calico Printing Industry of Great Britain', John Sherratt & Son, 1951, p.152.

(3) C. Ashwin. 'Art Education - Documents and Policies 1768-1975', Society for Research into Higher Education,1975, p.111.

(4) National Advisory Council on Art Education Second Report. 'On the Structure of Art and Design Education in the FE Sector', 1962, p.60.

(5) A. Buxton. 'Textile Design: Education and Industry', Royal College of Art, 1985, p.1.

(6) A. Buxton. 'Textile Design: Education and Industry', Royal College of Art, 1985, p.33.

(7) A. Buxton. 'Textile Design: Education and Industry', Royal College of Art, 1985, p.1.

(8) The Confederation of British Wool Textiles Ltd: Industrial Relations Council. Report and Recommendations of a Steering Committee on 'The Training of Designers', 1984.

(9) 'Changing Needs and Relationships in the U.K. Apparel Fabric Market', NEDO, 1982.

(10) 'Structure and Prospects of the Finishing Sector', NEDO, 1983.

(11) 'Designing for Success - Approaches to Managing Textile Design', NEDO, 1984.

Hunters Moon,
Dartington,
Totnes,
Devon,
England.

Leaders and Risktakers: Choosing the Unbeaten Path

G. Cooke and T. Altham

1. PART I

Risktaking is defined by Webster's Dictionary as 'taking the
chance of injury, damage or loss'. This brief presentation focusses on the concept that one cannot be a leader without being a
risktaker, and therefore being susceptible to injury, damage, and
loss. Inherent to the viability of a successful company - or
leader - is the element of risktaking. 'Maintaining the status
quo' is no longer a satisfactory or even viable method to sustain
growth - or even survival. The Macy's N.Y. Department Store in
1975 took a *risk* by throwing out an existing $40 million budget-
store business and replacing it with an up-scale lifestyle concept. Just two years before that, the *Wall Street Journal* had referred to Macy's Herald Square as 'the great white elephant doomed
to extinction'. Ed Finkelstein was a risktaker - and a successful
leader - and now, ten years after The Cellar was introduced, his
leveraged buy-out attempt is proof of that achievement. The Gim-
bels Department Store - on the other hand - maintained the status
quo, took no risks, and today is either going out of business or
being sold.

My company - Bloomingdale's - has, over the years, had the
reputation of being an innovator - of taking a chance - of being
the first to experiment or introduce something. Whether it be a
concept as crazy as the pet rock - or frozen ice from the Arctic -
or the introduction of an unknown tie designer from the Bronx
named Ralph Lipschitz (later to change his name to Lauren), Bloomingdale's is either dedicated enough - or crazy enough - to believe in a concept and run with it. We definitely believe in
'change for change's sake' and are obviously not afraid of suffer-
ing some failures in our efforts to be the best.

But even Bloomingdale's cannot go it alone: we are dependent
on the support - and the success - of our merchandising resources
and creative partners. To be a leader and risktaker, it is not
only very helpful but also essential to be in the company of other
leaders and risktakers.

In April, 1981, Marvin Traub, the Chairman of Bloomingdale's,

---

* Part I of the paper is by Gordon Cooke, Part II by Terence
Altham.

and myself were fortunate enough to be in Paris together to see an audio-visual presentation to the entire AMC buying organization by the International Wool Secretariat. The audio-visual was themed around the concept of French designers talking about their design techniques, their latest collections, and, of course - if they just 'happened' to mention it - their utilization of wool in the production of their garments. As only Marvin Traub would choreograph it, within one day we had the IWS fly over the marketing head of Womenswear from London and had initiated the concept of a joint promotion of international designers utilizing television for the Fall of 1981. Never before had any retail store in the United States attempted to promote regular-price designer RTW through television.

The International Wool Secretariat combined with Bloomingdale's and our vendors to support a series of eight separate international-designer television commercials featuring such names as Nina Ricci, Christian Dior, Anne Klein, Bill Blass, Jean Cacharel, and Kenzo. These commercials were filmed on location in Ireland, France, and the U.S.A. by Art Kane.

The creative conceptualization of these commercials was based on the IWS audio-visual we had seen in Paris and, in effect, had eight of the top international designers appearing on camera, commercially, and endorsing the qualities of wool.

In 1983, we once again approached the International Wool Secretariat to see if they would join us in our storewide Fête de France promotion. This time we wanted to concentrate not as much on the designers as on the clothing and thereby the qualities and subtleties of wool. We produced seven individual commercials on location in France by utilizing fashion photographer Jimmy Moore. A further innovation of this French promotion was to obtain the co-operation of Galeries Lafayette to present their Annual Festival de Mode within a Galeries Lafayette Department at Bloomingdale's. This brought together two great names under the emblems of the Eiffel Tower and the Statue of Liberty, another example of a marketing initiative with great style.

Not only were these commercials highly acclaimed for their creative excellence, but they also cemented the relationship of these top designers with both Bloomingdale's and the IWS. In fact, Bloomingdale's was able to convince both Kenzo and Sonia Rykiel to become Woolmark licensees in order to participate in these initial campaigns.

The creative excellence of the spots described was accomplished because of the great trust and co-operation between the various executives of both the IWS and Bloomingdale's. These commercials did not fit any pre-established guidelines and involved risks for both our companies. The monetary investment was significant, and the relationship with the designers of the world - most of whom were participating in their first television commercial ever - was on the line.

With two success stories behind us, we approached the IWS in 1985 with our most imaginative concept to date. To coincide with our Fall Ecco L'Italia promotion, we wanted to produce, in effect, a 60-second 'film' featuring five Italian designers. We presented this concept with the purpose of keeping Bloomingdale's and the IWS in the forefront and leadership position in the fashion-apparel industry. The reaction of the IWS was quick and simple: they said 'let's do it!'

This 60-second commercial won the NRMA's Best Retail Commercial of the Year and the Retail Advertising Conference Best Commercial of the Year and is a finalist for the Video Fashion Industry's award as Best Retail Commercial of the Year. Obviously, both the IWS and Bloomingdale's feel their investment in leadership and risktaking has paid off.

An extremely important ingredient to both the feasibility and success of many of the broadcast campaigns described above is the commitment and co-operation of both our partners and our resources.

The television spots featuring some of the world's foremost designers could not have been produced without the financial, organizational, and creative support of the IWS. Whereas the substantial financial investment may not have been justified *solely* by the next-day-sales results, I can assure you that the association of the IWS and Bloomingdale's with such designers as Kenzo, Cacharel, Sonya Rykiel, Chloe, and Christian Dior has helped maintain and solidify our mutual leadership positions. The long-term growth and market-positioning of companies such as Bloomingdale's relies greatly on the degree to which we can differentiate ourselves from our competitors through unique and innovative marketing techniques – in effect, through risktaking – and these commercials are only one example of how Bloomingdale's and the IWS have accomplished that distinction through their willingness to take a well-co-ordinated but untested step.

2. PART II

Now that is the past – what of the way forward and new ideas? I would like to tell you briefly of a recent design project, which also falls into the bracket of leadership and risktaking.

The IWS was approached by the Royal College of Art with a request to help the College celebrate its 150th birthday. Knowing of its high reputation in fashion design, we agreed to support it if it would participate with us in a totally commercial project. A collection for Autumn 1987 was designed by ten final-year students in close co-operation with the manufacturer, Stephen Marks of London. A showroom was built within the exhibition area of the College, and the IWS invited five leading international retail stores to see the collection when they visited Europe at the buying period.

The stores were Au Printemps (Paris), Bergdorf Goodman (New York), Harvey Nichols (London), La Rinascente (Milan), and Seibu (Tokyo).

They all came and were so impressed with the creativity and commercialism of the project that, not only did they buy, but all of them will also promote this story jointly with IWS for Winter 1987.

This design project has been extensively reported in both the trade and the national press. A video film was produced by the BBC for its weekly fashion report entitled 'The Clothes Show'. This story was screened at an important viewing time to more than eight million viewers.

I hope these examples of innovative and professional risktaking will stimulate some interesting discussion and consideration, both at the Conference and in later consideration of design and marketing strategy.

(GC) Bloomingdale's,
Third Avenue,
New York,
N.Y.,
U.S.A.

(TA) International Wool Secretariat,
Wool House,
London SW1,
England.

Note: This paper was illustrated by six television commercial films, five of 30 seconds and one of 60 seconds, and by a video film from the BBC programme 'The Clothes Show'.

Marketing and Controlling an International Designer Brand

J. Cousin

Abstract

The growth of the Daniel Hechter company reflects very closely the post-war development of the fashion industry. After the shortages of the War came the 1950s with their need to produce goods at all costs: the 1960s and the explosion of creativity, giving way to the more mature 1970s, where consumers were introduced to a more 'aesthetic' product, which attempted to achieve a harmony of colour, material, and shape. However, this 'aesthetic ideal' soon became jaded in the 1980s, and now something new is needed to give impetus to the fashion industry and push it beyond its normal boundaries. Perhaps this force is a concept for living, an attempt to create a more balanced environment in which to exist. Indeed, the 1990s will be the decade in which, at the end of the century, the consumer will be given an opportunity really to learn about the new art of living.

1. THE HISTORY OF DANIEL HECHTER

Daniel Hechter himself is a man of many parts, a leader and also a team worker, full of creative ideas and a consuming passion to succeed in major projects. The company was founded in 1962 with $3000. Today, 25 years later, it creates products for many different fields: ready-to-wear for men and women, sportswear, accessories, furniture, general household goods, and items for the office, for which a whole new range of design concepts is being developed. In 1986 Daniel Hechter had a turnover, at wholesale prices, of U.S.$330 million, with a growth rate of 20% per year. The company works with 120 licensees throughout the world and has 80 Daniel Hechter shops in Europe already. In the next four years, it is planned to increase this to 300 units. There are three main centres of activity for the company: Europe as a whole, North America, and the Far East, including Japan, in all of which the company maintains offices. The current good health of the company worldwide lies not only in its history and reputation but also in the strength of the design concepts that it launches onto the market.

55

2. THE MARKETING OF FASHION

2.1 Historic View

The textile sector is a comparative newcomer to the concept of marketing - twenty years later than consumer durables. For practical purposes, 1975 is probably the date when fashion discovered the marketing mix and its five major aspects:

name,
product,
price,
distribution, and
usage.

It started to become aware that an understanding and simultaneous balancing of all five were indispensable in the launch of a new product.

2.2 Educating the Consumer

During the last forty years, the way in which people in developed countries dress themselves has changed enormously:

clothes are much more responsive to the function they are asked to perform (to be warm, to be cool, to be washable);

clothes often co-ordinate and create a logical blend, such as shirts and trousers, for instance;

consumers now expect to be able to add a wide range of accessories, so that they can extend a total image, even as far as their home, where already they purchase the Daniel Hechter style in furniture, tableware, ceramics, etc.

If a consumer liked a certain style, he or she could firstly group a few objects and next redecorate a whole room and eventually the whole house. The same is already beginning to happen in offices, rooms in which so many of us spend a great deal of time. Without being really aware of it, the consumer may find himself in more and more of a homogeneous environment, quite different from his current way of life, and maybe a global concept is born.

2.3 Daniel Hechter: Passing from Ready-to-wear Clothing towards the New Style - a Total Concept in Fashion Living

The technical developments in communications are forcing fashion to become worldwide in its approach, because a worldwide consumer has appeared. It is no longer important whether this consumer is Japanese, European, or American; personality, purchasing motivation, habits, and fashion needs are more and more the same. It is therefore important to look on the developed world as one global 'whole' market, with a homogeneous concept of living. The new consumer has become jaded with just 'products'; he or she wants to buy products that conjure up global images that excite and convey an invitation to be part of a bigger universe. There is no longer any fashion left in just clothes - the new way is for fashion to be in everything. Daniel Hechter has stayed close

to this evolution, and the diversification of his products has
helped him to create a wealth of understanding between himself
and his consumers. It is a very modern concept, where the products, both innovative and expected, all with an active, sportive
style, mixed together in both the middle- and upper-price brack-
ets, are now sold successfully through the company's own shops;
retail outlets specially arranged by its licensees; and highly
selected speciality shops for men, women, children, sportswear,
and the home.

3. THE LICENSEE: FIRST OF ALL - A PARTNER

3.1 The Control of Policies and Reciprocal Strategies

Firstly, a prospective licensee must study the relationship between his existing brands and those of the licensor to ensure
that it is complementary, if he is to increase his market share.
If so, this means that the licensor will have confidence that his
trademark, his property, will be given a fair chance of success.
It is also important that there is a complementary blend of
skills, with the licensor supplying 'the label', his design flair
for concepts and products, his pricing policy, and his views on
distribution and performance, and the other party supplying his
technology, his production systems, and his knowledge of local
market conditions. Together they will be able to form a strategy
plan and create the best marketing mix. It is the only solution
for picking the right market-positioning and a successful launch
for the product.

3.2 Controlling the Product

The following are the vital steps in the control process:

    planning the collection;
    setting the timing;
    punctual supply of the creative work from licensor to
     licensee; and
    suitably rapid response back from licensee to licensor with
     the prototypes to allow for the house to modify, accessorize,
     and elaborate on the original collection.

3.3 Controlling the Price Structure

The company sets the optimum retail-price points, which are
decided on jointly with its licensees.

3.4 Controlling the Distribution

In the case of the opening of a Daniel Hechter retail shop, the
licensor is duty bound to supply this licensee with the best
information from his experience so that he can:

    site the shop in the most suitable area;
    be able to shopfit the site externally and internally
     according to the plans drawn up by the house architect;
    set up standard management systems;

57

set up staff-training programmes; and
create an effective local-advertising and public-relations
campaign.

The acceptance of such help makes for easier control, when it is
seen by the licensee, not as an interference with his approach,
but as confirmation.

3.5 Controlling the Communication of the Image

The company's main house retains its own independent and qualified public-relations consultancy in each country, which looks
after and promotes its image as it sees it itself and specifies.
In major markets, such as the U.S.A. and Japan, its own offices
in New York and Tokyo carry out this function as well as looking
after the commercial logistics of the licensing programme.

S.I.P.C. Daniel Hechter,
Hoche,
Paris,
France.

Criticism is Easy, but Art is Difficult:

A Nutshell Recipe for Combining Productive Design with Enlightened Technology in the Textile Marketplace

R.A. Donaldson

Abstract

The role and function of the textile designer/stylist in industry are enacted through a complex and diverse sequence of interrelationships and fast-paced interactions, not all of which are well understood, especially by the participants themselves.

If, as it has been stated, 'Art is a lie which points the way to the truth', then this paper may offer some reaffirmation of, or pointers towards, that important end!

1. THE NATURE AND FUNCTION OF DESIGN

The word 'design' is one of the most frequently used, yet least-understood, words in the English vocabulary, and therein lies a great deal of the cause of our anxiety in interpreting the role and function of the designer in the industrial setting. The old adage: 'Give a dog a bad name ...' applies most aptly in this case. Thus tagged, many designers are viewed by other agents of industry as nothing more than 'Cloud-9' artists whose sole ability lies in the realms of dreaming up glorified, two-dimensional finger paintings that the educated technologists have great difficulty in interpreting for production. Nor are such myopic interpretations encountered solely in the industrial domain, for academic institutions worldwide provide a perfect culture medium for the growth of this perfidy.

1.1 Design and the Human Perspective

In his book, 'Design Matters', Bernat Klein makes the following eloquent statement:

> 'The thesis of design is the physical world as we know it – people and their environment as they are and as they could be, with greater advantages all round. It is the attempt at the reconciliation of what we want with what we have; but more, it means making the best of what we have!'

1.2 The Nature of Design

Consider the following.

59

A mode of thought.
A scheme/plan.
Art with limitations.
The science of art?
An interdisciplinary science (in which designers are experts).
A catalyst!

The above brief summary indicates that the profession of design is non-specific but is goal-oriented and attitudinal in its process. Above all, design is the great catalyst; it is the canny science that makes ideas become reality, when they have been viewed from every perspective.

1.3 Design Begins with a Need

There are two types of need that may be identified:

(a) a need to fill some vacuum - call it *marketing*;
(b) a need to change or add to existing products - call it *sales*.

These highly simplified statements deal with the High Street world beyond the studio doors. This is the real world of the designer, and these needs must be recognized and reconciled.

1.4 Design is Performance Plus Aesthetics

Whole design, simply stated, is: the selection of the right materials and shaping of them to meet the needs of function and aesthetics, within the limitations of the available means of production.

Key words and phrases to consider are: selection, right materials, shaping, needs, function, aesthetics, limitations, available means of production - in other words, deliberate, purposeful planning! But many a competent person could accomplish the above objectives without necessarily being a professional designer. What is the key to the true designer's success? The key is the ability to understand people. People are any designer's greatest limitation: their likes and dislikes, their wants and needs, their emotions. People are the most unpredictable creatures on earth, but this is the very essence that makes the design profession so infinitely challenging and never-ending.

1.5 Design is for Other People!

1.6 Enlightened Design Adds to Ordinary Competence in Invention (Churchill)

Why? Design is often thought of as being merely a function of colour and pattern. However, this is certainly not the case, as is illustrated by the following list promulgated by the Council of Industrial Design in 1964. It presents nine aspects of good design in the 'engineering' of a consumer product:

(i) new concepts - satisfying the creative nature of design and the need for change;

(ii)   safety - for all conditions of use and misuse;
(iii) cost reduction - without adverse effect on other needs;
(iv)   ease of use - for the satisfaction of human physical
       and mental requirements;
(v)   reliability - giving efficient performance for a
       foreseeable future;
(vi)   rationalization - product variations at minimum cost;
(vii) ease of maintenance - keeping the product serviceable;
(viii) size reduction - for improved ease of handling and
       comfort; and
(ix)   good appearance - as an aid to sales, to better envir-
       onment, and to convey a feeling of well-being.

Ultimately, good design requires the integration of all of the
above factors. When one is looking at a product in relation to
any one aspect, all other considerations should be borne in mind.
This is the designer's job. In summary, a well-designed product
should be:

easy to make,
easy to use,
easy to look at, and
easy to buy.

So, the next time somebody suggests that design is a purely subjective quest of self-gratification, turn to this list, for it is
highly relevant in virtually every field of design work and projects the profession as a truly interdisciplinary science.

1.7 Good Design Saves; Good Design Pays

From the foregoing paragraph, we see that we should be able to
save time and money through rationalization of materials and a
well-planned approach to production and sales. As the people of
the Bauhaus would say, 'True simplicity tends towards sophistication'. But why should so-called good design be more expensive?
On the other hand, a primary skill of any professional designer
is to *add value* to the created product so that it will command
greatly increased value-in-exchange. In this opening section, it
is fitting to close with a most relevant quotation from John
Stuart Mill:

'That a thing may have value-in-exchange, two conditions
are necessary. It must be of some use; that is, it must have
a capacity to satisfy a desire or serve a useful purpose ...
but, secondly, there must be some difficulty in its attain-
ment.'

2. THE NATURE AND FUNCTION OF TEXTILE DESIGN

In the introductory section, we have had a brief look at the complex nature of design through an examination of design theory.
How, then, does this relate to the everyday practice of design in
textiles, and how might the various tasks and relationships be
better understood with advantages all around?

61

2.1 The Profession of Textile Design

The profession of textile design is concerned with the integration
of performance plus aesthetics in the manufacture of textile products. It involves the selection of the right material and its
skilful manipulation to meet the needs of function and appearance
within the constraints imposed by the available means of production. Textile designers must be aware of consumer requirements
and market influences. Above all, they must have 'flair', and, in
their work, they should not let themselves be limited by current
knowledge alone, but should constantly seek to develop new ideas.
As well as being artistically inclined, therefore, a good textile
designer must also be fully conversant with the economic and mana-
gerial aspects of the profession.

But it is not a matter of simply seeking out or creating/edu-
cating the new 'Renaissance Man', that extraordinarily complex
hybrid espousing both aesthetic sensitivity and techno-economic
savoir-faire, which is what I seem to propose as the ultimate
solution. After all, humans, through a variety of internal and
external reasons and societal pressures, are quite clearly divided
into two, almost mutually exclusive, camps in this industrial,
high-tech age: 'artists' and 'technologists' or, more simplisti-
cally, 'those who cannot' and 'those who can'!

This is certainly no new phenomenon. For as long as we have
lived in the machine age, the wiser ones in our midst have been
calling for a new breed of artist/craftsman, the person who could
bridge the gap between art and industry in an effective way. I
myself was the product of such an educational programme, which,
in the early 1960s, was unique for its time. As I wrote in 1976:

> 'The polarization of technological design and aesthetic de-
> sign in textiles is a bad thing and is mutually self-defeating.
> We do not need more and more of these same people, we need the
> person who can cope with and understand both technical and
> aesthetic aspects and, at a managerial, decision-making level,
> the "go commercial" level. There are too many "ideas men" and
> plenty of mill superintendents, but not enough total textile
> designers in this higher role, discharging their efforts with
> flair and over-all competency.'

2.2 Understanding the Designer and the Stylist

In the United States, where the mills have always tended to be
out in the provinces and rather remote from the large merchandising centres, the bipartite professions of designer and stylist
grew up. Their position, with respect to the textile-fabric industry, can be summarized as detailed below.

2.2.1 *Stylist: 'A Walking Wound Getting Infected Everywhere It Goes'*

The stylist is, first and foremost, an investigative reporter. He/
she is generally market-based and closely aligned to sales, marketing, and the account books. The stylist keeps abreast of what
is happening in the marketplace, at home and overseas, and has

his/her finger constantly on the pulse of the consumer. This person is usually extrovertly inquisitive and literate, one who will know exactly what are the currently 'in' art-shows, plays, television 'soaps', etc. - whatever is going to influence new fads and early fashion trends. The stylist keeps abreast of pronouncements in trade magazines and news releases, new-product showings, and so on. He/she will very often purchase artwork from studios or from individuals at home or overseas and will be the authority whose responsibility it is to conjure up next season's colour lines, chair the fabric-range meetings, and generally upset the production people in the mill with new and impossible product ideas! The stylist will also work in close consonance with the vice-president of sales and marketing (if they are not one and the same person) to set price points for the sale of each fabric quality and will determine whether items are open-line or for special customers.

The senior stylist in a big company is generally not an artist or designer (in the true sense) himself. Others, with more specific talents, will be hired for special jobs or to add some fashionable handwriting to a product line. Big-name personalities or other promotional 'gimmicks' will quite often be bought and used to endorse a line of goods.

Ultimately, it is the stylist's head that is on the block as far as the success or failure of a season's lines goes. If a line fails, then he/she 'will be laid out in clover' as the tradesaying goes.

2.2.2 Designer: The Interpretative Craftsman

The designer's job, in the trade parlance, is a technical, interpretative one and is generally mill-based. It is the task of this person to be thoroughly conversant with all the mill's materials and production equipment. The designer will be responsible for making all the fabric-layout sheets and for supervising the manufacture of experimental production runs, new colorations, finishes, etc. The designer is also responsible for coming up with complete cost specifications for the styling and marketing/sales people, on all new designs. Once a line is adopted, he/she is then charged with making sure that all necessary raw materials and associated production products are procured, that all fabrics are produced exactly to specification in terms of construction, coloration, and finish, and that they are shipped on time.

The stylist is thus not the only person with a weight of responsibility!

This designer will not usually be a person of great artistic talent either but will be a key member of the production team, concerned only with the actual manufacture of the cloth. Traditionally, where this division between designer and stylist occurs, there is very little sensitive dialogue between the two parties. Each is very apt to blame the other for problems occurring in manufacture because neither fully comprehends the other's job.

The author, having operated in both capacities, has viewed the prevailing attitudes from both ends. The solution in most cases, it would seem, lies in a more integrated approach to the subjects of technology and aesthetics at an early stage. For example, an integrated approach could be introduced at the tertiary education- al level, where good habits learned would tend to remain more firmly embedded in the psyche.

The key is communication and a healthy mutual respect by each for the other, each being cognisant also of the environment in which the other works. No one person can be all things and do all things equally well. However, we must all be prepared to learn the vocabulary of our counterparts so that we may communicate more intelligently and thus engender greater mutual respect and lower the lingering distrust that remains. The artists will, undoubtedly, function best in their specialized field of aesthetics - line, shape, colour, texture, and pattern - whereas the technologists will be best able to make a given idea work. In integrating the two, we must beware of compromised-hybrids, i.e., Jacks of all trades and masters of none!

However, the 'aesthetic designer' should be made well aware, at an early stage, of the relevant technical limitations of ma- terials and machine and should also be aware of the economic con- straints, which always seem to come along like a bucket of cold water just when a great deal of effort has been put into some wonderful new idea.

If design is indeed art with limitations, then these are a few of the practical limitations that any 'aesthetic designer' or sty- list should be willing, if not required, to master - indeed, that is what being a true designer is all about.

Having pointed out the gulf that can and often does exist be- tween the designer and the stylist, particularly in the larger U.S. and European companies, where my main experience lies, I should not want it to be assumed automatically that these rela- tionships are all marred. Certainly not. Divisions between the two appear to be found mainly in the apparel-fabric sectors, where mills are, indeed, rather remote from the markets.

However, the home-furnishings operation tends to be quite dif- ferent, since that marketplace is generally not within the con- fines of a large city but, as in the case of the world's largest home-furnishing manufacturing area, North Carolina, is located in the relatively small communities of High Point and Hickory, with many of the large mills in the immediate neighbourhood. There are therefore fewer stylists employed in areas remote from the mills, and, very often, those that are are employed as retained consult- ants to the home-design/styling group, resident in the same loca- tion as the mill. Hence, in these and similar situations, the tie- in between the two professional areas is much more effective and highly resolved.

3. THE 'THREE-LEGGED STOOL' OF TEXTILE DESIGN

We have looked, in general terms, at the respective roles of the designer and stylist. The fact is that they *are* different people and do have different roles to play, each one as important as the other. How do we, therefore, cement a truly meaningful and pur-

poseful relationship under the guidance of a kindred spirit, and
not simply by adding to the already frantic burdens of a vice-
president of sales and marketing?

Enter the grand ombudsman: the design manager.

3.1 Design Management: The Third Leg of the Stool

The discipline of design management in textiles is the youngest
of the major design skills and is less than fifteen years old.

In the early 1970s, the author was fortunate in being able to
develop, with skilled industrial and academic assistance, the
first tertiary-education programme in this area: the B.Sc.
(Honours) degree in Textile Design and Design Management at
U.M.I.S.T. in Manchester. The premise was that, in the new industrial state of larger and more complex companies, design would
always tend to be regarded as some sort of an enigmatic 'add-on'
to enhance sales unless a corporate-level design policy could be
adopted, and this would only be possible as a function of top
management. Hence there was the need to educate a very rare type
of high-level person: the design manager.

To illustrate, most simply and clearly, how it can and should
work, I have used the 'three-legged-stool' analogy because, without three firm points, balance cannot be achieved, and balance between the three major functions of the design process is what is
required. Professor Jack Willock, former Group Design Director for
Courtaulds plc, develops what he calls the 'three worlds of design' in the form of a design triangle, in which the two base
points are labelled 'life' (the arts), and 'technology' (interpretative craftsmanship), and the apex is entitled 'business'
(design management).

The following is a quotation from Professor Willock.

'(a) "Life"
The behavioural world of "life" embraces human emotions and
responses to the environment, social change, culture, the arts,
and fashion. From these influences, the designer is inspired
to capture, respond to, or reflect the mood of the times. This
world is a strong feature of design teaching, and especially
so in art schools.

'(b) Technology
The technology world ranges widely from the low end, with
simple tools and the crafts, through to the higher technologies with sophisticated equipment and on into the sciences,
computers, micro-electronics, etc. In educational institutions,
contact with this world is developed where there are both access to and understanding of the technology involved. Production and manufacturing methods, being a main feature, require
a strong mutual commitment between industry and education.
Summertime industrial placement for students plays an important role.

'(c) *Business*
The world of business covers trade, commerce, merchandising,
marketing, and distribution. Money in all its nuances, whether
on paper or in-hand cash, is a strong feature of nearly all
aspects of it. It is the understanding of relationships between
design and business that is the least well-researched and explored of the three worlds. It is also the least covered in
design education but is now beginning to appear in various
guises, one of which is called design management, an inadequate description for the activities involved.'

3.2 'Life', Technology, Business

3.2.1 *'Life'*

This involves dealing with people: their wants, needs, buying
power, emotions, politics and religion, peer influences, arts and
entertainment, fashion and fad, and, perhaps most of all, television, the single most important influence on our lives today.

This then, is the world of the stylist, who has to be able to
instil all of the human factors into basic design elements, the
most powerful of which is colour.

The stylist should be acutely aware of all the subtle symbolism
of colour and its effect on human emotions. At the same time, he/
she must thoroughly understand the interaction of colour and the
effects of one colour upon another, especially when perceived
under different lighting, from a distance, or when moving, as in
a flowing dresscloth. To have to choose from the countless possibilities only those 'sixteen' special colours that will ultimately
be used to form a line is a daunting challenge.

The stylist will also be responsible for organizing the promotional items to be used in advertising. This will probably be done,
in part, in-house, and usually also with the skilled professional
help of an outside agency. Neatness, skilful layout, and strong
visual impact are of the essence.

The ultimate skill of the stylist, however, may lie in the
ability to deal with people from all walks of life, from uncertain
meanderers to irascible egotists. Above all, the stylist has to
exude confidence in his or her decisions about the coming season's
fashion and style trends. In the knowledge that the customer is
always right, the policy of diplomacy must ever be to the fore:
that of 'letting other people have your own way!' Very often in
this field, we are asked to produce designs of which we do not
wholeheartedly approve. Our art backgrounds tell us it is a compromise and that we should react against it. However, it soon becomes evident that the more important aspect of our efforts, as
industrial designers, lies in keeping the mill in operation and
in keeping our fellow-workers employed. Once we have shown that
we have the capacity to do this, and to gain the company's confidence, it is amazing what we can do 'to show 'em' when the opportunities crop up. 'Innovation (design)', it has been said,
'consists not in doing extraordinary things, but in doing things
extraordinarily well!' - which comes right back to our opening
statement about 'making the best of what we have'.

3.2.2 Technology

In the context of this discussion, technology deals with the conversion of ideas into products, and these ideas come down (or across?) from the stylist to the designer. The expression often favoured by Professor Jack Willock, 'interpretative craftsmanship' is an excellent one and sums up well the mill designer's task. For this task is not only one of acting upon instructions but should also be regarded as an equally exciting and creative endeavour in the chain of events of placing a new idea on the textile market. Innovation in production is as much a key to the success of a product as is the initial concept of the stylist or artist, and this is where communication between the two areas is so crucial. The 'interpretative craftsman', or designer in this context, will be thoroughly conversant with the properties of fibres and with yarn development, commodity or novelty - and, most importantly, with the costs involved, whether produced in-house or purchased.

The laying-out of manufacturing specifications and the subsequent production of prototype samples will fall under the designer's area of responsibility, as will the dye-matching of fabric swatches for the new season's colours and the production of basic fabric swatches based upon forwarded textural samples, so that a base-line price and performance quality can be established early in the process. These, and many other day-to-day logistical details, fall within the designer's scope.

The same is true at a print converter's, dealing this time with selections of print base-cloth, inks, colour separations, repeat-matching, etc., all to come as close as possible to the studio-artist's gouache rendering.

3.2.3 Business

Especially today, the business 'leg' of the trio is the most crucial, and it is in this area that we find the design manager, the ringmaster. The design manager's task is to set the parameters and to develop and implement an over-all strategy for the efficient operation of all units relating to the design process. This person has to be the receiver and digester of many briefs, from both the styling/sales and production sectors. The design manager, in turn, will be required to develop a strong commitment to the company's major business objectives and be prepared to take the responsibility for change in these objectives as dictated by market fluctuations. This, in turn, infers a need for the creation of flexible production resources, so that a company might respond in the shortest time-frame to the needs of a changing market. A strong strategy is, of course, paramount in concert with the ethic that, to get ahead, *a progressive company must be in the business of making marketable goods and not merely trying to market makable goods!*

Financial-planning acumen will be the result of the design manager's strong background and sixth sense in economic affairs, commodity prices, consumer spending, national debt, interest rates, customer credit, government trade bills, overseas competition, etc., and the stock market, which, it is said, fluctuates in response to the current position of the hemline!

67

Whereas volumes have been written on the subject of design management in recent years, no magic formula has been developed for unlocking its special code nor, I suspect, will there be a specific handbook created in the foreseeable future. The education (or, perhaps better in this case, apprenticeship) of such people can only be half-accomplished within an academic institution. We can certainly introduce much more good economics and business groundwork into design curricula, provided that the theory is always backed up by illustrative and thoroughly demonstrative case studies – and these are rare, as yet.

And who might teach such an awesome new subject as design management in college or university? Scepticism that exists around this subject is centred less upon the nature of the subject and its undeniable importance to progress in our field than upon those who might teach it.

The key to successful design management is undoubtedly related to unlocking the supposed mysteries of the marketplace: people. And the earlier that aspiring young designers and stylists in the testile industry can be pushed out of their studio-classrooms and into the shopping malls and department stores, the better. They need to see what is being sold where, and for how much, and, most important, who is doing the buying! Yes, we must certainly continue to send our students to the art galleries and other centres of culture; that is implicit in the make-up of any worthy design education. We must encourage them to participate in industrial visits and in periods of extended work-study in the marketing/styling offices and in the mills. But let us not forget the High Street! A great deal is to be learned just from people watching people. As Henry Ford said, 'Sales begin on the drawing board'.

If, somehow, we could manage better to integrate the purist ideals of 'high art', where one must not become 'tainted' with commerce, with a better empathy for the needs of the masses, then we should all be better designers (in the broadest sense, inclusive of stylist). A good designer or design manager should be like a good shepherd. The shepherd does not bark around the heels of his flock, in the rear, nor does he race ahead, over hill and down dale, or else the flock will lose sight of him. The good designer, like a good shepherd should be constantly ahead of the masses, but not too far ahead, and drawing his flock along inexorably but in a mutually appreciative and understandable direction.

Continous exposure to marketing in all its facets, from haute couture to mail-order catalogues, is thus a primary prerequisite for the aspiring design manager. However, the design manager is also bound to have a plaque, secretly hidden away in the desk drawer, which proclaims, 'The only good design is one that sells!'. But then, assuming that the design manager really is in touch with particular markets and the price points prevailing therein, what is the problem with making the best possible design for that specific market? After all, good design transcends unreal values associated with specific price-tags.

Every management functionary, however naive and primitive in operation, knows that, unless a product can be sold for considerably more than the total cost of production, including all the ancillary overheads, then he/she will quickly become bankrupt.

68

Hence, for this reason, the design manager, as with every other member of the management team, must put the goal of financial solvency and, hopefully, ever-increasing profitability as the number one priority. After all, of what use is an exquisitely designed product if it commands no value-in-exchange.

The design manager, then, is the ultimate hybrid, being part stylist and part functional designer, as well as being master strategist. But, most of all, this person must come by way of the designing/styling roots to a corporate-level position of extreme sensitivity, shrewdness, and communicative skill. By the year 2000, I have no doubt that this position will have achieved a status of great respect and much clearer definition in all industry as today's trailblazers pave the way in education and in the field.

4. CAD/CAM AND THE DESIGNER

4.1 Computer-aided Design and Computer-aided Manufacture

The newest field of study and probably the greatest revolution in the textile-design function since the introduction of the jacquard loom in 1804, itself a fairly advanced form of mechanical computer, is that of computer-aided design (CAD) and computer-aided manufacture (CAM). Although we have been experimenting in this field for the past fifteen or twenty years, it is only within the past three years that CAD has truly come of age and is now recognized by everyone from craftspeople to corporations as an essential, everyday tool.

In the late 1960s and early 1970s, when prototype graphics instruments came on the scene, vast numbers of designers rebelled against the introduction of such a medium and claimed that it would do every bad thing from taking away creativity to making them all redundant. In fact, the more enlightened profession of today is able to see how the very reverse is true and how, in certain sectors, the computer is creating greater opportunities for designers than ever before, as on-shore manufacturing industries in the western world tend towards more high-tech service organizations, creating copious new product lines for manufacture in lower-cost countries.

But that, too, is only a temporary 'Band-aid', for the only real way ahead is to produce an excellent product!

It was unfortunate that the CAD/CAM insurgence of the early 1970s, when double-knits were flying high, was a boom-and-burst situation, which left a bad taste in many people's mouths. Now, we are on a fairly even keel and have almost everything at our fingertips.

Two years ago, we were awed at what the IBM PCjr could do with its tiny memory, low-resolution screen, and only dark and light variations of eight colours. Today, we expect prodigious desktop memory of up to 100 megabytes, or more; we are satisfied with no fewer than 1024 pixels of resolution per television screen, and it is such a pity that the now standard 16.7 million available colours do not include quite all of what we should be able to see.

69

Yes, and if we have to wait longer than 15 seconds for a multi-repeat pattern to appear on the screen (one repeat of which would have taken a good studio artist the better part of three days to execute just 24 months ago), we become restless and agitated because the machine is too slow!

Two years ago, decent hard-copy printouts on paper were virtually unknown. Today, at exorbitantly high cost, one can get high-quality screen image *and* printout. Even at moderate price levels, we can obtain an almost perfect illusion on the television screen on the one hand or we can get a bookplate-quality printout, with high colour-match accuracy but with a less-than-accurate screen image, on the other. In this latter case, the emphasis is placed upon programming a large colour inventory into the computer memory, obtaining a printout in the form of a colour catalogue, and matching the yarn colours directly against those already printed. Although a catalogue of some 2200 printed colours is no match for 16.7 million, at least the designer is guaranteed an accurate hard-copy document, rather than just a memory. For a little more money, it is possible to hook up a four-colour ink-jet printer, which will deliver, with great accuracy, over 200 000 different colours at the astounding resolution of 158 × 158 dots per square centimetre! This means that the designer today can afford to create novelty yarn effects, even stock-dye fibre blends, on the CRT screen at, say, eight pixels wide, type in a fabric construction, and still obtain an accurate hard-copy print at almost 20 ends and picks/cm (50 ends and picks/in.), if it is a woven fabric. About the only thing lacking in the quest for ultimate reality is the third dimension. Some of these new printers can actually print direct-to-fabric. So where do we go next?

4.2 What CAD/CAM Means to the Design Process

How does all this affect the role and function of the designer/stylist/design manager?

(i) QR, 'quick response', is the 'buzz-phrase', and that is certainly accepted, not only in the area of graphics, but also in all of the associated areas, such as computer-spreadsheet costing, which is instantaneous. The designer/stylist can cost while creating.

(ii) QV, 'quick variety', is surely a novelty for any designer/stylist. No more putting the same old 'hack' colours together just because you are afraid to take a chance at something new and untried. In an instant, colours can be swapped or substituted, new pattern effects loaded, different structural effects keyed in, and so on. But the QV begets a very real new need, and one very often alien to the designer's way of working.

(iii) That need is QD, for 'quick decisions'! One of the ironies of the new computer age is how much of our time computers consume. We can never leave them alone. We do not know when to quit.

(iv) Hence, more than ever before, *the new design process requires good editors*. This is another reason for advocating a strong background in aesthetics, for it is the true designer/

70

stylist who should make these decisions and not, as I have so
often seen in double-knit days, the local salesman!

(v) CE is cost effectiveness. We must never forget that our
final objective is to make cloth, not book prints - that the
CAD system is merely a sophisticated electronic paintbrush and
palette to enable us to develop more and better textile ideas
in much less time. It is not an end in itself. We can spend
relatively little or a great deal of money on different levels
of equipment sophistication, and against that has to be measured the cost of design staff, the QR advantages, the complexity and expense normally associated with the traditional execution of the final product, the cost of downtime and maintenance, and numerous other design-management decisions.

People, in many instances, have been hesitant to make purchases in recent years because of the initially high equipment
outlay. However, prices have fallen drastically, and performance has increased in proportion. There is probably a level-
ling-off very close at hand, and, when prices and performance
become more stable and predictable, there can be no stopping
the market. An equally sophisticated new breed of designer will
be needed, and many of them will be required.

(vi) J.I.T.: one could not take account of the role of computers in industry without alluding to the 'just-in-time' method
of manufacturing, in which we move towards the elimination of
all non-value-adding operations, equipment, and resources -
especially inventory. The implementation of J.I.T. philosophy
infers a thorough commitment to a strong marketing and product-
design strategy, not only in response to local market shifts,
but also on a global scale.

(vii) So we come back to communication, in grand style. Not
only is it possible now for the stylist in New York to be talking to the designer in the mill 500 miles away, and each to be
viewing the same design on a CRT screen and making, hopefully,
instant decisions, but the design manager can also be in similar communication with his counterpart in a huge mill in Taipei,
with a spinner in Yorkshire, with a printer in Como .... In
other words, GR is the new fact of life: global response, and
networking on a vast scale among stylist, designers, producers,
suppliers, merchandisers, etc., is possible.

This is why it is so critical that our 'three-legged stool' be
made to stand, and that mutual understanding and clear communication among co-operating agencies become ever more efficient.

North Carolina State University,
Raleigh,
N.C.,
U.S.A.

71

Design and the Future of Retailing

R.A. Fitch

1. INTRODUCTION

My experience over a wide range of retail projects - in fashion, furniture, and do-it-yourself - gives me a particular viewpoint concerning the importance of effective design in any successful contemporary retail formula. I shall try to demonstrate that design is an important, indeed essential, part of the retail mix, but I hope not to claim for it success it does not deserve, nor that design is an end in itself.

It does seem, however, that there is ample evidence to suggest that some retailers and their suppliers are missing market share, together with consumer loyalty, because they are failing to respond to, yet alone satisfy, the emotional, the subjective, what we might call the 'non-price', needs of their customers, those qualitative aspirations that a retailer's size, a manufacturer's investment in plant, or a product's price alone simply cannot satisfy.

2. CHANGE AND DESIGN

If the consumer is changing and if the market is changing, so too must the priorities of retailers and their suppliers change. To take advantage of today's marketplace, yet alone tomorrow's, all who would participate and operate in tomorrow's retail landscape must *want to change* - and to change with enthusiasm, for today's consumer measures change by quantum leaps rather than by cosmetic tinkerings. 'Change', as President Kennedy said, 'is the very stuff of life', and it has most certainly been the stuff of U.K. retailing in recent years. If the essence of this paper is about designing shops and stores of the future, what role is there for design in a changing retail landscape?

It can reasonably be said that shops, stores, and shopping centres in the future will fall into two categories: those that are successful and those that are not. Equally, it can be confidently assumed that those that are successful will have been 'designed'.

What then, is the essence of successful retail design? There are no doubt as many answers to that question as there are designers with clients! The Fitch approach, however, is centred on

knowledge. Only when we *know what to design* can we design successfully. Specifically, we need to know the following.

The customers. We must know and sympathetically interpret their
hopes and needs in order to serve fully their emerging aspirations.

The market. We must be aware of developing trends and emerging
opportunities so that our designs fully reflect the advantages
these changes present.

Society. Here we must understand the broad sweep of 'A Society
in Change' in order to benefit from society's changing attitude
towards design.

3. SOME IMPORTANT FACTORS

Market research enables us all to be aware of the statistics of
the marketplace. But what of some of the interpretive issues that
lie behind the statistics? There are five that call for special
consideration: children, health, quality of life, individuality,
and leisure.

3.1 Children

Children are the customers of tomorrow. They will use tomorrow
the shops and products we design today. This generation of children is the most visually aware and design-conscious ever. All
over the world, there is a preoccupation among the young with all
things *visual*, all things concerning *design*, and all things concerning *style*. There is more design in schools, and there are more
style and design magazines and more young people employed in de-
sign-related activities than ever before.

3.2 Health

This will be a preoccupation for future consumers, and it is not
only a matter of fitness. Health concern also gives rise to greater expectations of environment, of product information, of product
reliability, and the like.

3.3 Quality of Life

In all our recent research and experience, on a wide variety of
retail assignments, there is a particular (and increasingly consistent) trend that our customers are expressing, i.e., a substantial and significant shift by consumers, away from 'the need for
a better standard of living' to 'a demand for a better quality of
life'. This trend manifests itself in many ways, for example:

the consistent trading up by consumers (even among the less
affluent);

their demand for better quality;

their interest in environmental and product innovation; and

their rejection of sterile architecture, manifest in the U.K. by a wholesale rejection and subsequent destruction of high-rise apartment blocks.

In my view, no retail formula, indeed I go so far as to say no business formula, can be successful in the longer term if it does not wholeheartedly support our consumers' demands for a 'better quality of life'.

3.4 Individuality

This demand is demonstrated by a new kind of design-conscious consumerism. We find consistently in our research a new kind of individuality asserting itself. People increasingly cry 'Don't regiment me. Don't institutionalize me. Treat me as an individual'. One only has to observe personal fashion to see obvious examples of this. In other words, today's consumers take a more qualitative, more judgemental, more egocentric view. Our society will come to demand more and more to be treated as individuals, rather than as retail statistics.

3.5 Leisure

Increasingly, our consumers have available to them three valuable commodities:

more leisure time;

greater affluence and therefore more disposable income; and

greater mobility.

As people's use of their retail facilities begin to change - away from necessity and more towards discretion - design can help create a powerful interface between leisure and shopping. Retailers of all persuasions must use design to create shopping environments where people are happy to stay.

4. THE AIMS OF DESIGN IN RETAILING

Design deals in the issues that come closest to a human being's personal reality. Designing is about needs and desires. It is about social circumstances. It is about how far people can reach, bend, and see. Good design is about touching people in their hearts as well as in their pockets.

In retailing, designers must try to be expert in their clients' present and future markets in a way both broader and deeper than is possible through conventional market research in order to be knowledgeable about the realities of customer preference. We should be concerned with what people want rather than with simply what we can sell them.

From stores, those same people will demand more than just cheap prices. They are looking for *value*. Now, value has many dimensions, but, since 'lowest price' can belong to only one trader, everyone else must use the 'non-price factor' to express his version of value. In my view, non-price factors are to be found in this list:

environment;

intelligibility;

'stores are not just stores';

design as a resource;

design is practical.

4.1 Environment

The environment in retailing is as important as, indeed in some
markets more important than, the merchandise. One of Britain's
most important and successful retailers, Marcus Sieff, who led
Marks & Spencer for many years, used to say that he could sell
anything from a 'hole in the wall' as long as the merchandise was
right. In today's marketplace, I do not think he could, and I do
not think he would claim that he could.

Today, successful as they are, Marks & Spencer have discovered
the value dimension of the designed environment.

4.2 User-friendliness and Intelligibility

In today's complex retail world, design can unite the different
parts of a dispersed venture. Design can identify the venture as
a whole and act as a focus of its reputation as well as sharpen-
ing its impact in the marketplace. To do this, owners must treat
their customers in an adult way, whereas design must make stores
and merchandise presentation 'customer-friendly' and intelligible
in order to make them 'wantable'.

At Fitch, we never forget that, in a competitive democracy,
our customers and our clients have a choice. Neither do Brook-
stone in the U.S., where intelligibility has become a cult.

4.3 The Many Functions of Stores

We all know that it is relatively easy to gauge what customers
already like. What is more interesting, however, is to discover
what they *would* like once they were presented with fresh alternatives. The concept that stores are there only for shopping is, I
think, questionable. We find that people come to stores not just
to buy things but equally to be informed and entertained. Indeed,
in a recent survey in the U.S.A., it was discovered that 'to buy
something' was only sixth in a list of reasons given for being in
a shopping environment. More important reasons were to meet people,
to get ideas, to mix and mingle, and to be entertained. Covent
Garden in London - once derelict - is now a shopping Mecca, but
not only for the shops: it is a total entertainment!

4.4 Design as a Resource

The U.K. Prime Minister is an active design supporter. She knows
that, in the best companies, design resources are managed with all
the seriousness shown to marketing or finance. I know a company

that has a design director but no property director and another
that has several property people but no design champion. Both
firms do badly.

4.5 Design as a Practicality

Last, but not least, design is practical. At Fitch, we believe
good and bad design to be not only matters of opinion; they can
and should be measured and accountable.

Other consultant inputs may deliver endless reports to a hard-
pressed retail management. The designer delivers a practical working, exciting, store that can create a sense of place and be a
physical manifestation of his clients' management philosophies.
Concorde looks the way it does for purely practical reasons, but
it tugs at the heart too.

5. DESIGN IN THE FUTURE

In the context of 'stores of the future', the design factor can
deliver in all the dimensions I have mentioned in helping to create a unique retail proposition. But it can also help in other
areas, wherein I believe lies success for retailers.

Assuming the maintenance of free trade and democracy, the retail marketplace will grow increasingly polarized and competitive.
To be a winner in this environment, the successful retailer will
need to engage design in the following areas:

  differentiation;

  focus;

  positioning;

  excitement and an experience;

  stores as brands; and

  competitiveness.

In explaining my views here, I have chosen some practical examples.

5.1 Differentiation

All the U.K. banks, with 6000 branches between them, look exactly
the same. Yet to distance oneself from the competition by product,
environment, and positioning is essential. Design is the outward
manifestation of this. It keenly expresses management's determination to set one business apart from the competition.

Midland Bank is, with my company's help, doing just this in
the U.K. Our new branches express the Midland's difference from
the other banks in the retail-banking market. They provide a mixture of 'high tech, high touch' and customers are flocking to
these new designer branches.

77

5.2 Focus

Focussed retailing is an example of how design can help position
retailers within a market sector.

The Burton Group are my company's oldest clients and among its
most design-aware clients. Since we started to work together in
1977, Burton have become the U.K.'s most successful apparel retailer with nearly 10% of market share. This has been achieved
by a commitment to focussed retailing, expressed by design:

Burton Menswear appeals to the age 25–40 market;

Top Man appeals to the age 20–30 market;

Top Shop appeals to the age 15–25 market; and

Principles, launched in 1983 to compete with Next, appeals
to the more mature of the 25–40 age-group.

Each attempts to make an unequivocal design statement within its
market sector.

5.3 Positioning

Repositioning design can help move customer perceptions, and this
is what we are doing with ASDA. ASDA is a North-of-England-based
food-retailing company. At one time, its reputation was based
solely on selling branded goods at the lowest prices. To expand
into the wealthier South of the country, in a changing, more
quality-conscious market, however, required not only new product
development but also a new image that would better convey ASDA's
cultural change.

Great progress has been made, not only in foodstuffs but also
in non-food products, and, as the traditional 'pile it high, sell
it cheap' philosophy of Europe's superstore operators gives way
to a more consumer-led approach, I forecast a growing market share
in textiles.

5.4 Excitement and an Experience

Shops and stores are more than simply places in which to buy. The
well-designed store should be an experience, and it should make a
positive contribution to our customers' well-being and lifestyle.
An example is Debenhams, one of the U.K.'s largest department-
store groups, acquired by our clients, the Burton Group, in 1985.
We shall refurbish the entire chain, covering over $4\frac{1}{2}$ million ft^2,
over the next two or three years. Our brief is to make the stores
more efficient, more convenient, more exciting, and more glamorous
places in which to shop.

5.5 Stores as Brands

Strong retail brands are powerful factors in the shopping experience. Design can help support the brand.

I like to think of stores, not just as so much property, but as brands that need constant support to keep their reputations high. In a recent survey in the U.K., we attempted to identify some of the brands that were most 'front-of-mind' among a wide range of consumers. It was not surprising to discover that four of our leading retailers were in the top ten best brands.

This is a powerful position. Brand reputation is all a retailer really has. Consistently pursued good design can carry that brand through any number of changes. It can be not only the physical but also the spiritual and intellectual framework for a retailer's corporate culture. Benetton is an international example of this. Who knows or cares where the factory is? This retail brand, like some packaged goods, transcends geographical boundaries.

5.6 Competitiveness

Design creates the non-price factors. Design is less helpful for the low-price retailer, but, since only one trader can adopt the 'lowest-price' position, other traders must service the 'non-price' factors in order to achieve competitiveness. This is where design plays a significant role.

The well-designed store endows a business, its owners, and its products with premium values. Equally importantly, that store's customers themselves become a part of this premium-value relationship, creating self-respect and loyalty. Next is a good example of this. Its well-designed stores, selling good-value, co-ordinated merchandise, have, since their arrival on the U.K. scene in 1980, created a completely new self-awareness among the hitherto-ignored 'mature-fashion market'.

6. CONCLUSION

To conclude, one last dimension can be claimed for the design resource: Emotion. For too long, traders have thought only in numeracy terms - seldom have they thought from the heart. Too many buildings, too many stores, and too many developments deliberately try not to show open displays of emotion, wit, or humour. Popular taste and culture have been derided as vulgar by architects and critics alike. Perhaps that is why so many stores and other public places have in the recent past been built as 'temples to ordinariness'.

But this reserve must change, because increasingly today's more articulate customers, let alone tomorrow's, are looking for more than just price or comparative shopping. They are looking for pleasure, excitement, and hope. They are influenced by their hearts, their feelings, and their sensations, and design is the quickets way to the heart.

Design is a prime way of *communicating*. Design is sensory; people can touch it, feel it, experience it, criticize it. In other words, design 'talks' to people.

It is this communication with the customer, through the heart, through emotion, through the non-price factor, and through the establishment of a sense of place that is at the core of the designer's contribution to the stores of tomorrow.

Do not Best products, designed by James Wines, perfectly exemplify this emotional dimension to designed retailing? These humorous shopfronts appeal to people's hearts. They endow their locations, the products, and Best's customers with premium values that make them reach for their cheque books.

Long may this situation continue!

Fitch & Co. plc,
London W.1.

Product Development in Tune with the Market

J.F. Graham

Abstract

The paper will illustrate how the International Wool Secretariat, as an international fibre company, utilizes its worldwide infor- mation-gathering resources to read the market. This information, backed by detailed market analysis and consumer studies, is a major influence in deciding product-development programmes.

In recognition of a rapidly changing environment and consumer lifestyles, IWS has integrated its fashion and technical resources to ensure the most effective development of new products in wool. By adopting a case-study approach, the paper will illustrate how these activities and resources have been brought together to launch the 'Cool Wool' Spring/Summer campaign and re-establish wool jersey as a leading fashion fabric.

1. INTRODUCTION

Under the heading 'The Challenge of the Market Place', the Confer- ence brochure stated: 'Everyone recognizes that the production-led approach to textile manufacture is a thing of the past. What fewer people are able to say with any certainty is how to succeed in always getting precisely the right product to the right market in the right quantity at the right price and at the right time, and to present it in the right way.'

It is true that the time has passed when companies were able to impose a limited range of products, which suited particular manufacturing capabilities, on the market. Successful organiza- tions have become increasingly aware that a detailed analysis of consumer requirements, based on their emerging lifestyles and the environment in which they live, must be used as inputs to decide product mixes for specific market segments and geographical areas. There is a general acceptance on the part of the manufacturing industry and the retail trade that a major investment needs to be made in such studies.

Much has already been said and written about the emerging con- sumers who wish to exercise individualism in the way they dress and, in fact, to demonstrate independence and a degree of personal leadership. It appears that the age of this category of consumers is not as important a factor as was considered to be the case in

81

earlier years; they will not necessarily be in their teens and twenties, but what they will have in common is an affinity for contemporary living.

Whether or not this category of consumer becomes the major influence on the market is, of course, an important consideration but what is of more relevance in the first instance is the fact that he or she has been identified as both a specific influence and a specific target.

2. READING THE MARKET

This paper will attempt, firstly, to illustrate how the IWS, as an international fibre company, utilizes its worldwide information-gathering resources to read the market and to try to gain a clearer understanding of the expectancies of the various categories of consumers both emerging and traditional. Secondly, it will show how this intelligence, backed by an in-depth assessment of fashion trends and technological advances, is used to point the direction for research-and-development and product-development programmes that complement marketing opportunities.

3. IWS ORGANIZATION

Through its centrally co-ordinated information-gathering network, IWS is able to call on the qualitative and quantitative assessments of geographic markets made by a wide range of specialists based in headquarters and branch offices in over 30 countries.

To gain a full understanding of the results of economic and political trends, both branch and headquarters economists must be able to predict the events that could have a bearing on consumer-purchasing power and on the ability of specific countries to import or export, and to compete in international markets, taking into account considerations such as currency fluctuation, which has been a major factor in trading during the 1980s.

Farmers and agricultural economists in the IWS member countries in the Southern Hemisphere are in a position to indicate the availability of raw-material supplies and the qualities and types of wool that will be available to meet the demands of specific seasons in the main manufacturing and consuming countries.

Consumer researchers, from their analysis of consumer-lifestyle trends, are able to comment on likely threats and opportunities for traditional products and identify potential growth areas.

Fashion specialists are positioned to predict the types of new products in terms of style and colour that will be required to meet consumer demands.

Technical specialists provide information on trends in manufacture, production capabilities in various countries, and problems that can arise through over- or under-production.

Constant contact with the retail trade allows early warning to be given of consumer trends and the kind of responses required to

ensure that the right type of product is available at the right
time.

Over 15 000 Woolmark licensees, located in over 30 countries
worldwide, provide valuable production data to assist IWS in formulating its marketing strategy.

4. THE IMPORTANCE OF MAKING CORRECT DECISIONS

Essentially, everyone who has been involved in forecasting or in
trying to analyse data, such as those just described, will be
aware that it is still possible to make decisions that fall well
short of the target, and the judgement used in trying to find the
balance for future product initiatives from such wide-ranging inputs is critical:

hard facts have to be balanced against 'gut feeling';

source bias has to be balanced against objective perspective;

personality has to be balanced against practicality; and

wishful thinking has to be balanced against realistic recom-
endations.

Again, as implied by the theme of the Conference, emphasis
must be placed on getting the right product to the market at the
right time. Knowing what to do is only part of the exercise; knowing when to do it is equally important.

The decision 'when to go' with a particular product mix can in
some measure be based on studies of fashion cycles, etc., but, in
the final analysis, 'gut feeling' has to play a major role. To
some extent, the international-marketing approach provides some
opportunity for minimizing the risk, since different markets may
be ready to accept the same product at different times. However,
the inescapable requirement is that the product must be well conceived and be capable of providing a high measure of consumer satisfaction.

Accepting that everyone is convinced that his analysis or idea
provides the formula for corporate success means that multi-disci-
plined corporate thinking and appreciation of each other's views
are the best safeguard for arriving at sound operational strategies.

Having laboured the importance of market data and its analysis,
I consider it is equally essential that the two sometimes-opposing
influences of fashion and technology are balanced in attempting to
make available to the market products that carry high consumer
appeal. Fashion-right, image-enhancing, aesthetically acceptable
products will only emerge from an operating environment in which
design and styling specialists are aware of technical opportunities and limitations and technical specialists are totally sympathetic to the needs of the designers and specialists.

It is recognized that, to compete in the current and future environment, we need innovation in both product and marketing strategies. We need to stimulate interest with exciting new products and
with new ways of presenting them to consumers. Several discerning

manufacturers demonstrated clearly during the recession of the late 1970s and early 1980s that, even in a low-growth total market, there are always growth segments. There is always potential for shrewd people with imagination to identify growth areas and to conceive products that will be successful in them.

With these factors in mind, IWS, in 1983, amalgamated its fashion and technical groups within one department. This bringing together of central technical, statistical, design, and marketing services is not merely 'window dressing'. It is a very positive move, essential to the task of identifying and developing the kind of products required to keep 'wool in tune with the market'.

Simply bringing specialists of different disciplines together does not mean that they will interact positively and productively: it is essential to create an environment in which personal relationships, shared commitments, and shared objectives are totally accepted. There is also no guarantee that all sectors of industry will simultaneously want to discuss new ideas, and this particularly applies in the case of wool, which is regarded as an expensive material with which to take risks.

It is for this reason that IWS services to industry start early in the product 'pipeline', that is, at the yarn stage. It has been recognized that innovation at the yarn stage provides the platform for a wider variety of exciting end-products. Our yarn forecasts for Spring/Summer and Autumn/Winter incorporate yarns developed by IWS alongside selected commercial yarns, which are considered to offer an exciting new dimension for the achievement of identified fashion directions.

Before turning to two exmaples to illustrate how IWS has identified and approached two market opportunities for wool, namely, the Spring/Summer market and jersey fabrics, it would perhaps be appropriate to review the market position of various end-product categories.

5. WOOL'S SHARE OF WORLD FIBRE PRODUCTION

Wool accounts for only 5% of global fibre production (Fig. 1), a share that has remained unchanged for the last ten years. However, its influence on the apparel industry in particular far exceeds this figure.

6. THE APPAREL MARKET FOR WOOL

Two-thirds of global wool consumption is contained in apparel end-uses (Fig. 2). Of the total apparel-wool consumption, womenswear accounts for just under one-third, menswear almost one-quarter and knitwear one-fifth; together, these three end-uses consume around 75% of total apparel wool (Fig. 3). The total fibre market in each of these end-uses grew rapidly in the 1970s, but the 1980s have seen much less change. The recession year of 1982 actually saw a contraction in the total fibre market but the improved demand at retail level during the last two years has more than compensated for this fall.

84

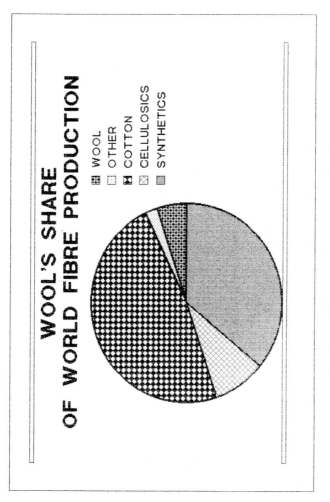

Fig. 1 Wool's share of world fibre production

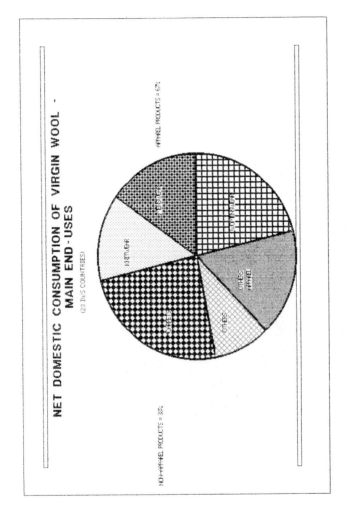

Fig. 2 Net domestic consumption of virgin wool: – main end-uses

86

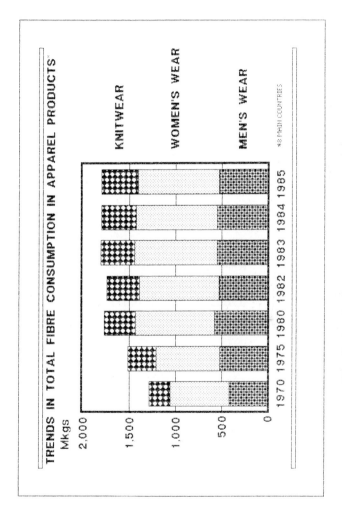

Fig. 3 Trends in total fibre consumption in
apparel products

87

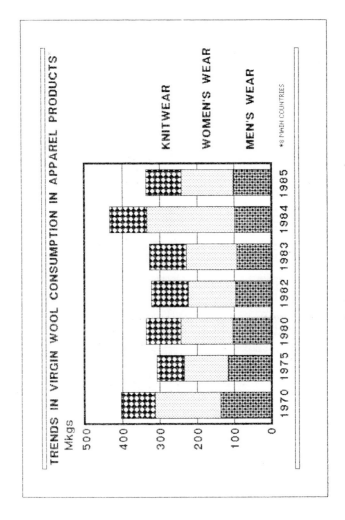

Fig. 4 Trends in virgin-wool consumption in apparel products

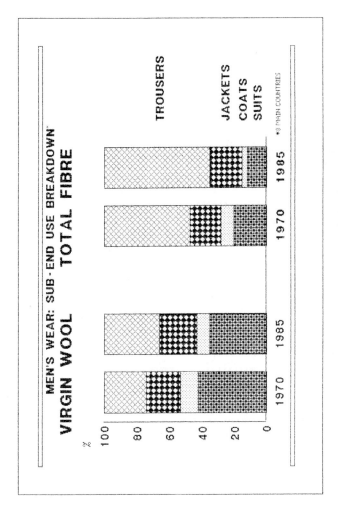

Fig. 5 Menswear: sub-end-use breakdown

89

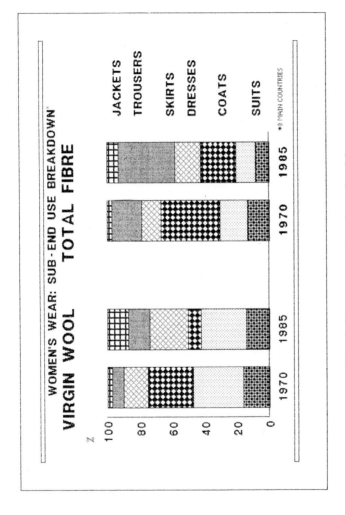

Fig. 6 Womenswear: sub-end-use breakdown

90

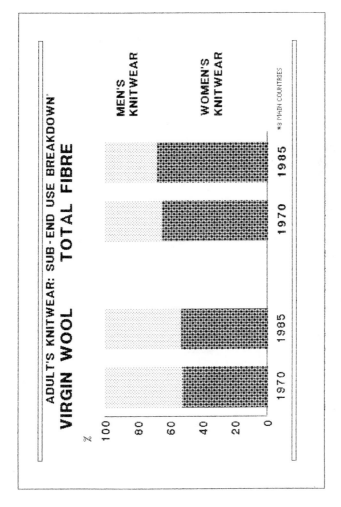

Fig. 7 Adults' knitwear: sub-end-use breakdown

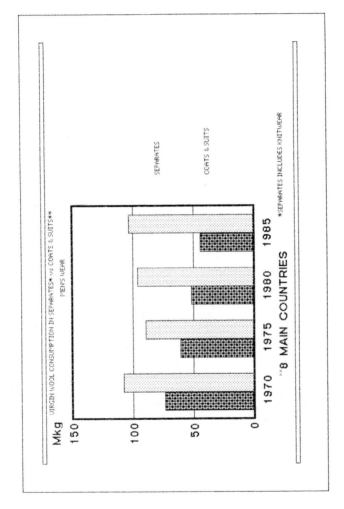

Fig. 8 Comparison of virgin-wool consumption in separates and in coats and suits: menswear

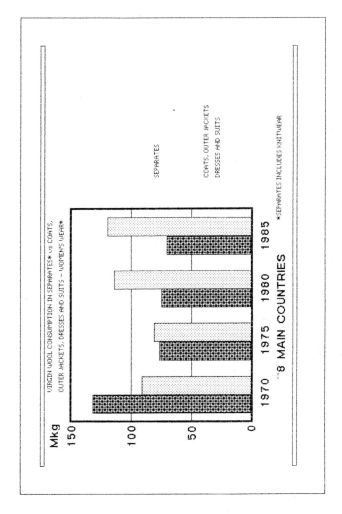

Fig. 9 Comparison of virgin-wool consumption
in separates and in coats, suits, and
dresses: womenswear

93

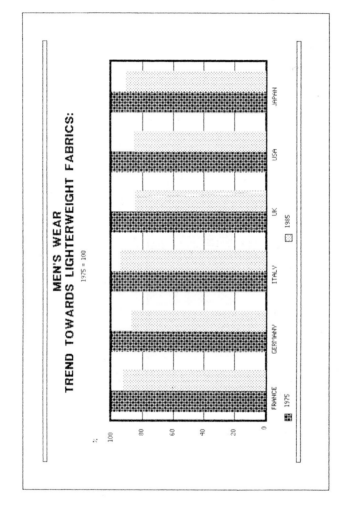

Fig. 10 Menswear: trends towards
lighter-weight fabrics

94

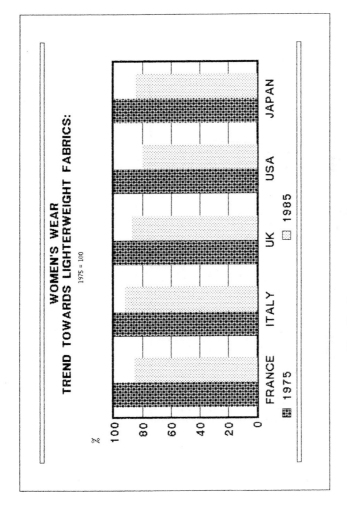

Fig. 11 Womenswear: trends towards
lighter-weight fabrics

95

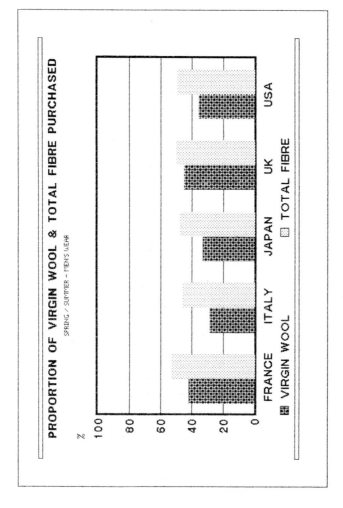

Fig. 12 Proportion of virgin wool and total fibre
purchased in Spring/Summer: menswear

96

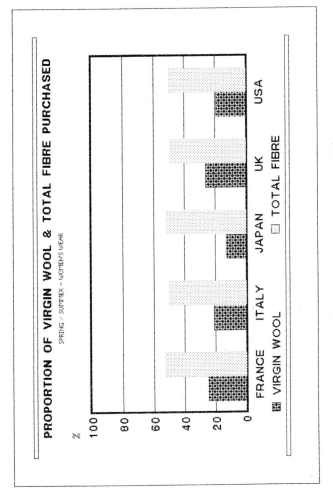

Fig. 13 Proportion of virgin wool and total fibre
purchased in Spring/Summer: womenswear

97

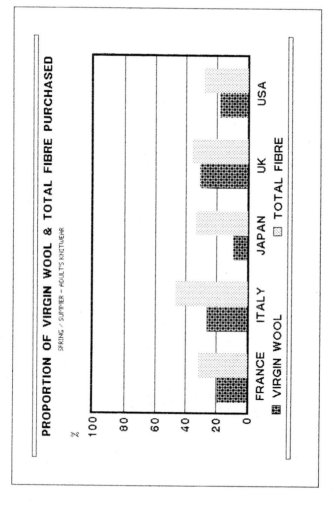

Fig. 14 Proportion of virgin wool and total fibre
purchased in Spring/Summer: adults' knitwear

98

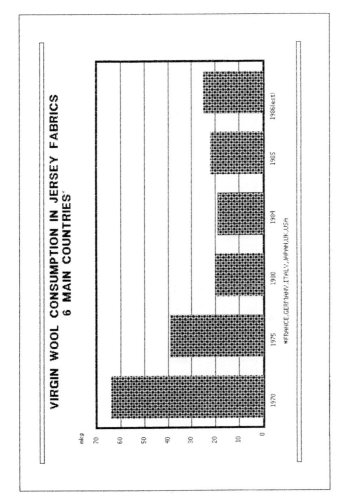

Fig. 15 Virgin-wool consumption in jersey fabrics
for six main countries

99

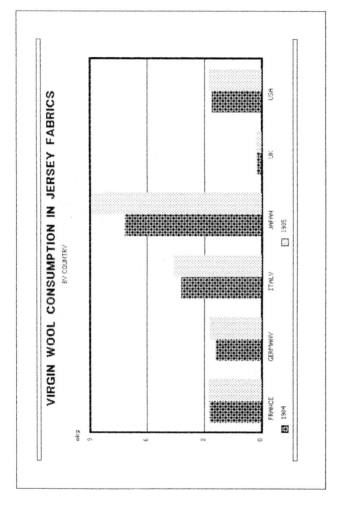

Fig. 16 Virgin-wool consumption in jersey fabrics
– by country

After the sharp fall in virgin-wool consumption in the mid-1970s, the situation has improved in both knitwear and womens-wear, with the latter now the most important apparel end-use for wool (Fig. 4). In the menswear market, consumption continued to fall until 1983, but the data for the last two years provide firm evidence that wool consumption in this end-use has passed its low point and is now gradually increasing. Suits are still the single most important end-use for wool consumption in menswear, although the once-dominant position of the classic, tailored business suit has been sharply eroded, and trousers now account for an increasingly large share (Fig. 5). On a total-fibre basis, trousers continue to account for the largest share and exceed consumption in the other three sub-end-uses combined. In total-volume terms, trousers have been the fastest-growing item.

In terms of virgin-wool consumption in womenswear, skirts and coats are of almost equal importance, and, whereas the volume of wool consumed in dresses has fallen sharply, on a total-fibre basis, trousers and dresses are the most important items (Fig. 6).

On a total-fibre basis, the knitwear market is dominated by women's sweaters, which account for just over two-thirds of the total market (Fig. 7). Men's knitwear accounts for just under one-third, a share that has marginally declined in recent years. In terms of virgin-wool consumption, however, the situation is very different. Here, wool's penetration of the men's knitwear market is higher than that of the women's market, with the result that virgin-wool consumption is fairly evenly divided between men's and women's products.

There has been a steady decline in wool consumption in suits and coats, which have traditionally been the two most important sub-end-uses for pure-wool consumption in menswear (Fig. 8). Whereas the more formal market has been declining, however, that for separates has been growing; the volume of wool consumed in jackets, trousers, and sweaters is now double that contained in suits and coats and is only marginally lower than the peak figure of 1970.

In womenswear, too, the situation is broadly similar. After a sharp decline at the beginning of the 1970s, wool consumption in the larger budget items of coats, dresses, and suits has been rather flat. At the same time, wool consumption in separates has grown strongly, so that the relative position of coats, suits, and dresses to separates in 1970 had been almost completely reversed by 1985 (Fig. 9). The separates market now accounts for a significantly larger share of virgin-wool consumption than the more traditional-type items.

7. WOOL FOR SPRING

In the Spring market for wool, the IWS information system provided the awareness of why IWS needed a strategy for lighter-weight outerwear. There was irrefutable evidence that manufacturers and consumers in all major markets were moving towards lighter fabric weights. During the last ten years or so, average menswear fabric weights have decreased substantially (Fig. 10). In Italy, where fabric weights were already lower than average, this trend is at least apparent, but in Germany, the U.K., and U.S.A., fabrics have decreased in weight by around 15%. In womenswear, too, fabrics have become lighter, though here the degree of variation is somewhat greater than that in menswear (Fig. 11). In the U.S.A., for example, fabrics are now around 20% lighter than they were ten years ago, whereas in Italy, which again started from a lower base, the fall has been only around 8%.

Our decision to adopt a Spring/Summer marketing programme was strongly influenced by the fact that, in the menswear market, whereas around 50% of total fibre purchases are made in the Spring/Summer season, wool's share is generally much lower. In Japan and Italy, for example, only around one-third of wool purchases are made in the Spring/Summer season (Fig. 12). In womenswear, the situation is more extreme. Again on a total-fibre basis, around 50% of purchases are made in Spring/Summer. For wool, however, the situation is even less satisfactory than it is for menswear. In Japan, only 13% of wool purchases are made in the Spring/Summer season, and even in the U.K. and France this proportion rises to only a quarter (Fig. 13).

In knitwear, the situation is more variable, though here too wool is generally under-represented in the Spring/Summer season. With the exception of Italy, where almost half of the total fibre purchases are made in that season, only around a third of all purchases are made in the warmer season of the year. At best, less than a third of wool purchases are made in Spring/Summer in the U.K., and, at the other extreme in Japan, this proportion falls to under 10% (Fig. 14).

The reasons why demand for lighter, comfortable clothing has increased are well documented and include living-environment factors, such as improved central heating and air-conditioning, with similarly improved atmospheric control in automobiles and other transport. Incidentally, this conscious and sub-conscious pursuit by consumers of comfort is now extending from apparel into furnishing products, including carpets.

A second factor was the emergence of the *trans-seasonal concept*:

the possibility of selling mid-weight products in nine months of the year in the North-European and U.S. markets was recognized; and

the concept was welcomed by the industry, since it allows a more balanced share of merchandise between seasons.

A third consideration was the *February-April market gap*:

for example, bikinis were being shown in the displays of leading retailers when the ground was covered in snow; and

retailers also saw an opportunity to recapture a lost season; one of the reasons put forward for this loss was a decline in the celebration of Easter, which traditionally involved Easter parades and a requirement for new outfits.

Clearly IWS needed to develop a strategy that encouraged the use of wool throughout the year, although avoiding high summer in extreme climates. It was recognized that wool had all the necessary properties: the major problem was how to communicate them.

Wool was traditionally associated with the Autumn/Winter season in its main consuming countries, mainly on the basis of considerations of warmth. This attitude was even entrenched in the language of various countries. In English-speaking countries, the first snap of Winter was a time to pull on a 'woolly', and conversely, at the first hint of Spring, the 'woolly' was once again confined to the dark recesses of the wardrobe. In French, the term 'woolly' loosely translates into *'petite laine'*. Presumably there are equivalents in other languages.

It was clearly understood at the outset that our advertising programmes would have to encourage traditional consumers to reappraise wool in the context of Spring/Summer conditions. The strategy was devised and constructed in 1984 on the basis of the following key factors.

(i) It was recognized that appropriate conventional lighterweight products did exist at the top end of the market in the shape of fine fabrics woven from fine yarns spun from superfine wools. In fact, during the 1970s, the highly successful 'Merino Extrafine Programme' had been devised to increase demand for fine-micron wools.

(ii) New technology had become available with the successful introduction of the CSIRO/IWS Sirospun double-rove spinning system, which allowed wool to be spun economically to finer counts on the worsted system than previously.

(iii) Sirospun and other improved spinning techniques allowed an increasing range of wool micron categories to be spun in singles-yarn qualities, which thus expanded the supply position.

(iv) In fashion, there has been a positive demand for luxury, ideal for superfine wools, and the demand persists and involves other luxury fibres, such as cashmere and silk.

(v) Again on the fashion front, there is renewed interest in crinkled textures in lighter fabrics. In this context, the properties of wool lend themselves superbly to creative experimentation, which provides added opportunities for product innovation.

8. THE SUCCESS OF 'COOL WOOL'

The challenge to IWS was how to exploit fundamental market changes and shorter-term fashion movements with traditional and new products.

The response has been:

(i) consolidation of merino extrafine wool at the luxurious top end of our menswear ranges, representing our 'flagship' qualities;

(ii) the introduction of 'Cool Wool', an idea conceived in

Germany and based on products developed in both Germany and
Italy, which received worldwide promotion; and

(iii) the Cool Wool womenswear campaign, aimed at changing
attitudes to wool.

The outcome has been as follows.

(i) In volume terms, 38 million m^2 of Cool Wool were used in
1985 in Italy and Germany alone. Figures for 1986 have yet to
be confirmed but will almost certainly be an advancement on
1985.

(ii) In terms of image, wool is confirmed as a quality fashionable fibre, and traditional wool ranges have been enhanced
by beautiful top-end-quality products, manufactured at the
right time for the right market.

(iii) The lightweight trans-seasonal theme has been adapted
by IWS branches in various countries to suit the local market
requirements and climatic conditions. In Italy, the March
edition of *Menswear Vogue* focussed on Spring 1988 wool fabrics
taking the theme of fabrics that simulated the physical characteristics of sea and land.

(iv) Also in Italy, a new project to promote Cool Wool yarns
for Spring and Summer knitwear was launched by the IWS and
fourteen leading Italian spinners at Pitti Filati in Florence
in February, 1987.

(v) With the slogan '*Lana Fredda, una Nuova Stagione per la
Maglia*' (Cool Wool, a New Season for Knitwear), the project
highlights the special qualities of light, fine-worsted wool
yarns initially to the knitwear industry and later, in the
Spring, 1988, season, to consumers through a publicity campaign
for cool-wool knitwear in fashion publications.

(vi) The Lana Fredda project was initiated by IWS after market
research among consumers and leading designers, manufacturers,
and retailers indicated there was potential for new Woolmark
products. Although many of the spinners have been selling Cool
Wool yarns successfully for several Spring and Summer seasons
- and some also for the Autumn and Winter - they welcome the
IWS Lana Fredda project and are optimistic that, coming at a
time when there is a return to classic, natural-fibre styles,
it will reinforce the appeal of these fine and light, pure-
wool yarns.

9. WOOL'S REVIVAL IN JERSEY FABRICS

Moving on from the Cool Wool concept, I would now briefly like to
describe how IWS contributed to the revival in interest in wool-
jersey fabrics. It probably does not need me to remind you that,
in the 1970s, the jersey market declined fairly rapidly from what
appeared to be a reasonably healthy position.

Following consumer dissatisfaction with jersey fabrics after
the boom of the early 1970s, wool consumption fell sharply and

reached a low point in the early 1980s. Since 1984, however, wool consumption in this market has shown some improvement, and current indications are that the popularity of wool jersey will continue to increase (Fig. 15). Wool-jersey consumption has grown in each of the main consuming countries except the U.K., where it remains substantially below that of the other main consuming countriès and, as yet, shows little sign of increasing (Fig. 16).

On a basis of market data, it was evident that, in the case of knitwear, the market had grown steadily during the past five years and had averaged around 4% growth per year, which is not surprising in view of the increased consumer awareness of comfort and the trend to more casual forms of dress, including 'body-hugging' styles. It therefore appeared that, with wool's established up-market image, coupled with the consumers' desire for self-expression, this was an appropriate time to reappraise wool jersey. As a preliminary step, it was considered necessary to analyse the reasons for the decline in the early 1970s, and it was concluded that the major causes were:

(i) the adverse consumer reaction to all fabrics in jersey constructions, particularly double-jersey, and the down-market image created by double-knit polyester-fibre fabrics;

(ii) the decline in popularity of the traditional two-piece wool double-jersey suit; and

(iii) the unwillingness on the part of many leading manufacturers to present wool in more adventurous styles, which appealed to younger consumers, wool being felt to be too expensive a fibre with which to take risks.

The message from most of the major IWS branches was that these consumer perceptions could be overcome and that, with improved design and styling, wool jersey could be successfully relaunched.

Against this background, the goals were simply:

(i) to increase the range of attractive contemporary products available in wool jersey; and

(ii) to make available merchandise in jersey structures that would appeal to the younger market as well as the traditional wool purchaser.

A survey of manufacturing and finishing potential in 1985 had revealed that the relevant skills, although diminished, were still available in the U.S.A., Italy, and France and that, given an increase in demand, extra wool-production requirements could be satisfied. In fact, the operations available today are much broader than was previously the case, and the IWS development programme has highlighted these through the use of yarn variations and surface effects produced by either physical or chemical finishing techniques. The availability of more sophisticated patterning systems has also widened the design possibilities. Information bulletins with samples prepared on double- and single-jersey knitting routes have demonstrated these yarns and techniques in various structures. Each sample is backed by technical detail on yarn selection and fabric construction. Several hundred such designs have been circulated to the trade.

The outcome of the IWS wool-jersey initiative has been:

(i) a rediscovery of wool jersey by many of the world's leading designers, who have applied it with great success to the modern consumer's requirements;

(ii) the depth of penetration of Woolmark jersey in the Autumn/ Winter 1987-88 collections, in Milan in March, which suggests that the trend is destined to continue for many seasons; and

(iii) the confidence of designers that its success is due to the fact that it not only looks good but also feels good, since it is a supple, forgiving fabric that moves with the body to give real ease and comfort in wear.

10. CONCLUSION

In conclusion, what I have attempted to demonstrate in this presentation is how IWS relies on information from the market to decide its product-development and marketing strategies.

Internationalism is undoubtedly emerging as one of the most important elements in ensuring long-term success in the textile industry, and, in this context, IWS, with 50 years' experience, is well positioned in its jubilee year to support its licensees in all the important markets.

Product development is also an essential component of the total package, but programmes must be market-led and based on a sympathetic understanding of emerging consumers and the constantly changing environment in which they exist.

International Wool Secretariat,
Development Centre,
Ilkley,
West Yorkshire,
England.

Creating a Successful Apparel Line
Merchandising for Targeted Consumer Markets

K. Greenwood and M. Jenkins

1. INTRODUCTION

The solution to problems confronting the apparel manufacturer is
dependent on the solution of problems existing at the supplier's
level. Proactive (future-oriented) textile and apparel companies
recognize the importance of networking within the various industry segments. A coalition must be forged for the mutual good of
the various segments of the fashion industries, which are invisibly linked by the marketing and merchandising goals focussed on
serving the ultimate consumer.

In recent years, progressive apparel manufacturers have made
significant changes in management and technology, as illustrated
by: (1) elevating the merchandiser to vice-president and a member of the management team; (2) implementing new techniques, such
as fashion-market segmentation and 'quick response', in order to
gain a consumer-oriented focus rather than the traditional product-oriented approach; and (3) formalizing the company's strategic plans, along with detailed marketing and merchandising calendars to guide and control seasonal events.

For the purposes of this paper, a brief summary of these three
significant changes in apparel manufacturing precedes the Case
Study, which focusses on 'How to Merchandise an Apparel Line' and
includes a discussion of each of the four phases of events leading
to the successful creation of a line: (1) developing fashion ideas
for advanced seasons; (2) working with textile suppliers; (3) fi-
nalising seasonal lines; and (4) formulating promotional strategies.

2. STRUCTURE OF THE FASHION INDUSTRIES

Competitive pressures in the fashion industries continue to accelerate owing to economic conditions, import problems, and changes in consumer markets. The fashion industries encompass a wide
range of companies involved in providing consumers with fashion-
oriented goods, fashion being defined as the accepted style of a
product at any given time. Highly segmented industries operate at
the supplier's level, the manufacturer's level, and the distribution level, as depicted in Fig. 1. Sales efforts are participated
in at each level to expedite the marketing process and form an
invisible linkage within the fashion industries.

107

The complex network of component segments must function as a whole to enable the giant fashion industries to fulfil the marketing 'rights' and thereby provide the ultimate consumer with a varied assortment of fashionable apparel on a highly seasonal schedule.

3. APPAREL-MANUFACTURING TECHNOLOGY

Today, many progressive apparel firms recognize the merchandising function as the key to achieving the goals of manufacturing in the highly competitive environment of fashion. The apparel manufacturer's goals focus on 'developing and delivering products in a system that will minimize total inventories, out of stock, risks and markdowns; and, at the same time, achieve maximized sales, return on investments, and customer services' (Frank (1)).

3.1 The Merchandising Function

Changes in the organizational structure of apparel companies have occurred in order to achieve the manufacturing goals in today's competitive environment. The anatomy of an apparel company is depicted in Fig. 2. As one of the vice-presidents in the management team, the merchandiser is responsible for co-ordinating the fabric inventory with the production flow, market promotions, and delivery schedules, and at the same time increasing the return on investments and profits. 'Integral to the merchandising function is the counter-balancing of the demands of sales on the one hand and those of manufacturing on the other' (Frank (1)). Elevation of the merchandising function to top-management level enables the company to move from the traditional product orientation to a merchandising-guided marketing orientation.

3.2 Merchandising Techniques

A multiplicity of techniques and tools are being used by merchandisers in apparel firms to achieve the goals of management. Highly acclaimed consumer-driven market-oriented strategies are being adopted by management and utilized in the development of strategic plans that influence the marketing and merchandising calendars. Several consumer-focussed techniques are being implemented by merchandisers in proactive apparel companies. Two concepts are explained in the following discussion.

3.2.1 Fashion-market Segmentation

An understanding of fashion cycles and market segmentation is basic to making effective 'fashion judgements' in merchandising products with a high degree of fashion influence. An integration of the fashion-cycle concept with the theory concerning the time of adoption for new products provides a quantitative fashion-market-segmentation model, as shown in Fig. 3 (Greenwood and Murphy (2)).

Fashion leaders, composed of innovators and early adopters, represent approximately 16% of the consumer market responding to

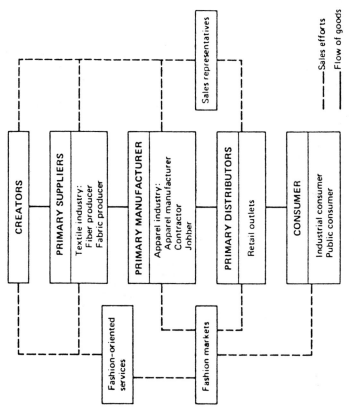

Fig. 1 Flow chart for the fashion industries

109

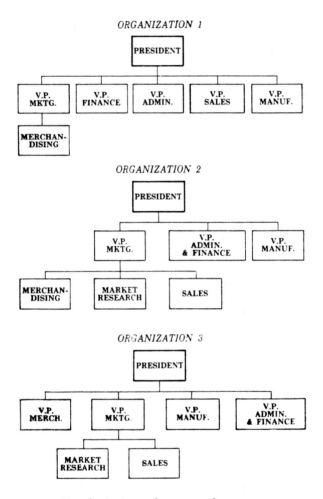

Fig. 2 Anatomy of an apparel company

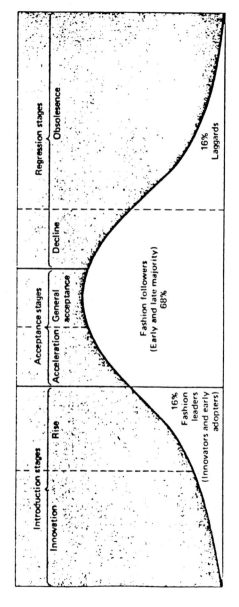

Fig. 3 Market segments for fashion merchandise

111

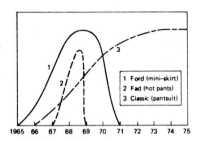

Fig. 4.1 Variations of acceptance patterns
in fashion cycles

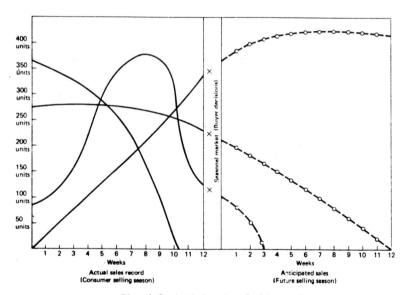

Fig. 4.2 Anticipating fashion sale

new styles during the introductory stage of a fashion cycle. Fashion followers make up an estimated 68%, the largest group of consumers, including the early and late majority in the acceptance stage of the fashion cycle. The laggards make up the remaining 16% of consumers, who resist changes of any nature, particularly in fashion.

Buying behaviour differs for the consumers in each market segment. The apparel merchandiser makes 'fashion judgements' in advance of each season on the basis of understanding of the targeted market segment gained from both informal and formal market-research techniques.

Sales forecasting for each season can be made on the basis of expected sales of fashion goods. Trends in fabrics and styles vary and can be traced as indicated by the diagrams in Figures 4.1 and 4.2.

3.2.2 The Strategy of 'Quick Response'

In today's economy, the concept of 'quick response' and other techniques, such as 'short-cycle' manufacturing, have become high-tech planning strategies. The goals of 'quick response' focus on the following points: (1) providing products and services for targeted customers in the precise quantities and variations (the right product and price); and (2) delivering products and services in the time frame required by the customer (the right time and place).

The apparel merchandiser is responsible for achieving these goals on a continuous basis. The key to successful merchandising is maintining a minimum dead time and risk for the product development and supply, while retaining maximum competitiveness and increased return on investments (Salmon (3)). The 'quick response' mode of operation is ideally suited to fashion-influenced markets, and can therefore be used by apparel merchandisers to improve performance in highly competitive environments where rapid change is constant.

'Short-cycle' manufacturing is an important component of the quick-response mode. Two other controls and scheduling techniques are a part of the state-of-the-art high-tech operations: 'Just-in-time' computer-aided manufacturing and 'computer-integrated' manufacturing (Salmon(3)).

3.3 Planning Tools

Planning is the accepted approach to successful marketing and merchandising today. Effective planning by the management team includes the following advantages: maintaining management control; minimizing mistakes by avoidance of diverging work and targets; and decreasing the element of risk involved in the delegation of responsibility. However, planning is time-consuming, it has an element of risk, and it is difficult to obtain consensus and agreement at the management level. (Vanhonacker (4) lists three planning tools used by progressive apparel manufacturers, which are described in the following discussion.)

113

3.3.1 Strategic Plans

Today, strategic planning is used to co-ordinate objectives and set goals that integrate the activities of top management. Strategic-planning meetings involve the president and the vice-presidents of key management functions: marketing, merchandising, and manufacturing.

Plans may be projected five or ten years out and should define the following: (1) the company image in terms of what it wants to stand for in the market place, i.e., the type of garments to manufacture; the merchandise assortments; size ranges; price points; (2) the target market and who the consumer is in terms of market segmentation, i.e., the customers' buying habits; their needs and wants; their likes and dislikes.

Decisions regarding these and other questions must be clarified prior to developing the marketing and merchandising calendars. The management team must understand and be committed to what the company wants to represent in the market place.

3.3.2 Marketing Calendar

After the strategic-planning meetings, the marketing calendar is developed as the 'central mechanism from which all other plans evolve. A concise document, it sets out in concrete terms the company objectives on an annual basis' (1). The components of the marketing calendar are included in the following list.

(1) Seasonal objectives by units and dollars.

(2) Seasons in which the product line will be offered.

(3) Dates for line release and preview.

(4) Dates shipping is to commence.

(5) Shipping by month for each season.

(6) Dates by which each season should be shipped complete.

The responsibility for the marketing calendar is shared by the management team in order to achieve total agreement from each function represented. After completion and approval, the marketing calendar should be published and used by each member of the management team in directing and controlling seasonal events.

3.3.3 Merchandising Calendar

The responsibilities of the merchandising function are specific with regard to the development and execution of a product line.

The merchandising calendar usually spans four or five months and may include 30-50 events. Some important components are described in the following list.

(1) Merchandising-plan meeting: review and analyse current market situation and the line's past performance.

(2) Market research and fabric-order placement: select basic colours, fabrics, and special trims.

114

(3) Line-plan meeting: develop line-plan summary and reconfirm or adjust the season objectives in units and dollars.
(4) Style development: prepare patterns and construct garments approved on line plan.
(5) Garment-costing: estimate 'quickie cost' or costing for sale or both.
(6) Line-adoption meetings and final adopt session: reaffirm commitment to previously approved original garments and release for duplication.
(7) Forecast adopted styles: estimate sales for each style.
(8) Finalize original patterns and grade: review garment specifications.
(9) Duplicate salesmen's samples: authorize duplication of adopted styles for line release.
(10) Manufacturing-planning meetings: develop weekly plant-load schedules and shelf stock.
(11) Receive production fabrics and trims: check inventory for production, 'cuttable' cuts.
(12) Production authorization and control: confirm the 'mix modules' of finished garments and confirm patterns.
(13) Line adjustment: decide on discontinued styles, modified styles, and/or new styles.
(14) Season critique: review the results of season informally.

Adherence to timing is extremely important once action is underway for a particular season. The merchandiser must exercise discipline in checking key deadlines; which thus ensures minimum inventory of fabrics with a maximum flow of goods. This is one of the major benefits of the merchandising calendar.

The advent of the merchandising calendar 'signals the change in apparel manufacturing from an unconstructed merchandising environment to a highly disciplined one' (1). However, it must be remembered that the calendar is only a tool and enables the merchandiser to control the mix of goods and production schedule for a given period.

These merchandising techniques and tools work best for 'time-sensitive' products, such as women's wear, which has from four to six seasonal-product lines. However, the key to success is gaining co-operation between the three levels of the fashion industries. 'Linkage systems' must be improved between the fabric suppliers, the manufacturer, and the retailer in order to tighten up the total sequence. 'The basic idea is that by working closely together in using marketing intelligence and in planning for a season's business, consumer demand can be better satisfied with less inventory and that the supply pipeline can be shortened dramatically' (5).

The previously discussed merchandising techniques and planning tools make it possible for today's apparel merchandisers to direct and control the advanced events involved in creating seasonal lines on schedule. The following Case Study demonstrates how the vice-president of merchandising for an apparel company in the United States applied some of these previously discussed techniques and tools in the creation of a successful line.

115

world. Art ideas for screen prints or fabric prints for confined
use in apparel lines may be collected. Store windows, street
scenes, and other activities may generate unique ideas. A sketch
pad and a camera are necessities for informal market research,
since it is important to make more than just mental notes in conducting informal research.

Attending trade shows in the United States is a 'must' for merchandisers. Apparel markets in New York, Atlanta, Dallas, Chicago,
Los Angeles, and other regional locations should be visited on a
regular basis. In addition to visiting the showrooms of competitive companies, the merchandiser should schedule time to be in
the company showroom during seasonal markets in order to observe
the reactions of retail buyers viewing the line. The Bobbin Show
is held in Atlanta annually and offers many technical ideas for
advancement, along with fabric and trim presentations.

The Dallas Apparel Mart is the largest in the world under one
roof, housing 2000 showrooms with over 14 000 lines of women's
and children's apparel, and has five scheduled markets a year. An
entire market complex has been developed in Dallas, including the
World Trade Mart, the Home Furnishing Mart, the Men's Wear Mart
adjoining the Women's Apparel Mart, and the latest development -
the first Info (computer) Mart in the country. The Southwest consumer offers manufacturers an ideal test market for forecasting
purposes.

Another component of informal market research is visiting
stores and shopping centres in various areas of the country, as
well as attending events that the targeted customer frequents and
activities in which certain age groups, lifestyle groups, and
other market segments commonly participate.

A vital source of formal market research is available within
the company, such as last year's sales, the top ten best-selling
styles, heavy reorder numbers, and trends evident in the current
line. Competitive shopping reports and catalogues from other manufacturers are valuable as the market-research process continues.

In-depth focus groups, interviews, and field-sampling studies
can be used to explore the 'wants' of the target customer. Both
retail buyers and fashion consumers can be included in this type
of formal market research.

The apparel merchandiser must interpret market research judici-
ously, since it points the way to merchandising decisions, 'fashion judgements'. The risk is great at best, since advance season's
forecasts are aimed at 'hitting a moving consumer target' (1).

4.1.2 Projections and Plans

The strategic-planning goals of the company along with the market
research provide a guide for the merchandiser to use in making
fabric projections and plans. Fabric trips to New York are usually
arranged three times a year. In addition, sales representatives
will call and show new fabric lines. In working with confined
prints, three months' advanced scheduling is necessary. (This
scheduling will be discussed in detail later.)

116

4. CREATING AN APPAREL LINE: A CASE STUDY

The merchandiser first reviews the company's strategic plans and the marketing calendar prepared by the management team. For example, the company strategic plan states:

> 'It is the mission of Shirey Company to provide children's sleepwear, underwear, and related-quality fashion products for the medium-to-high-priced infants'-through-junior market.'

Next, the merchandiser finalizes the merchandising calendar with careful adherence to the key seasonal dates designated in the marketing calendar. An example of a six months' merchandising calendar is included in the Appendix, along with the merchandising cycles depicting the timing for five seasonal lines. Key events are listed and the monthly deadlines indicated, along with designated responsibilities for the management team. The merchandiser uses this planning tool to guide and control events involved in creating an apparel line.

The creation of each seasonal line involves a number of phases. Fabric and style ideas must be researched, plans must be presented for adoption, fabric orders must be placed, sample garments must be constructed, costed, and duplicated for the salesmen, and promotional materials must be prepared.

4.1 Phase I: Developing Fashion Ideas for Advanced Seasons

Apparel merchandisers are sensitive to the market and constantly diagnose conditions and use market research as a backdrop. The preliminary activities of market research, projections, and plans are actually on-going responsibilities of the merchandiser. Accumulative knowledge is drawn on in the first phase of the line creation. However, changes in the buying behaviour and the 'wants' of the targeted consumer may be detected season by season. Timing is important in this first phase in order to keep on the 'quick-response' schedule established by the marketing and merchandising calendars.

4.1.1 Market Research

Apparel merchandisers actually conduct market research 24 hours a day, wherever they may be. Their eyes become trained to look for ideas and trends related to the selected target market. However, as the advanced season approaches, both informal and formal research must be scheduled for completion. Some of these techniques are suggested in the following discussion.

Informal market research may include trips to Europe to give an international flavour to apparel lines produced in the United States. Interstoff, the international textile show in Frankfurt, the European Apparel Mart in Zürich, and visits to other showrooms in Milan and Paris may be scheduled by the merchandiser, if time and money permit.

During trips such as this, the merchandiser can gather ideas from the advanced showing of colour and fabrics from all over the

117

The apparel merchandiser shops many lines of fabric from converters, textile mills, and print houses before making decisions on a complete line layout. Fabric groups can be used to tell a seasonal fashion story.

4.1.3 Fabric-board Presentation

Fabrics being considered should be swatched and displayed on a fabric board for each season's line so that they can be viewed easily. Presentation boards should depict the fabric stories and designate groups being used to create styles for the apparel line. Screen-print ideas and various kinds of trims, such as lace, ribbon, rosettes, and piping, can be shown on the fabric boards.

At the appropriate time, according to the merchandising calendar, the fabric boards should be presented to management for adoption. The designers use the fabric swatches to create the style ideas for the line. From time to time, a particular style demands a certain fabric, but most of the time fabrics are selected first, and styles are derived from them.

4.2 Phase II: Working with Textile Suppliers

The second phase is concerned with the creation of fabric concepts and the placement of orders. The merchandiser works with textile producers and converters to continue gathering ideas to finalize the selection of fabrics for the advanced season.

4.2.1 Creation of Fabric Concepts

The merchandiser works with the confined-print resources first. Paintings on paper or design-print ideas gathered in market research are used in working with confined prints. Converters who produce confined prints will have a collection of artwork. Original painting ideas may be with a black background, or the colours may be different from the colour range desired for advanced seasons. The converter will usually have an artist on staff to create a painting by using the new colour presentations for approval of the merchandiser.

In establishing confined prints, it may be necessary to match a colour story. The print method that is best used by a converter for a particular type of apparel line may determine the type of prints available from that resource. With the merchandiser's approval, the converter has the rollers engraved and the sample fabric printed. The colour match may need to be approved by the merchandiser at the first printing, or colour swatches can be given to the converter to assure a colour match with the proposed fabric story.

Timing is of essence with confined prints and is usually as follows: four weeks are allowed for artist revisions of layout, after the artwork selection; two to three weeks are allowed for rollers to be engraved; six to eight weeks are allowed for print time on fabric; a total of twelve to fifteen weeks must therefore be allowed for finished fabric on confined prints.

In working with confined prints, the original garment samples have to be 'sewn up' in a substitute fabric, since the entire minimum has to be printed at the same time. The first stock run is at the same time as the samples for duplicates are being printed. The minimum run ranges from six to twelve thousand yards, according to various textile converters. Often orders can be placed and sample duplicate yardage shipped earlier than the stock shipment is released, but the apparel company is liable for the balance of the entire printing, unless special terms are agreed on in advance.

4.2.2 Placement of Orders

Fabric-purchase orders must specify properly all information pertaining to style numbers, weight and yield of the fabric, the yardage desired, fibre content, price and colours designated, and square yards or linear measurements. The purchase order should also include any quality requirements established from past experience in dealing with particular converters or mills. An example of a purchase order for fabrics is included in the Appendix.

Delivery dates are specified on the purchase order at the time that it is placed. Nevertheless, follow-through actions are essential on sample orders as well as stock, in order to meet the deadlines established by the merchandise calendar.

The merchandiser is responsible for co-ordinating the fabric inventory with the production flow, the market responses, and the completion dates for the apparel line. The 'quick-response' technique enables the merchandiser to maintain a minimum fabric inventory by utilizing the phasing technique for long seasons, such as Fall I, Fall II, and Holiday. This allows a flow of fabric purchases as the season phases, and fewer dollars are therefore involved. Thus, the merchandiser can work closer to the order rather than to the forecast (1).

4.3 Phase III: Finalizing Seasonal Lines

The third phase involves the preparation and adoption of style sketches and the construction of sample garments. Line-planning is scheduled closer to the start of the selling season as the 'quick-response' mode is implemented by the management team. The merchandiser supervises the translation of sketches into patterns and the making of sample garments and authorizes the duplication of samples after the final adoption of the line.

4.3.1 Style Sketches

The entire line should be sketched on one large sheet of paper. The appropriate scale should be used in order to present the entire line at one view. The merchandiser views the line and notes any duplications of yolks, collars, or collar types and other undesirable elements. The final sketches reflect the ideas and projections developed during the market-research process. Important trends in fabrics, styles, and trims are incorporated into the sketches.

This approach eliminates making up many patterns and garments
that are never included in the line. Planning at this point reduces the cost of fabrics and labour used in producing excessive
samples.

The fashion-market-segments concept can be used to guide the
merchandiser in terms of the number of new-style ideas to introduce each season and the number of previously accepted styles to
repeat each season. For instance, the continuation of the best-
selling styles from previous seasons may be a risk if the trend
has peaked.

4.3.2 *First Adopt Session*

The merchandiser presents the proposed sketches to the management
team in the first of the adoption sessions. By utilizing 'quick-
response' techniques, styles that have a consensus of opinion at
the first adoption meeting can be approved, and samples can be
started. A second and third adopt session may be scheduled closer
to the line release if the merchandiser needs to adjust certain
styles.

4.3.3 *Sample Garments*

The preparation begins on the patterns for the sample garments,
and the first garments are made for each approved style. The designer reviews each style as it is completed to see if the sketch
has been correctly adapted in real life. Proportions are very important but often are not interpreted uniformly from the sketch
to the actual pattern. Screen-print ideas should be sketched and
coloured in roughly to interpret the general concept. The colour
of the trim or a bow may change the entire garment from success
to failure.

The merchandiser makes a final review of each sample garment
before the entire group is presented at the second adopt session.
Construction techniques can be corrected from the first pattern
and better adapted to the production-assembly process in the factory. However, the merchandiser should be familiar with the production capabilities, so that the first patterns can be made by
techniques as close as possible to the methods used by the manufacturer. Additional adopt sessions can be set up to review the entire
line of the first samples. Interval-scheduled meetings may be arranged for specific groups, if needed for a fashion or fabric story.

4.3.4 *Costing Garments*

Accurate 'costing-out' of a garment has been elevated to the
realm of a science; however, pricing for optimum profits remains
an art. Straightforward arithmetical pricing, derived from the
simple addition of labour, materials, overheads, and mark-up,
continues to be appropriate for the base. But the opportunities
are growing, as is the need, for the frequent use of subjective
pricing, that is, pricing according to what the 'market will

120

bear'. According to Frank (1), the merchandiser, with close ties to the market and with access to marketing expertise, 'is in the best position to determine when subjective pricing is appropriate'.

'Quickie' costing ensures that proposed styles for adoption meetings are within the appropriate price structure. A quick cost, projected at the time at which the initial sketches are made, can accelerate the adoption process and help the merchandiser to meet the deadlines established by the marketing and merchandising calendars. 'Cost for sale' is usually based on the original sample garment. 'Accurate cost calculation here is critical to profit, for, in most apparel companies, the mark-ups to selling price tend to compound any errors made in the base costs' (1). After a careful study of subjective pricing, the final selling cost can be set. An example of a cost sheet is in the Appendix.

4.3.5 Final-line Adoption

After the adopt sessions for the first garments, corrections are made and styles discarded. By utilizing the 'quick-response' mode, the final adopt session for the management-team review can be scheduled closer to the market-line release, when more is known about the season ahead. Prior to the final adoption, additional market research may be needed. Selected retail buyers can be asked to review the line and indicate general opinions and likes or dislikes of particular styles in question. However, in doing so, it is important to keep the ultimate consumer in mind rather than the reactions of individual buyers.

After the final adoption, the merchandiser, with the aid of the management team, estimates the sales for the various styles, and a forecast by sales is made. The results are reviewed and the post-adoption administrative actions are taken by the merchandiser.

4.3.6 Duplicate Garments

The merchandiser authorizes the manufacturing of the duplicates for the salesmen at an appropriate time to maintain the deadlines for line release established on the marketing and merchandising calendars. The duplication of samples begins under the supervision of the merchandiser in co-operation with manufacturing.

The line list of the finalized styles is prepared and computerized so that the necessary information on the new styles will be available for analysis. From the instigation of each style, the processes for the entire plant are initiated. The computerized line list integrates the master file, and the material utilization is calculated.

Raw-material needs are made and updated constantly as projections are changed. Formulae have been programmed into the computer by 'weeks out' to project quantities needed according to the amount sold at a particular time of the season. Thus, the fabric purchases and usages are calculated. 'Cuttable' cuts determine the production flow; cuts are 'cuttable' only if the fabric, findings, and trims are in stock. The merchandiser continues to monitor the fabric flow in order to co-ordinate the fabric inventory with the

121

production flow, market promotions, and delivery dates.

4.4 Phase IV: Formulating Promotional Strategy

The fourth phase in creating an apparel line is concerned with communications with retail buyers and consumers. The catalogue production, logos, hang-tag designs, and other point-of-sale ideas are the remaining responsibilities of the merchandiser.

4.4.1 Catalogue Production

Catalogues are selling tools, and the market demands a current offering. When the apparel line has been finalized and adopted for the advanced season, the freelance artist begins sketching each of the adopted styles for the catalogue production. With the approval of the merchandiser, the type is set for the catalogue production by using the computer-generated list, and the entire mechanical process of the paste-up is completed.

Catalogue production is one element of the industry that demands changes in response time. Photography, editing, and publishing have forced merchandisers to make samples available at earlier dates. Once again, 'quick-response' techniques may be dependent on technology. Typically, the catalogue-production time is about four weeks for the artist and/or the photographer, one week for the paste-up, and then two weeks at the printers for actual printing time.

4.4.2 Promotional Messages

Special motivational messages for logos and hang tags can be developed to create added interest and provide image identity at the point of sale. Consumer appeal is very important in determining the success of each style. Consumer acceptance or rejection is the key to the success of an apparel line.

Other promotional media are being used in merchandising apparel lines. Video production is gaining in popularity and is a potential tool for the future. Consumer markets may be tested through the use of cable television, and merchandisers can respond directly to consumer demand earlier in creating seasonal apparel lines.

As the season arrives, the merchandiser will review actual orders with the management team; the line may be adjusted, styles discontinued or modified, and new styles added. When each season is over, the merchandiser reviews the success of each style and makes an informal critique for use in planning and implementing future apparel lines.

5. CONCLUSIONS

Apparel-manufacturing technology is still in the infant stage; nevertheless, it has come a long way from the traditional 'seat of the pants' operations. One of the significant changes has been the recognition of the importance of the merchandising function and the advent of the apparel merchandiser as a member of the management team.

Progress is being made in solving some of the problems inherent in the fashion industries. Market-segmentation strategies enable apparel companies to become more consumer-oriented in focussing the goals of the strategic plans. 'Quick-response' techniques make it possible to eliminate some of the risk involved in minimizing inventories and maximizing sales.

The apparel merchandiser has solved a number of problems by serving as a counterbalance between sales (marketing) and manufacturing. Strict adherence to the marketing and merchandising calendars has enabled the merchandiser to control the flow of fabrics with the flow of production and thus gain additional stock turns and profit for the company. Disciplined actions by the merchandiser have eliminated some of the risk involved by working to order rather than working to forecast.

Extensive market research on the part of the merchandiser has made it possible to obtain confined prints for seasonal apparel lines and thus ensure the company of a competitive edge in the market. By working co-operatively with fabric producers and converters in creating seasonal apparel lines, merchandisers have made considerable headway in improving the networking between textile suppliers and apparel manufacturers.

Each segment of the fashion industries is painfully aware of the problems that must be faced in order to forge a coalition between textile suppliers, apparel manufacturers, and retailers. The realization of finding solutions to the major problems demands that the industries band together in the quest for success. Each segment is invisibly tied to the other, and the success of one is dependent on the success of the other.

REFERENCES

(1) B. Frank. 'Profitable Merchandising of Apparel', National Knitwear and Sportswear Association, New York, 1982.

(2) K.M. Greenwood and M.F. Murphy. 'Fashion Innovation and Marketing', Macmillan Publishing Co., New York, 1978.

(3) K. Salmon. 'Questions and Answers about Quick Response', Kurt Salmon Associates, New York, Sept. 1986.

(4) W.R. Vonhonoacker. 'Marketing: Core Business Program', Facts on File Publications, Mike Morris Productions, New York, 1983.

(5) K. Salmon. 'Restructuring in the U.S. Apparel Industry' (excerpts from a speech by the Chairman of the Board, Kurt Salmon Associates, at 1986 Conference of International Textile Manufacturers Federation, Helsinki, Finland), Kurt Salmon Associates, New York, Nov. 1986.

(K.G.) Center for Apparel Marketing and Merchandising,
Oklahoma State University,
Stillwater,
Okla.,
U.S.A.

(M.K.J.) Shirey Co. Inc.,
Dallas,
Tex.,
U.S.A.

EXHIBIT 5. MERCHANDISING CALENDAR

KEY EVENT	MERCH	SALES	PROD	DESIGN	MISC	Jan 8	Jan 15	Jan 22	Jan 29	Feb 5	Feb 12	Feb 19	Feb 26	Mar 5	Mar 12	Mar 19	Mar 26	Apr 2	Apr 9	Apr 16	Apr 23	Apr 30	May 7	May 14	May 21	May 28	Jun 4	Jun 11	Jun 18	Jun 25	Jul 2	Jul 9	Jul 16	Jul 23
1. Market Evaluation	X	X				F1	F1																	H2										
2. Initial Projections	X	X				F1	F1		F2							H1									H2									
3. Preliminary Manufacturing Plans	X			X		F1			F2								H1								H2									
4. Shop Fabric and Trim Market				X			F1			F2								H1								H2								
5. Order Sample Fabrics and Trims	X			X			F1			F2								H1								H2								
6. Receive Sample Fabrics and Trims				X					F1		F2									III H1							H2	H2						
7. Formulate Line Concepts	X			X								F2								H1								H2						
8. Review Line Plans	X	X							F1			F2								H1								H2						
9. Start Samples				X					F1			F2								H1								H2						
10. Initial Griege Fabric Buy	X								F1			F2								H1								H2						
11. Preliminary Costings	X									F1			F2										H1						H2				
12. Initial Line Adoption	X	X								F1			F2										H1						H2				
13. Complete Line Concepts				X						F1			F2										H1						H2				
14. Complete Samples	X			X							F1			F2											H1						H2		
15. Complete Costings	X										F1			F2											H1						H2		
16. Final Line Adoption	X	X									F1			F2											H1							H2	
17. Finalize Garment Specifications				X							F1			F2											H1							H2	
18. Line Release	X	X										F1			F2												H1						
19. First Orders Booked	X	X												F1			F2										H1						
20. Purchase Production Fabrics	X													F1			F2										H1						
21. Purchase Production Trims	X													F1			F2										H1						
22. Make First Pattern and Factory Sample				X										F1			F2										H1						
23. Receive Production Fabric and Trim			X											F1			F2										H1						
24. Issue First Cuts	X															F1		F2															
25. Grade Patterns Make Markers		X															F1		F2										H1				
26. Cutting		X																		F2													
27. Sewing		X						S2	S2										F1	F1										H1	H1	H1	
28. Finish		X						S2	S2											F1	F1									H1		H1	H1
29. First Goods on Shelf		X							S2												F1	F2										H1	H

EXHIBIT 6. SEASONAL MERCHANDISING CYCLES

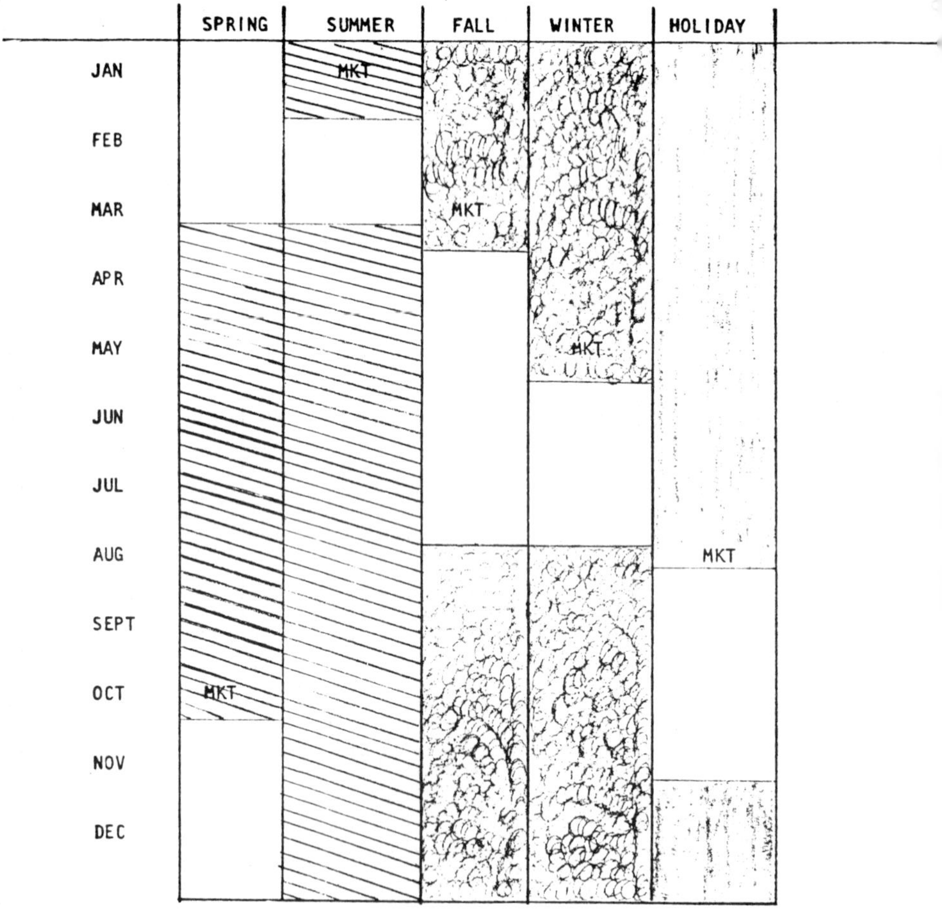

	SPRING	SUMMER	FALL	WINTER	HOLIDAY
JAN		MKT			
FEB					
MAR			MKT		
APR					
MAY				MKT	
JUN					
JUL					
AUG					MKT
SEPT					
OCT	MKT				
NOV					
DEC					

126

SHIREY COMPANY, INC.

1917½ STANFORD STREET
P.O. BOX 1038
GREENVILLE, TEXAS 75401

SALESMAN _Ray Dawson, Sr_

PHONE _212-889-5440_

DUNS #733-1671

To _Northbury Textiles_

ADDRESS _233 Madison Ave_
New York, New York 10016

SEASON _F '87_

OUR ORDER NO. **M 0828**

DATE OF ORDER	_1/20/87_				
WHEN SHIP _3/1 for Samples_		BILL EACH ORDER SEPARATELY			
CANCEL IF NOT COMPLETED BY _see below_		**SHIPPING INSTRUCTIONS**			
OUR PERMISSION MUST BE OBTAINED TO EXTEND CANCELLATION DATE		UP TO 50 LBS. UNITED PARCEL SERVICE			
VENDOR A/C NO. _448_		OVER 50 LBS. VIA _Roadway_			
		F.O.B. _North Carolina_			

QUANTITY	STYLE	WIDTH	YIELD	COLOR	DESCRIPTION	FIBER CONTENT	MIN. YDG.	PRICE	UNIT
6,000	3452	60"	7½ oz	Pink/white	Check (Karinda) Knit	100% Polyester	6,000	2.15	yds
6,000				Blue/white					
6,000				Yellow/white					
				Match colors to attached swatches.					
				Ship 500 yds per color for samples by Mar. 1 – Hold balance for Purchasing to call out as needed for stock cuts.					
				Must be flame retardant for Childrens Sleepwear					

127

BUYER _M Jenkins_

DESIGN DEPT.   SHIREY COMPANY, INC.

EXHIBIT 8. **GARMENT COST SHEET**

SEASON: *Spring 81*

Garment: Bow Pontie   Selling Price: 30.00   Sug. Retail 6.00   Style: 2174   Design No. DW-21

Colors/   On Hangers: _____

Color No. Pastel, Bright   Pack: 4/12 DZ per SZ   Box: ✓   Sizes: 2,3,4,5,6

    15   32   per color

FABRICS

Fabric/ Fiber Content	Component Number	Mill	Style No.	Width	Cost	w/frt.	Yardage Estimate	Yardage Actual	Cost Estimate	Cost Actual
65/35 Poly/Cotton	2Mo-960	Grnwd	Batiste	60		1.369	2.933		4.41	
							Waste %	.4		
							Total Fabric Cost		4.41	

TRIMMING

Item	Component Number	Source	Style No.	Unit	Unit Cost	Yardage Estimate	Yardage Actual	Cost Estimate	Cost Actual
Eyelet	3LO-320	Unired	32389	Y	.142	14		1.99	
Attach Elastic	4CE-803	RI	8828	Y	.040	9		.36	
Insert Elastic	4CE-506	FF	3/8"	Y	.018	6.667		.12	
Pre-ties	3RO-806	Brick	3/8"	Dz.	.392	5		1.95	

SKETCH

5 Bows

3170 Block

Trim Colors for stock: Pre-Ties

Pastels - Pink, Blue, Yellow, Lilac

Brights* Brt. Pink, Green, Red, Gold & Royal

Screen print Information:

Others:

Care Code: X
Label 1

Thread: White Perma Spun Image 52

* Use Nylon thread to tack Bright Bows

Sub Total	4.42
Waste %	.44
Total Trim Cost	4.86
Packaging: CHB	
BOX	30
LTT	
LT	13
Handling:	
Manufacturing Cost	8.50
TOTAL COST	18.20

MU% __	Total per DZ	32.03	Total Each	2.6

Special MU% __	Total per DZ		Total Each	

Prepared by: E.B.   Date 7/10

Approval: _____ Date _____

FR test pass: _____ Date _____

Colour-Measurement Applications in Textile Design and Marketing

J.D. Hudson, Jnr

Abstract

Colour is a vital ingredient in the marketing and design of many textile products. Recent technical advances in instrumentation and in high-resolution graphics now provide new approaches to the design and control of colour in fabrics. An understanding of the fundamentals of colour science is necessary in order to apply this modern technology in a useful way.

1. INTRODUCTION

Perhaps one reason for holding a conference on design and product-marketing of textiles is that today's textile industry is being affected by economic pressures, more ecological requirements, rising quality demands, and complex domestic and international business factors.

So we need all the help we can get! Where do we look?

1.1 Customers

Hopefully, we look to our customers, to maintain sensitivity to their changing needs.

1.2 Suppliers

We also look to our suppliers, for expert assistance in using their products as wisely as possible.

1.3 Employees

We should always look to our employees for their innovative ideas. This needs to encompass all levels of the organization (from clerk to vice-president) and all departments (not just research and development).

1.4 Technology

But we are all inclined to look to technology most of all.

Computers have permeated every area of our lifestyles. It is fair to say that we expect a great deal from technological improvements in general, and computers in particular.

2. COLOUR

2.1 Relationship to Appearance

First of all, before beginning a brief discussion of the psychophysical aspects of colour, it should be noted that appearance and subjective effect to the human observer include properties other than colour.

2.1.1 Texture

One example would be texture. Those who do not recognize this might spend many hours and dollars in the laboratory in adjusting a shade, when texture and surface-effect differences are the source of visual discrepancy.

2.1.2 Lustre

Contrast gloss, which we in textiles usually refer to as lustre, is another nonchromatic attribute of appearance. Hunter (1) refers to properties such as texture and lustre as geometric attributes of appearance.

2.1.3 Colour Surrounds

Surrounding colour can also influence the effect that is perceived. This should be kept in mind in matching shades for print patterns and fancy yarn-dyed fabrics.

2.2 Quantifying Colour

Colour is a sensation resulting from visible light from a particular source reflecting from a coloured object into the eye of an observer. The visible spectrum includes wavelengths in the approximate range of 400-700 nm.

2.2.1 Light

A particular light source, E, has a spectral-energy distribution curve, which represents its characteristics.

2.2.2 Objects

The way in which an object reflects light is given by the reflectance curve for this object, R. Mathematically, the light reflected to the observer is the product of the spectral-energy distribution curve of the light source, E, and the reflectance curve of the object, R.

Two reflectance curves, R_1 and R_2, might be shaped such that the products $E_W \times R_1$ and $E_W \times R_2$ are reasonably close (E_W being white fluorescent energy). When the light source is changed to E_A (incandescent), the products $E_A \times R_1$ and $E_A \times R_2$ might then be considerably different.

This phenomenon is known as *metamerism* and is sometimes referred to as *flare*. Special viewing booths are used to examine the metameric properties of proposed matches. The degree to which apparent matches under one light can mismatch under another illuminant is sometimes surprising. One advantage of computer colourant formulation is that the degree of metamerism for each alternative recipe can be calculated and considered before any trial dyeings are made.

2.2.3 Observer

The third component required in representing colour quantitatively is the human element, that is, the eye and brain of the observer. Experiments have shown that a viewer's sensitivity to blue, green, and red stimuli varies across the visual spectrum. The curves depicting this variation are called *tristimulus functions* or colour-matching functions. They are meant to represent the responses of a typical observer based on experimental data.

2.3 Communication and Colour-order Systems

Measuring colour quantitatively permits communication in objective terms. This facilitates better internal communication and control within an organization as well as between customer and supplier. There are many ways in which attributes of colour may be expressed, and colour comparisons can be described by a potentially long list of adjectives. To simplify matters, we need an organized concise rationale for systematic representation of colour.

Many different colour-order systems have been devised over the years, and a wide variety are in use today. They all express colour as a three-dimensional quantity, and most have a way of combining these three components into a single number representing total colour difference.

2.3.1 Munsell

The Munsell system defines the three dimensions of colour as hue, value, and chroma. It is probably the best-known of all colour-order systems and is based on equal visual perception of small colour differences.

2.3.2 MacAdam

One system was developed from experimental data to define the threshold of perceptibility, this theoretical unit being called the MacAdam unit.

2.3.3 Hunter

Another widely used system is the Hunter L,a,b solid, which partitions colour into a lightness component, a red-green component, and a yellow-blue component (1).

2.3.4 CIELAB

Eleven years ago, the Inter-Society Colour Council held a conference called 'Instrumental Colorant Formulation, 1976' in Williamsburg, Virginia, U.S.A. Keith McLaren, of ICI, Mancester, England, presented a paper entitled 'The Case for CIELAB', in which he proposed a system similar to the L,a,b system. This system, also known as Starlab, transforms the chromatic parameters $a*$ and $b*$ from Cartesian co-ordinates to the cylindrical co-ordinates H and C. The resulting three parameters L, H, and C correlate with the value, hue, and chroma attributes, respectively, of the Munsell System.

This system has gained wide acceptance on an international and inter-industry basis. Use of this rationale permits any description of colour difference to be definable by using just three adjectives from the following eight: light or dark; dull or bright; red, green, yellow, or blue.

Standardization of colour terminology in this way reduces the ambiguity in oral and written communication.

2.4 Colour Instruments: 'Unbiassed Observers'

Tristimulus colorimeters are designed for psychophysical analysis yielding measurements (e.g., L, a, and b) to correlate with the impressions of the eye-brain. Spectrophotometers measure the physical properties of light reflected by objects, for example, percentage reflectance relative to a white standard. Spectrophotometric measurements can be converted to psychophysical scales, but colorimeters cannot measure reflectance curves.

Recent improvements in modern instruments include more speed (typically less than two seconds of measurement time) and microprocessor intelligence to aid calibration and simple functions such as averaging. More important, most of this new instrumentation is specifically designed for colour measurement.

2.5 Applications

2.5.1 Colour-matching (Formulation)

Colour-matching is a term for a process that usually involves two steps. The first step is a selection of a combination of dyes or a recipe. The second is the determination of the amounts of these colorants required to match a shade satisfactorily. The objective of computer colour-matching is usually reduced dyestuff cost. A considerable investment in laboratory effort is required to dye the primaries that are measured to produce the data that are stored in the computer. The importance of obtaining reliable and representative primary data should be emphasized strongly. Statistical and colour analysis of primary data is necessary to fine-tune the model for optimum results.

2.5.2 Colour Correction

Correction of shades in the laboratory or in production is just as important as formulation. The opportunities for increased throughput and shorter lead times are considerable with a well-designed instrumental approach to colour adjustments.

2.5.3 Shade-sorting

Consistent shade-sorting by instrument is now a reasonable way to avoid variability in visual judgements. Better instrument precision and rapid data-handling systems have become available recently. This has allowed the establishment of numerical colour tolerances for acceptability. In addition, shade groups can be assigned with a simple three-digit code for each category. Groups with similar sort codes can then be sewn together without an objectional mismatch. This technique also provides valuable feedback for control in the dyeing process.

2.5.4 Summary of Classical Applications

A more comprehensive review of traditional applications is given in an earlier paper (2).

Experience in colour control is still a valuable asset, but educated guesses are sometimes insufficient for today's needs. By blending this experience with proper application of colour science and modern technology, we can better meet current challenges and those in the future.

2.5.5 New Applications

There are several very recent developments that should be of interest.

One company in the United States has integrated a spectrophotometer with a high-resolution colour-graphics display. This provides the capability of measuring swatches, paint chips, yarn, or any reflecting object and the automatic accurate representation of the colour on the screen. The spectrophotometer also allows the proper calibration of the monitor, which is required to maintain reproducibility. A third use is the control of colour output in a printer.

Another exciting new product is a colour printer with solid-ink-jet technology. Designed in the United States and manufactured in Japan, it can produce over 250 000 shades and does not require special paper.

REFERENCES

(1) R.S. Hunter. 'The Measurement of Appearance', John Wiley &
    Sons, New York, 1975.

(2) J.D. Hudson, jun. *Text. Chem. Col.*, 1978, 10, No. 3, 17.

Advanced Data Technology, Inc.,
Danville,
Va.,
U.S.A.

134

Marketing 'Lifestyle' in the U.S.A.

The Anne Klein II Approach

M. Kawakami

1. HISTORICAL OVERVIEW

Anne Klein & Co. is one of Seventh Avenue's most prestigious
firms. Anne Klein became known as the 'mother' of American
Sportswear. During its nineteen-year reign as one of America's
foremost designer-sportswear houses, the cost of designer apparel
has escalated to such a point that the market base has eroded to
a rarified percentage, which currently caters to the privileged
and wealthy. An average outfit from Anne Klein would retail at
between U.S.$1500 and $2000.

It was in the Fall of 1983 that Anne Klein II was conceived
to fill the market void that was created by the high prices of
designer sportswear compared with the more volume-oriented
'better'-sportswear market, where an average outfit would retail
for approximately $250. This gap was not a 'step-up': it required
an elevator to span those price-point margins. This is where the
term 'bridge' sportswear came into existence. In 1983, an outfit
from Anne Klein II would retail for about $300.

We entered that market with a concise focus on the customer.
We knew who she was, and we had a clear marketing programme, and
that programme continues today. We are a company that is driven
by its merchandising and marketing concepts. We believe that:

(1) Anne Klein II had to represent the same level of designer
    direction and sophistication;

(2) Anne Klein II must produce a garment that represented in-
    trinsic value, not only from the use of quality fabrics
    but also as to how well it was constructed;

(3) after satisfying style and quality, price then becomes an
    issue - not before - and hence the price point at retail
    was positioned to be from one-half to one-third of the
    cost of Anne Klein & Co. and other designer lines, bridge
    prices being selected to allow for the use of better fab-
    ric, i.e., pure wool, pure cotton, pure linen, etc.

2. IDENTIFYING THE MARKET: WHO IS THE CUSTOMER?

Let me introduce the Anne Klein II target audience - the Career

Woman. She is between the ages of 25 and 49. She enjoys a minimum household income of $35 000 or more per year.

The 'career woman' is a substantive and viable market. Anne Klein II focussed on her, in the belief that this market evolved from economic necessity and is therefore not as affected by the fluctuations in the economy. For this customer, her image is an integral part of her career. For Anne Klein II, she represents a stable base upon which to build a business.

Almost one out of every two women in the United States today is employed full-time. In the 1970s and 1980s, two-thirds of all new jobs were occupied by women.* As we broadly focus upon our 31 372 000 women who are potential Anne Klein II consumers, we realize that, as a group, they exercise an incredible discretionary clout.

Mr Ike Lagnado, Director of Research at Associated Merchandising Corporation, has projected that the 'career consumer' will account for $10 billion in retail sales for the year 1987.

The career market continues to grow with an impact generated by the famed 'baby-boom' generation of 'yuppies' born between the years of 1946 and 1965. They are now between the ages of 22 and 41 and are just reaching their career and income peaks. They are better educated; they prefer working in order to maintain the better lifestyle with which they had grown up; they are both married and single; and they work not only for the financial rewards, but also for personal fulfilment and growth. We know that these 15 million women with a minimum HHI of $35 000 will purchase: 12 071 000 blouses or shirts yearly; 13 000 sweaters daily; 337 000 skirts monthly; and 6 340 000 pairs of slacks yearly. This will give you some way of measuring the size and scope that the career 'bridge' market represents.

The woman in whom we are interested represents a market of women who are as intelligent about their clothing purchases as they are about running their own companies, selecting their own stock certificates, or taking a case to trial. These women understand quality not only as an aesthetic but also as a necessity. They understand that the image they create upon first impression establishes their socio-economic position, education, and lifestyle. They are bright enough to understand that clothing and their appearance allow them to merchandise themselves into a new job, a promotion, a title, and independence.

3. FOCUS: LIFESTYLE PROFILE

Our career market is a female who is challenged by the balancing of roles between wife, mother, single parent, single person, wage earner, and career. She has a multi-dimensional profile, within which, in terms of an index against population, we can examine a range of topics from education to investments to luxury-goods consumption, athletics, and the influence over the man in her life.

---

* Bureau of Labor Statistics.

Women today enjoy a high-profile lifestyle. They are optimistic about the world's future, and they feel strongly that they will get ahead politically, economically, and socially. The outlook is bright. Women believe they have a promising future and that they will play a larger role in shaping it.

4. DEVELOPING A MARKETING STRATEGY

In developing our marketing strategies, we used certain assumptions as guidelines.

(1) The woman who is our objective is interested in fashion but not obsessed with it.

(2) She has fashion constraints - the career woman's apparel must reflect her mind, her ambition, and her success. She cannot appear as a dizzy, feline fashion victim.

(3) Her apparel needs vary depending upon her chosen career path - Corporate, Classic, Creative. Anne Klein II had to accommodate the needs of the lawyer, real-estate agent, Wall Street banker, advertising executive, interior designer, or writer; she is both urban and suburban, and she runs the gamut from the very conservative to those who are more fashionably flamboyant. Her clothing has to work for her by reflecting her goals and position.

(4) She requires quality, which, along with style, gives her a sense of self and reflects her socio-economic and career positioning.

(5) Apparel needs vary depending on the climate zone in which she lives. Our dual-line concept of North-South - hot and cold - has therefore been developed. Because of the vast size of the United States and its diverse seasonal differences we produce collections that provide apparel for both climates. We produce a line that could satisfy the needs from Sweden to Sicily. This was a challenge, since most designers design from a Northern, urban point-of-view. Anyone who would review our collection today would find light wools, cotton sweaters, silks, silk blends, and silk/wool Challis on the line for Fall for the South as well as the classic flannel and heavier-weight wools. He would find woollens on the line for the Northern climates from November to March, when we also have linen, silks, and lightweight warm-weather fabric for the Southern region.

(6) Most designer apparel is believed to be targeted for taller women. However, the average height for women in the United States is 5 ft 4 in. or 160 cm, with a great number of women under this height. Anne Klein II maintains a fashion attitude but has scaled down fashion to compliment the average figure. We have also developed proportioned fashion sportswear for special-sized women under 5 ft 4 in. - now known as Anne Klein II Petites. We knew we were successful when we could view a model of 5 ft 9 in. and a model of 5 ft 2 in. at a distance and find they looked identical. We knew we had accomplished our goal.

(7) Because of the multi-dimensional profile of this consumer, she has limited personal time available. That time which is spent in shopping establishes a new criterion for the retailer. Shopping must be EASY, FAST, and CONVENIENT.

   (*a*) Visual display and merchandising are imperative to attract the consumer to the Anne Klein II shop.

   (*b*) An Anne Klein II shop provides a consistent location, exciting presentation, and promotional events supported by trained sales associates.

5. IMPLEMENTING THE ANNE KLEIN II MARKETING STRATEGY

The collections we present are expansive to cover the needs of our target audience. The attitude and direction have never veered off course - we feel that we know what she wants. Our major objective is letting her know what she wants and who will provide it to her.

Our marketing philosophy was simple: that Anne Klein II would assume the responsibility of taking our product directly to the consumer, where we should be able to control our marketing and image.

5.1 Print and Television Campaign

We planned not only an extensive print campaign but also one for television. The print campaign reached a select audience that covered all the up-market major fashion publications and career magazines. Print was a complement and gave us a broad reach in the market place. Spot television is used for in-depth market penetration. Key retail markets are capable of providing a disproportionate amount of sales. The seven cities where we used television as an additional advertising vehicle delivered over 25% of our target audience nationally. Utilizing both print and television, we found that the results were:

   45% of our national target is reached an average of $3\frac{1}{2}$ times;
   86% of the local target is reached an average of 9 times;
   the potential number of people exposed to the print message is 23 826 000 (gross impressions);
   the potential number of people exposed to the spot-television message is 85 325 000 (gross impressions).

Key markets for spot television are: New York, Chicago, San Francisco, Los Angeles, Dallas, Atlanta, Washington D.C., Boston, and Detroit. In a very short period of time, we had customer recognition of the Anne Klein II label. We were the first and remain the only fashion house that has used television as a successful vehicle for clothing other than the blue-jeans companies.

5.2 Introducing the Mailer

We believed that we should let the customer know who we were, and it was the retail store's responsibility to let her know where to buy what she wanted. This was a fine concept, but the fact is that

Table I

Broad Demographic Overview*

	Number	Percentage
Total women (in the United States)	90 265 000	100
Total women aged 25-49	42 230 000	46.8
Total women employed full-time	38 030 000	42.1
Total women in professional, managerial, administrative, sales positions	31 372 000	34.8
Total women aged 25-49 with HHI $35 000+ **	15 675 000	17.4 (1 of 6 women)

* Simmons Market Research Bureau, New York, N.Y., 1986.
** The Anne Klein II Target Audience.

Table II

Apparel Purchase*

Professional/Managerial Women Aged 25-49 with HHI $35 000+

	12 months	1 month	Daily
Blouse/shirt	12 071 000	1 006 000	34 000
Sweater	4 541 000	378 000	13 000
Dress	6 277 000	523 000	17 000
Skirt	4 047 000	337 000	11 000
Suit	1 812 000	151 000	5 000
Coat	1 507 000	125 000	4 000
Slacks	6 340 000	528 000	18 000

* Mediamark Research Incorporation, New York, 1986.

Table III

Women 25–49 with HHI $35 000+ Index against Total Adults 18+	
Socio/Economic/Domestic	Index
Graduated college	214
Single	49
Married	136
Live in: Northeast	109
Midwest	107
South	83
West	111
Children in HH: under 2 years	130
2–5 years	133
6–11 years	150
12–17 years	173
no children	59
Own home	123

Investments	
Owns common/preferred stock in company work for	235
Has tax-sheltered annuities	211
Has investment property	183
Acquired U.S. Savings Bonds/12 months	203
Has an IRA	157
Has a brokerage account	152
Owns securities (excluding U.S. Savings Bonds)	147
Has/uses store credit cards	215
Has/uses bank credit cards	165

Ultimate Consumer of 'New Technology' and Luxury Goods	
Bought an answering machine/last 12 months	221
Owns a foreign car bought new	207
Owns an all-terrain vehicle	173
Bought fine-china dinnerware/12 months	170
Bought a cordless telephone/12 months	168
Owns a VCR	167
Bought wine by the case/12 months	164
Bought merchandise from a catalogue/12 months	150
Owns a microwave oven	148

Table III (contin.)

She is Socially/Politically Conscious	Index
Actively participates in local civic issue/past year	195
Engaged in fund-raising/past year	175
Actively worked for a political-party candidate	165
Actively worked as a non-political volunteer	164
Written to an elected official regarding public business	
Written something that has been published	137

She is Athletic

Participates in aerobics	237
Belongs to a health club	189
Participated in a physical fitness programme outside home/past year	164
Participated in horseback riding/past year	163
Owns a tennis racquet	156
Bought a bicycle/past year	163
Owns a stationary bicycle	163
Owns jogging/running shoes	159

She Enjoys Her Home and Likes to 'Share It'

Shopped at a gourmet food store/12 months	195
Bought custom-made draperies, curtains/12 months	190
Gives dinner parties	179
Gives cocktail parties	175
Gives barbecue or cook-out parties	131

She is Culturally Involved

Belongs to a book club	164
Attends classical concert/12 months	182
Attends live theatre performance/12 months	176

She Indulges Herself

Uses perfume, cologne or toilet water	197
Took a foreign-destination vacation	174
Drinks imported wine	166
Drinks reduced-calorie 'light' domestic table wines	178

Table III (contin.)

And Indulges the Man in Her Life	Index
Bought a suit for a man/past year	390
Bought sports coat/blazer/past year	359
Bought neckties/past year	333
Bought dress/sports shirt/past year	330
Bought sweater/past year	298

Source: 1986 SMRB.

most retailers used newspapers or their own catalogues as their
primary vehicles for reaching the customer. Newspapers, we believe, are ineffective, since television news and radio are used
for information - much faster and efficient - and the store catalogues give a store image only. Many stores' advertisements are
not up to the professional impact levels that we seek.

Anne Klein II continued to assume the marketing responsibility,
and we started to produce our own direct-mail piece. We introduced
the 'mailer' to the retailer. The mailer is a marketing tool that
has the effect of a rifle - targeted directly to the consumer. We
utilized store computer lists that focussed on specific customer
groups that either purchased goods to a specific number of dollars
yearly or purchased similar merchandise of comparable price points.
This method is much more cost-efficient than retail newspaper advertisements, which are a shotgun approach. We now produce six or
seven mailers yearly, and, as a result of distribution by the retailer directly to the Anne Klein II customer, between seven and
nine million copies were circulated last year.

We now have effectively reached our target audience - the
Career Woman - through print, television, and the Anne Klein II
mailers. She knows what Anne Klein II represents, and she wants
the product. It is here that we run into a wall, since major retailers run their business from computer sheets. Buyers do not
visit their stores, and the retail-selling staff is scarce on the
selling floor: they are there to guard the inventory, not to sell
it. Lack of buyer travel and shortage of selling staff are generally the result of budget cuts.

We had to develop a way that would ensure us of visual presentation with impact, exciting sales promotions to keep selling
staff and consumers turned-on and develop responsible, enthusias-
tic, and well-trained retail-sales associates. The Regional Sales
Executive programme (also known as RSE) was conceived. The RSEs'
sole meaning to life is 'retail sell-through'. They merchandise,
arrange floor presentation, train, sell, do shows, do stock, or
deliver merchandise. They do whatever is necessary to achieve
success at retail.

They are also the key link from consumer to manufacturer. They
feed back information as to what is successful and why - as well
as what is not performing and why.

They produce pertinent information for Anne Klein II and the
retailer as to the needs of our customer. Our focus is fine-tuned
door by door, city by city, region by region.

The feedback from our RSE programme is used by our design staff
to refine our collections and by our selling staff to work with
the retailer. That information is used to adjust store purchases
and to tailor each order to its respective door - taking into account the particular customer profile and regional needs. Today,
our major stores will not complete an order without first having
the Anne Klein II RSE approve its over-all content. The RSE programme was an integral part of the original concepts and business
plans. I believe we needed to have some input into our destiny:
since most products at retail sell by accident, we needed to feel
we could orchestrate our own success at retail with strong visuals,

143

signed locations and shops, exciting promotions, and trained selling associates, all of which would make it easy, fast, and convenient for the career consumer. Our RSE programme is now 50 women
strong, ensuring the success of Anne Klein II throughout the
United States.

In order to maximize the RSE programme, our New York-based
group augments various programmes and generates a continuous information flow as well as developing new ideas to stimulate business. We also produce, every season, 'how-to' videos to be used
for training and to create a strong visual impression as to how
our collection is to be put together. The Anne Klein II how-to
videos are made possible through a co-operative venture with the
Wool Bureau.

6. CLOSING REMARKS

6.1 Identification of the Target Audience and Her Lifestyle
    Profile

We have now identified our target audience. She can be defined
as follows.

(1) She is the career woman, aged 25-49.

(2) She enjoys a minimum HHI of $35 000.

(3) She has a high discretionary income and is an active pur-
    chaser projecting $10 billion in retail sales for 1987.

(4) She is interested in fashion, but not obsessed by it.

(5) She is multi-dimensional and has a limited amount of time
    for clothing purchases.

(6) She requires apparel purchases to be easy, fast, and con-
    venient.

(7) She is both short and tall.

(8) She lives in both hot and cold climates.

Her lifestyle profile is upscale; she is educated; she is involved in her investments; she has a social and political con-
science; she loves the new technology; she is athletic; she is
culturally active; and she indulges herself.

6.2 Marketing Strategy

Our marketing strategy successfully encompasses the following.

(1) Fashion, style, and quality with a designer attitude that
    is broad enough to span professional women's needs from
    the very conservative to the 'fashion-forward'; from dressy
    to casual; from various geographic regions - semi-tropical
    to temperate; from the fashionably tall to figures under
    5 ft 4 in. or 160 cm; and to make fashion shopping easy,
    fast, and convenient.

(2) The marketing philosophy is one of assuming total respon-
    sibility for taking our product direct to the consumer via:

144

(*a*) television;
(*b*) print;
(*c*) mailers;
(*d*) retail training and promotional programmes;
(*e*) the Regional Sales Executive programme; and
(*f*) 'how-to' videos and promotional ideas.

Anne Klein II,
Seventh Avenue,
New York,
N.Y.,
U.S.A.

Design of Complex-Shaped Structures

F. Ko and C. Pastore

Abstract

This paper presents a broad interpretation of industrial textile-product design in terms of the ancient art of braiding. By the creative use of the computer to link design and manufacturing, the feasibility of engineering design and formation of complex structural shapes for advanced composites is illustrated.

1. INTRODUCTION

While the growth rate in apparel and home-furnishing markets in the Western world has slowed considerably in recent years, the opportunity for continued growth in high-performance textiles has never been greater as a result of the materials/processing revolution triggered by the advances in high technology.

High-performance textiles are *highly* engineered fibrous structures with *high* specific strength, *high* specific modulus, *high* fatigue life, and *high* damage-tolerance properties, designed to perform under *high* temperature, *high* pressure, and *high* corrosive environments as well as other extreme conditions. What makes high-performance textiles more attractive commercially than tradition-al textiles is undoubtedly their *high* profit margin.

The applications for high-performance textiles range from human-body replacement parts to space vehicles and space stations. High-performance textiles are used for marine ropes, reinforce-ment of dykes, containment of hazardous waste materials, high-temperature filters, and thermal barriers. Composites of high-performance textiles in resin, metals, or ceramics matrices have found uses as structural components in automobiles, aircraft, and spacecraft. High-performance textile-reinforced composites are being evaluated for engine components such as turbines, piston rings, and numerous other energy-generating devices.

Because textile structures are being used increasingly as en-gineering materials, there is a greater need for engineering analysis and modelling of the performance of textile structures. With the aid of the computer, the complex material/geometry inter-actions of textile structures can now be analysed. The growth of high-performance textiles has also given rise to the rediscovery of many older textile structures and the development of new ways

147

of making textile structures. A case in point is the revival of
interest in braided structures. In this paper the design and formation of complex-shape structures is illustrated in terms of the
braiding process.

2. FORMATION OF COMPLEX SHAPES BY BRAIDING

Traditionally employed as decorative items, braids have evolved
from industrial applications such as cables and electrical sleeves
to the reinforcement of high-performance complex-shape composites.
With large diameters, taking advantage of the conformable nature
of braided structures, a wide variety of complex-shape structures
ranging from coupling shafts (see Fig. 1) to automobile bodies
(see Fig. 2) have been designed and fabricated with a 144-carrier
braiding machine as shown in Fig. 3. The integrity of the structure provided by the intertwining of yarn systems in the opposite
directions facilitates the subsequent resin infiltration of the
braided complex-shape preforms to form composite structures.

Expanding the traditional braiding technology into three-dimensional displacement braiding as described by Ko (1), a large
family of complex structural shapes have been demonstrated as
shown in Fig. 4. The 3-D braid is formed by the alternate displacement of yarn carriers in the X and Y (or r and Θ) directions
as shown in Fig. 5. The formation of shapes is accomplished by
the proper positioning of the carriers and the joining of various
rectangular or annular groups through selected carrier movements.

3. CAE OF COMPLEX-SHAPE STRUCTURES

Although there is no substitute for imaginative conceptual design,
the use of a computer greatly facilitates the translation of design concepts to product-manufacturing. Successfully proven in
the manufacturing industry, it is our objective to illustrate the
application of computer-aided engineering (CAE) to textile-product
design, braiding being used as an example. The CAE system for complex-shape structures includes three components: computer-aided
design (CAD), computer-aided manufacturing (CAM), and computer-
integrated manufacturing (CIM).

3.1 Theoretical Basis

With the identification of constitutive equations relating fabric cover factor to machine-control parameters, a computer-aided
design (CAD) system can be created which directly manufactures a
fabric based on the designer's specifications. The development of
these relationships is purely geometric in nature and is based on
an understanding of the geometry of the braided unit cell. Fig. 6
shows the fundamental unit cell for the 1/1 braid.

The cover factor, K, of a fabric is defined as the projected
yarn area in the unit cell divided by the area of the unit cell:

$$K = A_y / A_f ,$$ (1)

where K = cover factor,
      A_y = projected area of yarn in the unit cell, and
      A_f = area of the unit cell.

If the unit cell has length x and width y, as shown in Fig. 7, the area of the unit cell can be given simply as:

$$A_f = xy. \tag{2}$$

By geometry, the projected area of yarn consists of the area of the two yarns, minus the overlap at the intersection of the two yarns, and the overhang at the corners. This is shown in Fig. 8 and can be expressed mathematically as:

$$A_y = 2w(x^2 + y^2)^{1/2} - (w^2/\sin 2\theta) - \tfrac{1}{2}(w^2\tan\theta + w^2\cot\theta) \tag{3}$$

where A_y = projected area of yarn in the unit cell,
      w = yarn width (in.),
      x = unit-cell width (in.),
      y = unit-cell height (in.) = 1/picks/in., and
      θ = fibre orientation with respect to machine direction.

By taking yarn orientation into consideration, the unit-cell height, y, can be expressed in terms of θ and x:

$$y = x/\tan\theta. \tag{4}$$

By using this identity, Equation (4), and suitable algebraic manipulation of Equation (3), the projected yarn area can be simplified to:

$$A_y = (2xw\cos\theta - w^2) \; / \; \sin\theta \cdot \cos\theta , \tag{5}$$

and the area of the unit cell is:

$$A_f = x^2 \; / \; \tan\theta . \tag{6}$$

From Equations (1), (5), and (6), the cover factor can be expressed as:

$$K = (2xw\cos\theta - w^2) \; / \; (x^2\cos^2\theta). \tag{7}$$

Typically, the designer identifies the cover factor and the mandrel size, and the orientation is to be determined by the CAD system. The unit-cell width, x, can be expressed in terms of the machine and mandrel as follows:

$$x = 2\pi R/N ,$$

where R = radius of the mandrel, and
      N = number of carriers on the braiding machine.

Thus, the orientation that will produce the desired cover factor can be calculated as:

$$\theta = \cos^{-1}[\{Nw/(2\pi KR)\}\{(1 + \sqrt{(1-K)})\}]. \tag{8}$$

149

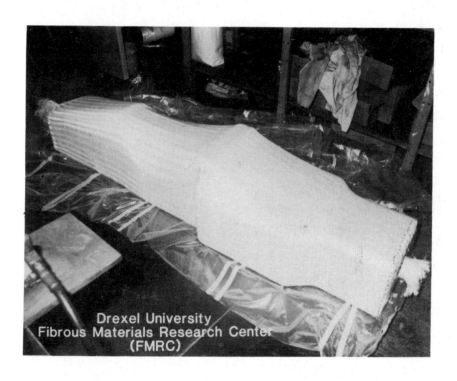

Drexel University
Fibrous Materials Research Center
(FMRC)

Figure 3. FMRL 144 CARRIER TRIAXIAL BRAIDER

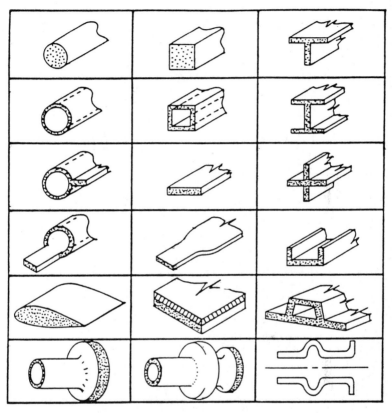

Figure 4.

Net Shape Structures
Produced by 3-D Braiding at the
Fibrous Materials Research Laboratory

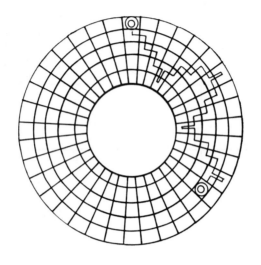

Figure 5. FORMATION OF TUBULAR AND
RECTANGULAR 3-D BRAID

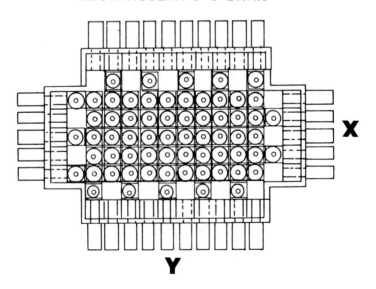

154

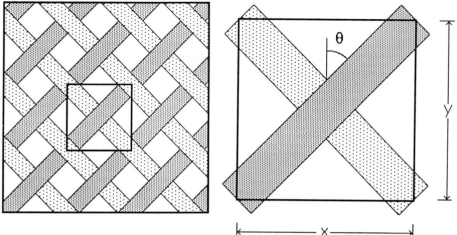

Figure 6. Geometry of a Braided Fabric

Figure 7. Unit Cell of the Braided Fabric

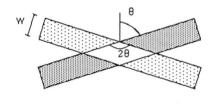

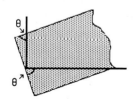

Figure 8. Overlap and Overhang of Yarn in the Unit Cell

155

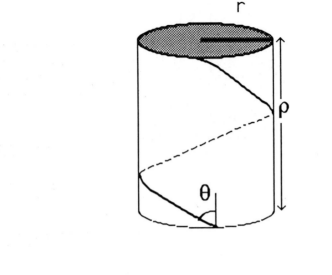

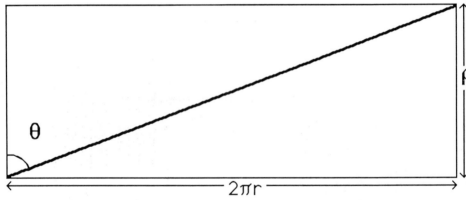

Figure 9. Geometry of a Braided Yarn Helix

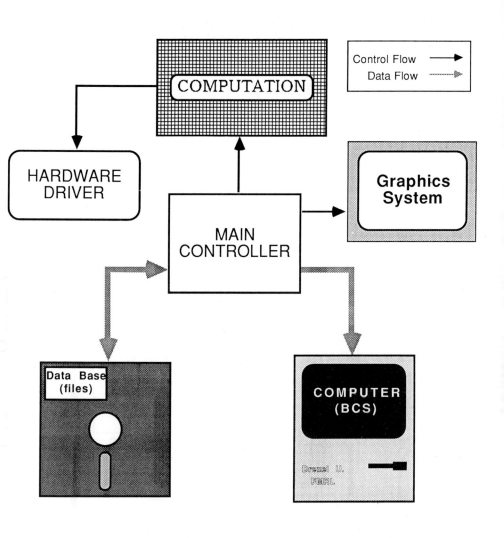

Figure 10. Flow Diagram of CAD Program

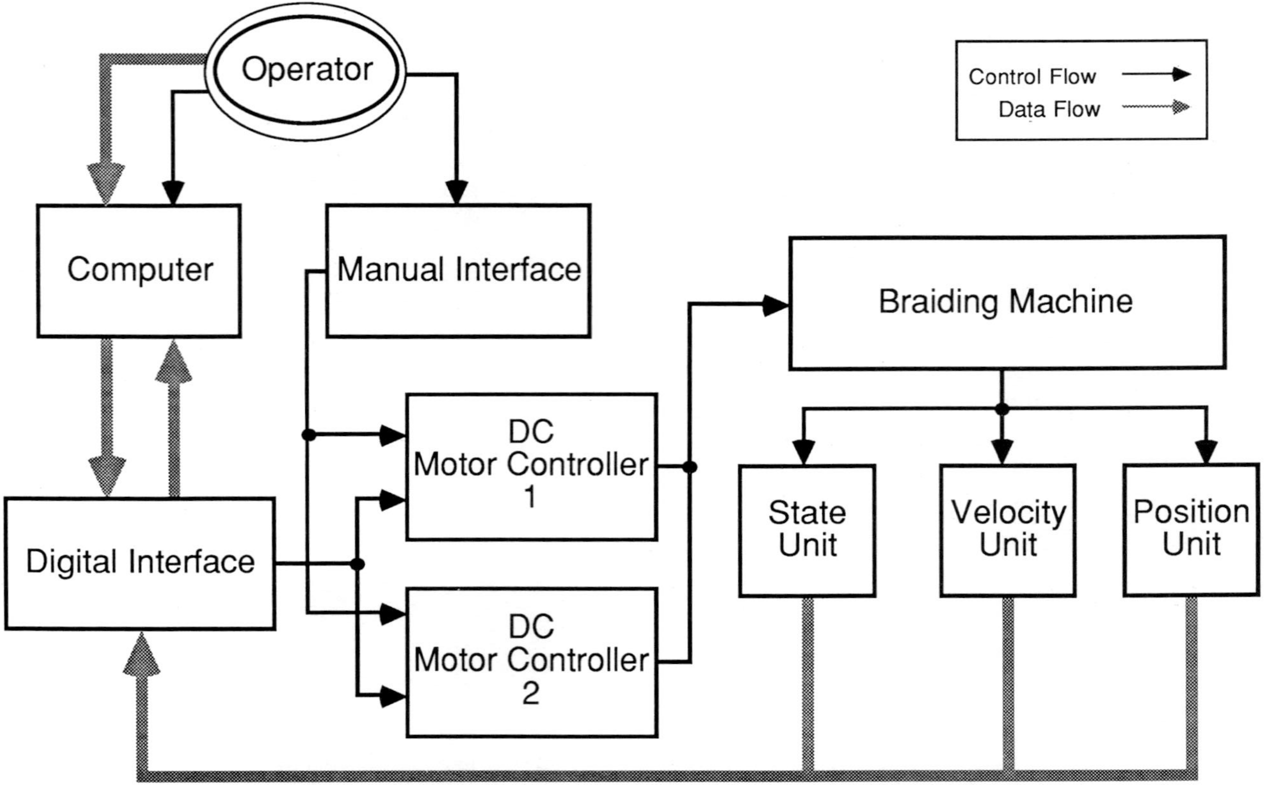

Figure 11. Flow Diagram of BCS

If the mandrel is a complex shape consisting of concentric circular cross-sections, the radius can be given as a function of the length of the mandrel:

$$R = R(t), \tag{9}$$

where R = instantaneous mandrel radius, and
t = length along the mandrel.

Thus, the orientation is also a function of length along the mandrel and can be given directly from Equation (8) as:

$$\Theta(t) = \cos^{-1}[N\omega/\{2\pi KR(t)\} \; \{1 + \sqrt{(1-K)}\}]. \tag{10}$$

3.2 Control Parameters for Braiding

The computer-aided manufacturing (CAM) of the braid is the process of determining the machine-control parameters and sending them to the braiding machine on the basis of the design criteria established previously. With the relationships identified in the previous section, an algorithmic model can be developed to control a braiding machine in order to manufacture a desired fabric. In a simple 1/1 braided fabric, the orientation of the yarn can be related to the machine-control parameters. As shown in Fig. 9, the orientation of the yarn is related to the fabric as:

$$\tan \Theta = 2\pi R/\rho \; , \tag{11}$$

where ρ = length of fabric braided in one carrier rotation (in.).

If the braiding machine has a rotational velocity of v_r (r/s) and the mandrel has a traverse velocity of v_t (in./s), then the distance travelled in one revolution is:

$$\rho = v_t \; / \; v_r. \tag{12}$$

Rewriting Equation (11), we have:

$$\rho = 2\pi R/\tan \Theta . \tag{13}$$

Previously, a relationship was established to find Θ (Equation (8)) and R is known. Thus, ρ can be found at any point. As in Equation (11), ρ can be found for complex mandrel shapes as:

$$\rho(t) = 2\pi R(t) \; / \; \tan \Theta(t). \tag{14}$$

The parameter ρ relates rotational velocity to traverse velocity as shown in Equation (12). Thus the manufacturer has one degree of freedom in controlling the machine operation. Typically, the rotational velocity will be fixed, and the traverse velocity determined as a function of distance along the mandrel:

$$v_t(t) = v_r \cdot \rho(t). \tag{15}$$

The rotational velocity and traverse velocity can be controlled by a variable-speed motor. Thus, the necessary voltages can be calculated and sent to the braiding machine to complete the process.

159

3.3 CIM of Braiding

Computer-integrated manufacturing is the joining of CAD and CAM into a unified package that can take the designer's data and directly control the braiding machine to produce the desired fabric. The CAD aspect of the BCS takes designs in the form of data and links them with a graphics system, computer software, and a hardware driver. The logical flow is illustrated in Fig. 10. The information sent to the hardware driver is processed and executed by the CAM package.

The CAM package is composed of eight parts: a computer, a digital interface, a manual interface, d.c. motor controllers, a position unit, a velocity unit, a state unit, and the braiding machine. The logical flow is illustrated in Fig. 11. With this methodology and the equations developed previously, a coherent, unified system has been developed to bridge the gap between composite design and braided-fabric manufacturing.

4. CONCLUSIONS

This paper illustrates the possibility of the creation of new applications and new marketing opportunities by the development of complex shapes. By employing a relatively obscure textile technology - braiding - it has been shown that computer hardware and software can be adopted to establish an effective and integrated network of design and manufacturing system. By coupling this computer-aided design and manufacturing strategy with a suitable textile-manufacturing process, products with various forms and functions can be developed to meet the ever-changing marketing needs.

REFERENCE

(1) F. Ko. 'Development of High-damage-tolerant, Net-shaped Composites through Textile Structural Design', *Proceedings of the Fifth International Conference on Composite Materials*, (edited by W.C. Harrigan, J. Strife and A.K. Dhingra), AIME, 1985.

Fibrous Materials Research Laboratory,
Department of Materials Engineering,
Drexel University,
Philadelphia,
Pa.,
U.S.A.

The Engineering Design of Suiting Fabrics

T.J. Mahar, R.C. Dhingra, and R. Postle

Abstract

The concept is presented of using engineering principles as an
aid to the design of fabrics with desirable aesthetic characteristics (though fabric colour and pattern are not considered in
this context). Fundamental to this approach is the use of objective measurement of basic mechanical and physical properties of
fabrics, e.g., fabric tensile, shear, bending, lateral-compression,
and surface properties. Relationships are reviewed between these
basic properties of fabrics and fabric aesthetic characteristics,
e.g., fabric handle, fabric drape, fabric tailorability, and garment appearance. Examples are cited of the use of the engineering
approach to fabric design, particularly in relation to selection
of both fibre quality and fabric-finishing routine. Results are
presented that quantify the effect on basic fabric properties of
the individual steps in a commercial fabric-finishing routine for
worsted-type fabrics.

1. INTRODUCTION: ENGINEERING DESIGN

Engineering design of suitings is a two-stage process. The first
stage is to translate the aesthetic properties of the suit required by the consumer into a set of specifications. In the second stage, a product is designed that meets these specifications.

   The aesthetic properties of suits important to the consumer
are comfort, fabric handle, drape, tailorability, and garment
appearance.

   By using this approach, it is technically feasible for a fabric designer to alter measurable physical and mechanical properties of fabrics in order to optimize for a given end-use the
functional and aesthetic performance of a fabric in garment manufacture and in subsequent wear.

2. OBJECTIVE MEASUREMENT OF AESTHETIC PROPERTIES

Objective measurement of the aesthetic qualities of fabrics is
not new. Peirce (1) pioneered work in this field with a paper in
the *Journal of the Textile Institute* in 1930 entitled, 'The Handle
of Cloth as a Measurable Quantity'. Since then, several research

161

groups have made contributions towards objective specification of specific aesthetic characteristics of fabrics, e.g., Cassie *et al.* (2), circa 1955, physiological comfort of fabrics; Lindberg *et al.* (3), 1960-65, fabric tailorability; Kawabata *et al.* (4), since the early 1970s, fabric handle, etc.

Table I lists basic physical and mechanical properties of fabrics that can be objectively measured and a series of related fabric-quality and performance characteristics. Much progress has been made in accurate and reproducible measurement by using laboratory testing instruments to determine those properties listed on the left-hand column of the table because of the essentially objective nature of basic physical and mechanical properties. These advances have culminated in the availability of a system of commercially manufactured instruments, the Kawabata Evaluation System for Fabrics (KESF) (5), which can be used to measure, either directly or indirectly, the properties listed in Table I, with the exception of fabric settability, relaxation shrinkage, and hygral expansion.

The characteristics of fabrics listed in the right-hand column of Table I are largely subjective in nature, and their assessment therefore depends at least partly on our sensory perceptions. These characteristics are difficult to test directly. However, relationships have been established between these fabric characteristics and combinations of basic physical and mechanical properties of the fabric, which can be measured on the KESF (2-4).

3. INTERACTION OF OBJECTIVE MEASUREMENT AND DESIGN OF FABRICS AND GARMENTS

Objective measurement of fabric physical and mechanical properties is being used as an aid to fabric design by both industrial companies (6,7) and research-and-development organizations (8-10). Major areas of application are fibre selection and fabric-finishing. Specific examples of these applications are:

(i) fibre selection - the development of a range of men's summer-suiting fabrics based on blends of New Zealand wool types and Australian merino wools to produce a stiffer, crisper handle for the Japanese market (8);

(ii) addition of chemical additives during finishing - assessment of the effects of surfactants, setting agents (9), and specific treatments such as bleaching (9) and polymer shrink-resist-resin application (10) on the mechanical and aesthetic properties of fabrics; and

(iii) evaluation of fabric-pressing (11) and setting (12) during finishing.

Sponging, a process that is sometimes used in the manufacture of suitings, is also being evaluated in the U.S.A. by using objective-measurement technology (13).

Combinations of physical and mechanical properties of fabrics have been isolated (14) to characterize the fabric handle/quality of broad groupings of winter suiting-type fabrics, e.g., flannel,

Table I

Basic Physical and Mechanical Properties of Fabrics
and Related Quality and Performance Characteristics
of Fabrics and Garments

Physical and Mechanical Properties of Fabrics	Fabric Quality and Mechanical Performance
Uniaxial and biaxial tension	Fabric handle and drape
Fabric shear under tension	Fabric formability and tailoring properties
Pure bending	
Lateral compression	Garment appearance and seam pucker
Longitudinal compression and buckling	Mechanical stability and shape retention
Surface roughness and friction	Wrinkle-recovery and crease-retention
Specific volume	Dimensional stability
Settability	Abrasion- and pilling-resistance
Relaxation shrinkage	
Hygral expansion	Mechanical and physiological comfort

163

Table II

Construction and Finishing Details for Test Fabrics

	Fabric 1	Fabric 2	Fabric 3
Construction			
Wool-fibre diameter (nominal average)	22.5 μm	22.5 μm	22.5 μm
Polyester-fibre linear density (dtex)	–	3.3	3.3
Yarn linear density (dtex)	R44/2	R40/2	R52/2
Singles twist (turns/m)	600	650	550
Folding twist (turns/m)*	560	728	630
Fabric sett (finished) ends/cm	25	35	17
picks/cm	21	25	18
Weave	2/2 twill	3×1 satin	plain
Mass (g/m²)	275	290	212

Finishing

Fabric 1	Fabric 2 & 3
Soap-milling	Heat-set
–	Singe
Scour	Scour
Brush/crop	Brush/crop
Open-decatize	Open-decatize
Paper-press	Paper-press
Pressure-decatize	Pressure-decatize

serge, and more subtle variations, i.e., coarse or fine flannel, and slight variations in texture, firmness, and fullness of basic plain and twill constructions.

The effect of individual stages within a worsted-fabric-finishing routine and the importance of fabric formability in garment manufacture are discussed in the following sections.

3.1 Fabric-finishing

The dramatic effect of fabric-finishing on fabric shear (under tension) and bending properties is well documented (15). During finishing, both the fabric shear and bending stiffnesses are greatly reduced, the reduction resulting in a more supple fabric. Fabric shear and bending hysteresis are reduced to an even greater extent, which enables the fabric to recover more fully from deformation or crushing.

In this paper, a study is reported in which a series of three worsted and worsted/polyester-fibre suiting fabrics was sampled after the following steps of a commercial finishing operation:

    (i) weaving - loomstate:
    (ii) heat-setting - wool/polyester-fibre fabrics only;
  (iii) scouring;
   (iv) pressing; and
    (v) pressure-decatizing.

The construction and finishing details for these fabrics are given in Table II.

Measurements were made of the fabric mechanical and surface properties (including fabric shear and bending properties) of these samples taken at each step in the finishing.

The results of the full set of KESF measurements on these samples can be summarized as follows:

(i) there is a dramatic effect of scouring, and heat-setting where appropriate, on the shear, bending, and some tensile properties of the fabrics, and a small effect of the other finishing steps on these properties; and

(ii) there is a dramatic effect of pressing on fabric-surface properties and fabric compressibility and thickness, and a small effect of the other finishing steps on these properties.

The effect of the fabric-finishing process on each group of properties tested by the KESF is discussed below.

3.1.1 Tensile Properties

The effects of fabric-finishing steps on fabric extensibility are shown in Fig. 1. A large increase in fabric extensibility for the pure-wool fabric occurs during fabric-scouring, namely, from 5.6% to 11.6% in the warp direction and from 3.2% to 6.6% in the weft direction. This is followed by much smaller decreases in extensibility in subsequent finishing steps. Since this increase in extensibility is common to both principal fabric directions, it is unlikely to be due to a simple interchange of warp- and weft-yarn crimp during scouring.

Fabric tensile resiliency increases during finishing much more in the case of the two wool/polyester-fibre fabrics than for the wool fabric, but the final value for the two blended-fibre fabrics is approximately the same as that for the pure-wool fabric.

3.1.2 Shear Properties

Fig. 2 demonstrates the dramatic effect of scouring on the shear rigidity (Fig. 2(a)) and on shear hysteresis (at 5° shear strain – see Fig. 2(b)). These reductions are as much as 76% of the original value (e.g., for shear hysteresis of the pure-wool fabric) and are indicative of the greatly reduced inter-yarn pressures in fabrics after scouring.

3.1.3 Bending Properties

Similar dramatic changes in the values of fabric-bending parameters are also evident after scouring or heat-setting/scouring as shown in Fig. 3. Both the bending rigidity and bending hysteresis are greatly reduced during scouring or heat-setting/scouring, e.g., the reduction in bending hysteresis after scouring is 79% of the pre-scour value for the pure-wool fabric.

3.1.4 Compression Properties

The compressibility of each fabric decreased with progress through the finishing routine as shown in Fig. 4. However, the greatest decrease occurred during fabric-pressing, where reductions in compressibility of from 32% to 38% were observed. There was also a large increase during finishing of compressional resilience for the pure-wool fabric, and relatively unchanged resilience for the wool/polyester-fibre fabrics.

3.1.5 Surface Properties

The variation in fabric surface roughness is depicted in Fig. 5. Here again, fabric-pressing is shown to have the greatest effect of the various finishing operations. These results quantify the effect of pressing on the surface roughness of these three different fabrics. The much greater roughness of the plain-weave fabric, 9.5 μm compared with 2.6 μm for the 2/2 twill and 3.0 μm for the 3/1 satin, is also highlighted in Fig. 5.

3.1.6 Structural Properties

Fabric specific volume is also greatly affected by pressing, and heat-setting where appropriate, for each of the three fabrics, as indicated in Fig. 6. The characteristic bulkiness of pure-wool fabrics is evidenced by the slightly higher specific volume of the finished pure-wool fabric, 2.7 cm^3/g, compared with the two wool/

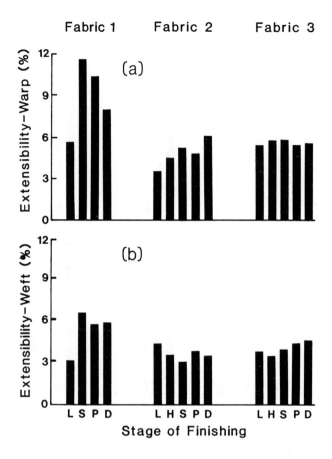

Fig. 1 Fabric extensibility in the warp (a) and weft (b) directions after various stages of fabric-finishing, namely,
L: loomstate; H: after heat-setting; S: after scouring;
P: after pressing; and, D: after pressure-decatizing
(note the increase in extensibility after scouring in
the case of the pure-wool fabric, fabric 1)

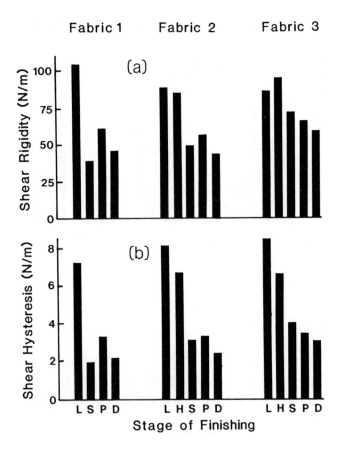

Fabric 1   Fabric 2   Fabric 3

Fig. 2   Fabric shear rigidity in the warp (a) and weft (b) directions after various stages of fabric-finishing, namely,
L: loomstate; H: after heat-setting; S: after scouring;
P: after pressing; and, D: after pressure-decatizing
(fabric scouring has the greatest effect on shear rigidity of all the finishing operations)

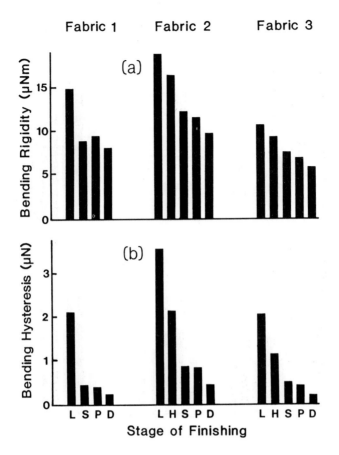

Fig. 3 Average fabric bending rigidity (a) and bending hysteresis (b) after various stages of fabric-finishing, namely,
L: loomstate; H: after heat-setting; S: after scouring;
P: after pressing; and, D: after pressure-decatizing
(fabric-scouring, and heat-setting where appropriate,
have a great effect on fabric-bending properties)

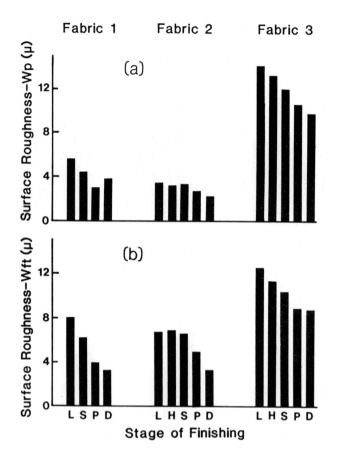

Fig. 5 Fabric surface roughness in the warp (a) and weft (b)
directions after various stages of fabric finishing,
namely, L: loomstate; H: after heat-setting; S: after
scouring; P: after pressing; and, D: after pressure-
decatizing (the shorter weave floats of the plain-weave
fabric, fabric 3, contribute to an over-all rougher surface for this fabric)

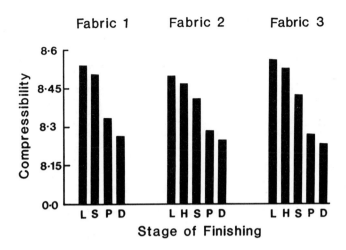

Fig. 4 Fabric compressibility after various stages of fabric-
finishing, namely, L: loomstate; H: after heat-setting;
S: after scouring; P: after pressing; and, D: after
pressure-decatizing (in this case pressing has the greatest effect on fabric properties)

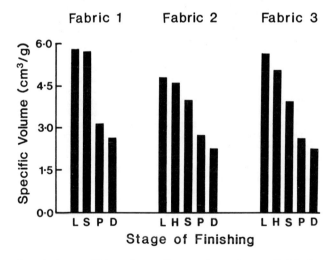

Fig. 6 Fabric specific volume after various stages of fabric-
finishing, namely, L: loomstate; H: after heat-setting;
S: after scouring; P: after pressing; and, D: after
pressure-decatizing (fabric specific volume is most
strongly influenced by fabric-pressing)

polyester-fibre fabrics, 2.3 cm³/g in each case. These differences occur despite the different weave constructions in the three fabrics.

The major influence of fabric-pressing on important fabric surface and compression properties, including fabric thickness, highlighted in this report demonstrates the scope for the application of engineering-design principles in this process. Indeed, recent work (16) in which objective measurement was used has quantified the effect of pressing-wrapper pressure, fabric regain, and machine-setting conditions on wool-fabric surface properties.

3.2 Fabric Formability

Fabric formability refers to the ease with which an essentially two-dimensional fabric can be made to conform smoothly to the complex three-dimensional shapes required in a tailored garment, e.g., a suit coat. A measure of fabric formability along the major thread directions of the fabric has been defined (17) on the basis of measurements made on the KESF. The amount of 'ease' or fullness that a fabric can accommodate in the major thread directions without puckering near the seam has been shown (18) to be related to this measure and to fibre type/fabric settability.

Measurements were made of fabric formability in the warp and weft directions for 40 summer-weight suiting fabrics. These fabrics were make up into suits, and suit-coat appearance was assessed by a panel of experienced staff from a major Japanese suiting manufacturer (19). Results indicate that it is difficult to tailor suits of acceptable appearance from fabrics with values of formability in either thread direction of less than 20×10^{-4} mm² (17).

4. FABRIC DATA BASE

On the basis of the establishment of relationships between fabric physical and mechanical properties and various aesthetic characteristics of fabrics, a number of researchers have established fabric maps, which set out zones of acceptable or optimal combinations of these fabric properties in order to achieve desired aesthetic characteristics in the final product, e.g., Lindberg et al. (3), van Krugten et al. (20), Kawabata et al. (21), and Postle et al. (22).

More recently, the increased availability and sophistication of computers has led to the concept of using data-base systems (23) and even an expert-system approach (24) in order to provide a 'user-friendly' interface for designers and technicians within the textile and clothing industries to apply this knowledge.

5. CONCLUSION

Developments have been made, and are continuing to be made, in both the measurement of fabric mechanical and physical properties and their practical application. The use of these developments by suiting-fabric designers and manufacturers is an application of the principles of engineering design to the production of apparel fabrics with aesthetic properties acceptable to the consumer.

Research is in progress that will, for example, provide an objective basis for the establishment of finishing-machine parameters during worsted finishing. This, and other such work, will lead to the possibility of more precise engineering of the aesthetic properties of fabrics. Progress in information technologies, especially data-base and expert-systems approaches, should ensure that the benefits of this area of fabric research are available in a suitable form for commercial application.

ACKNOWLEDGEMENTS

The authors gratefully acknowledge the co-operation of Shri Dinesh Mills Ltd, India, in supplying the three suiting fabrics at various stages of finishing. They are also indebted to Mr J. Galea and Mrs Z. Peselson for undertaking the necessary technical work for this paper.

REFERENCES

(1) F.T. Peirce. *J. Text. Inst.*, 1930, 21, T377.

(2) A.B.D. Cassie. *J. Text. Inst.*, 1962, 53, P739.

(3) J.L. Lindberg, L. Waesterberg, and R. Svenson. *J. Text. Inst.*, 1960, 51, T1475.

(4) S. Kawabata in 'Objective Specification of Fabric Quality, Mechanical Properties and Performance' (edited by S. Kawabata, R. Postle, and M. Niwa), the Textile Machinery Society of Japan, Osaka, 1982, p.31.

(5) S. Kawabata in 'The Standardisation and Analysis of Hand Evaluation' (edited by S. Kawabata), the Textile Machinery Society of Japan, Osaka, 2nd edition, 1980.

(6) M. Mori in 'Objective Evaluation of Apparel Fabrics' (edited by R. Postle, S. Kawabata, and M. Niwa), the Textile Machinery Society of Japan, Osaka, 1983, p.55.

(7) Y. Matsui in 'Objective Evaluation of Apparel Fabrics', (edited by R. Postle, S. Kawabata and M. Niwa), the Textile Machinery Society of Japan, Osaka, 1983, p.301.

(8) G. Carnaby, S. Kawabata, M. Niwa, M. Mori, K. Saito, and R. J. Walls in 'Objective Measurement: Applications to Product Design and Process Control' (edited by S. Kawabata, R. Postle, and M. Niwa), the Textile Machinery Society of Japan, Osaka, 1986, p.75.

(9) E. Finnimore in 'Objective Specification of Fabric Quality, Mechanical Properties, and Performance' (edited by S. Kawabata, R. Postle, and M. Niwa), the Textile Machinery Society of Japan, Osaka, 1982, p.273.

(10) A.G. de Boos in 'Objective Specification of Fabric Quality, Mechanical Properties and Performance' (edited by S. Kawabata, R. Postle, and M. Niwa), the Textile Machinery Society of Japan, Osaka, 1982, p.285.

(11) S. de Jong, J.W. Snaith, and N.A. Michie. *Text. Res. J.*, 1986, <u>56</u>, 759.

(12) A.G. de Boos, F. Harrigan, and M.A. White in 'Objective Evaluation of Apparel Fabrics', (edited by R. Postle, S. Kawabata, and M. Niwa), the Textile Machinery Society of Japan, Osaka, 1983, p.75.

(13) F. Fortess. Private communication.

(14) A.E. Stearn, R.L. D'Arcy, T.J. Mahar, and R. Postle in 'Objective Measurement: Applications to Product Design and Process Control' (edited by S. Kawabata, R. Postle, and M. Niwa), the Textile Machinery Society of Japan, Osaka, 1986, p.557.

(15) R. Postle, in 'Objective Evaluation: Applications to Product Design and Process Control' (edited by S. Kawabata, R. Postle, and M. Niwa), the Textile Machinery Society of Japan, Osaka, 1986, p.1.

(16) D.H. Tester and S. de Jong. 'The Effect of Pressing Process Variables on the Physics and Mechanical Properties of Wool Fabric' (in preparation).

(17) T.J. Mahar, I. Ajiki, R. Postle, and R.C. Dhingra in 'Objective Evaluation of Apparel Fabrics', (edited by R. Postle, S. Kawabata and M. Niwa), the Textile Machinery Society of Japan, Osaka, 1983, p.359.

(18) T.J. Mahar, R.C. Dhingra, and R. Postle in 'Objective Specification of Fabric Quality, Mechanical Properties and Performance' (edited by S. Kawabata, R. Postle, and M. Niwa), the Textile Machinery Society of Japan, Osaka, 1982, p.301.

(19) Melbo Clothing Company, Ohte Dari 1-37, Higashi-ku, Osaka 540, Japan.

(20) J. Westerveld and F.J. van Krugten. TNO Report No. 13030 (1226-030)-13, 1967.

(21) H. Morooka and M. Niwa. *J. Text. Mach. Soc. Japan*, 1978, <u>24</u>, 105.

(22) V.L. Gibson and R. Postle. *Text. Res. J.*, 1978, <u>48</u>, 14.

(23) R. Postle, T.J. Mahar, and R.C. Dhingra. *Proc. Int. Wool Text. Res. Conf. Tokyo*, 1985, III-90.

(24) R. Postle, J.I. Curiskis and O. Zubzanda in 'Objective Measurement: Applications to Product Design and Process Control' (edited by S. Kawabata, R. Postle, and M. Niwa), the Textile Machinery Society of Japan, Osaka, 1986, p.11.

174

(TJM) CSIRO Division of Textile Physics,
Ryde,
New South Wales,
Australia.

(RCD and RP) Department of Textile Technology,
School of Fibre Science and Technology,
University of New South Wales,
Kensington,
New South Wales,
Australia.

Designer's Guide to Computer Graphics

L. Miller

Abstract

Computer graphics now offer a degree of flexibility in image creation and manipulation that cannot normally be matched by traditional methods, and designers in all fields are now looking at
this technology with increasing interest and awareness. The paper
sets out to explain the general concepts of computer graphics and
concludes by looking at the barriers that have to be crossed before a major new leap forward can be taken.

1. GRAPHICS

Although the origin of the word 'graphics' in the strictest sense
means 'to write', common acceptance of the word has now been extended to mean visual writing with lines or colour, covering drawing, painting, and etching, and the key part of today's dictionary
definition is the phrase 'having the facility of vivid description'. In the world of computers, the term has come to apply to
the process of creating visually descriptive images on a colour
monitor, images that simulate reality ... or fantasy.

Traditionally computer graphics evolved as a better means of
displaying numerical data, with histograms, pie-charts, and graphs
providing an easier way of assimilating the indigestible mass of
numbers being spewed out by the world's business computers. In
the late 1950s and 1960s, the only available display device was
the vector refresh tube, and, although this provided a useful system for line-drawing, it suffered the disadvantage of being capable only of very limited colour, and realistic images were difficult to generate.

It was the arrival, in the late 1960s, of raster-display systems that provided the major breakthrough needed by the computer-
graphics industry. Adapted from television technology, the raster-
scan system provided a new graphics device that was inexpensive
and opened the door to realistic full-colour images.

1.1 Thanks for the Memory

In order to appreciate how a raster image is created, we must
first consider what is meant by memory. All computers have an
area of memory. Essentially, this can be considered as a work-

space, the area in which the computer handles the program that
it is currently running, and the amount of memory built into a
computer governs the size of program it can handle.

Memory can be usefully thought of as masses of pigeon-holes,
into which information or instructions are passed. When you type
something at the keyboard of a computer, the letters you type are
passed into areas of the computer's memory for immediate - or
subsequent - processing, rather like the sorting office of the
postal service. Similarly, when you load a program from a floppy
disc into the computer, the program is copied piece by piece se-
quentially into the computer's memory. When the program is being
run, it is being handled entirely within the computer's memory.
This gives a certain sense of security, as you can rest safe in
the knowledge that any mistakes you make will not affect the original program, since this stays safely on the disc and is no
longer used once it has been loaded into memory.

1.1.1 Screen Memory

One special area of the computer's memory-space is referred to
as 'screen memory', and this is of particular interest in considering graphics. Screen memory is the work-space in which the
computer stores the information that is to be displayed on the
screen.

In a business computer system that is concerned only with
words and numbers, and which does not have any graphics facilities, the screen will probably display up to 25 lines of writing,
each line holding up to 80 characters across its width. To hold
this display in memory, the computer must allocate one 'pigeon-
hole' for each possible position, and into this box (or memory
location) it will place a representation of the letter or number
to be shown on the screen at that point. Such a system will therefore require a screen memory of 80 × 25 units. Each letter in the
alphabet, as well as the digits from 1 to 0 and the various other
keyboard characters, is identified to the computer by a special
numeric code, and it is this code that is stored in screen memory.
Screen memory is scanned by the computer 25 or 30 times per second, and any values found in these screen locations are passed
to a 'character generator', which recreates the letter at the correct place on the screen. The shape of the letter is created as
a pattern of tiny dots in a grid, usually about 7 × 9.

The standard code in use today is the ASCII code, and in this,
for example, the letter A is given the numeric code of 65. If you
type the letter A into a computer, the value 65 is placed into
the screen-memory location corresponding to the current cursor
position. On the next scan (1/25 second later), this value is
found in memory, and the letter is generated on the screen, dot
by dot. By extending the range of characters to cover more than
those shown on the keyboard, simple graphics shapes can be added,
each within the size allocated to one letter. These can be used
in place of letters or numbers to build up very simple graphics
images, as can be seen in any Teletext display. Such graphics
displays are referred to as block graphics since the images are
built up by using simple block-shapes, and they are generally restricted to the normal 80 × 25 blocks per display. The amount of

detail that can be generated by using block graphics is obviously
very limited.

1.2 Pixel Graphics

Pixel graphics follows the same concept, but takes the potential
much further. Rather than use blocks to display characters or
shapes, the image is created out of individual dots, each dot
being referred to as a pixel (short for picture element). This,
of course, means that the screen memory has to be large enough
to allow each individual dot to be held separately in memory, so
that, if we require an image to be generated with 600 dots across
and 400 dots high, then we need an area of screen memory with 600
× 400 units (or boxes) to hold the display information for each
point on the screen.

The display information held in memory is no longer an ASCII
code, but an indication of whether the particular pixel is illu-
minated, together with any colour information. In order to keep
the image steady and constant on the screen, the image must be
regenerated every 1/25 second. In a graphics system with 1000 ×
750 pixels, the computer must scan three-quarters of a million
memory locations, ascertain the colour for each, and generate the
correct colour for each pixel on screen - all in 1/25 second.
This process of scanning the screen memory (i.e., the raster scan)
gives its name to this type of system.

A graphics system will therefore contain two distinct areas of
screen memory - one area 80 × 25 to hold the normal alpha-numeric
display, data from which are processed to the screen via the character generator, and a separate area equivalent to the total number of pixels, which is scanned and processed to the screen via
the display controller. This area of graphics memory is sometimes
referred to as the 'frame buffer' or 'refresh buffer'. These two
areas may be displayed independently on separate monitors, generally a monochrome monitor for the alpha-numeric display, and a
colour monitor for the graphics. Alternatively, they may both use
the same monitor, with an 'overlay' system of windows to separate
the two displays.

The number of pixels provided by any graphics display is referred to as the *resolution* of the system, and typical figures
for today are 768 × 576, 1024 × 768, and 1280 × 1024. The higher
the resolution, the more detail can be included in the image, but
the *fineness* of detail is influenced by the *density* of the pixels
when displayed on the monitor, rather than the resolution. It can
be seen that, if a system has a resolution of 768 pixels in the
width, and if it is shown on a monitor with a 10-in. display, the
resulting image will have a pixel density of 76.8 per inch. A system with a higher resolution of 1024 pixels, but shown on a monitor of 13-in. display width, will result in the *same* pixel density. The image will not have any finer detail, but, of course,
there will be more of it.

1.3 Bytes

In order to understand the basic concepts of computer graphics,

179

it is necessary to appreciate the meaning of one essential computer term, the word BYTE.

Computers work entirely in minute electrical pulses, and every
instruction or piece of information given to the computer has to
be interpreted into simple pulses. A pulse is either ON or OFF -
either it is there or it is not there - and the computer uses the
pulse to represent the two numbers Zero and One; no pulse means
Zero, a pulse means One. Although we are used to counting in tens
(Decimal), using the ten digits from 0 to 9 - for the simple and
convenient reason that we were born with ten fingers - it is
equally possible to count by using only two digits. Numbers represented by using only Zero and One are known as Binary Numbers,
and Table I shows some equivalent Decimal and Binary Numbers.

Each unit in a Binary Number is known as a Binary Digit, and
this is shortened to a BIT. As can be seen from Table I, if four
bits are used to create a number, then any number from 0 to 15
can be represented. To depict a number greater than 15 needs more
bits. Similarly it can be seen that eight bits can represent numbers from 0 to 255.

The movement of data internally within the computer is normally
done in blocks of 8 bits, and a unit of 8 bits is known as a BYTE.

A byte can therefore be used to represent any number from 0 to
255. If each location of screen memory is capable of holding one
byte, then up to 256 different characters or letters can be selected from the character generator, as any character can be being
represented by a single byte. When the capacity of a computer's
working memory is referred to as 512K, this means that the area
of memory can accommodate 512 000 bytes, or half a million characters.

2. SCREEN COLOUR

In the early days of colour graphics, the allocation of limited
screen memory was usually a matter of compromise between screen
colour and resolution. For example, if the system was based on
69K bytes of screen memory (i.e., 60 000 locations), this could
give a resolution of 300 × 200 pixels, with one byte to each
pixel. This in turn meant that 256 colour numbers could be stored
and allocated to each pixel, giving a display capable of showing
256 colours on screen at any one time, with a 300 × 200 resolution.

Alternatively, if each memory location held only 4 bits (or
half a byte), then the 60 000 bytes could be spread over twice
as many locations (i.e., 120 000 pixels), giving a resolution of
400 × 300. But, since each pixel can only be allocated a 4-bit
number rather than a byte, this only permits a choice of up to
16 colours for the display. Similarly, if colour is not required
at all, then a black and white display needs only one bit per
pixel (it is either ON or OFF, zero or one). This means each byte
of screen memory can correspond to eight pixels, giving 480 000
pixels or a resolution of 800 × 600. These alternatives are given
in Table II.

Such considerations originally gave rise to the appearance of graphics systems with alternative options - you could have medium resolution with lots of colours, or you could have higher resolution with fewer colours. More recently, with memory chips becoming cheaper, larger allocations of screen memory are eliminating the need for compromise, and most serious graphics systems are now based on one byte per pixel, giving a 256-colour display, although in engineering applications there is still a leaning towards 16 colours with any extra memory being allocated to even greater resolution. The original compromise is resolving itself into a clearer division of function, with full-colour systems being aimed at the graphics and simulation market, and high-res 16-colour systems for the CAD-CAM market.

In considering screen colour, we must also pay regard to the variation of colour that can be provided. If the display can show 16 or 256 colours at one time, to what extent can each of these colours be varied ... if at all? To appreciate this, we must first consider how colours are generated on the monitor.

Colour monitors, like television sets, create colour by additive mixing of red, green, and blue lights. The colours in question are created by red, green, and blue phosphor dots on the back of the glass tube. Beams of electrons from three separate guns are directed at the back of the tube, and these pass through a thin metal shadow-mask just behind the glass. The mask permits the beam from each gun to strike only the correct colour of phosphor dots, one gun for each colour. As the dots are bombarded by their respective guns, they glow brightly for a brief period, but, since the entire sweep takes less than 1/30 second, they are recharged continuously to give a bright steady picture.

Each group of three phosphor dots is known as a triad, and there must be several triads on the monitor for every pixel in screen memory. For this reason the monitor must have a 'triad resolution' capable of handling the system's pixel resolution, and colour monitors are usually specified in terms of the pixel resolution they are capable of displaying.

The brightness of any phosphor dot on the screen is governed by the intensity of the electron beam at that point in the raster scan. The actual colour of the pixel on the screen depends on the relative intensities of the red, green, and blue dots in the clusters of triads that make up the pixel, and is therefore a combination of these three values, known as the RGB values for the pixel.

Referring again to screen memory, with one byte stored in each location, this gives up to 256 values or colour numbers that can be allocated to each pixel. Screen memory therefore only stores the colour number (any value from 0 to 255) and does not give any indication of the actual colour specification. This is stored separately in a Colour Look-up Table, which is simply another specific area of memory. The table allocates three bytes of memory to each colour number, one byte for each of the red, green, and blue values. Since one byte can represent up to 256 values, such a system permits 256 brightness values for each of the red, green, and blue electron beams. This gives 256 cubed possible colours that can be generated on the system, which is 16.7

million colours.

This number of colours is obviously a theoretical figure; the electron beams may be capable of generating 16.7 million variations in relative intensity, but it does not follow that the phosphors will respond with such precision in a strictly linear way. However, as the human eye is not capable of distinguishing 16 million colours anyway, the argument may seem slightly irrelevant. Nevertheless, the point should be remembered that the final colour is very much dependent on the monitor used in the monitor and on the way they respond to the varying intensities of the electron beams, and it does not necessarily follow that different monitors will behave in the same way.

A system such as that described above, using one byte for each pixel, is described as an 8-bit system (one byte = 8 bits), and the byte that corresponds to each pixel can only indicate a colour number between zero and 255. (The actual colour is then found from the Look-up Table.) The screen display can therefore only contain a maximum of 256 colours at any time, although these colours can be varied individually over the theoretical 16 million possible shades. If, however, the screen memory is expanded to three times its size, so that each pixel can be allocated THREE bytes, these bytes can now be used to represent the red, green, and blue values directly. This means there is no longer any need to go via 256 colour numbers to a Look-up Table to establish the colour. Instead EACH pixel memory contains its own colour data within the full range of 256 values for each of the red, green, and blue, so that each pixel can be ANY colour out of the 16 million palette. Such systems are referred to as 24-bit systems, as there are three bytes per pixel in screen memory.

These 24-bit systems are used mainly for video work, particularly where frame-grabbing from a video camera is required in full colour.

3. GRAPHICS SYSTEMS

A standard personal computer may contain no graphics facilities at all, or it may have some limited graphics with its corresponding area of screen memory allocated accordingly. For most serious graphics, however, the extra screen memory (or frame buffer) must be added to the host computer together with the associated display controller. This can be done by inserting a suitable graphics card (or circuit board) into one of the expansion slots of the host computer, and coupling a high-resolution colour monitor to the output terminals of the graphics card. This type of arrangement is normally referred to as 'on-board' graphics.

Alternatively, the graphics card can be housed in its own separate box, making it more independent of the choice of host computer, as separate interface cards are then produced to fit a range of hosts. The interface card is inserted into an expansion slot in the host, and a cable connects the interface card to the graphics box. The monitors are then connected directly to their respective units, the monochrome monitor for alpha-numeric display to the host computer in the normal way, and the colour monitor directly to the graphics box. A further advantage of such boxed graphics systems is that they are more capable of expansion, allowing, for example, for the addition of a video 'frame-grabber', which enables images from a video camera to be loaded into screen memory, and subsequently manipulated by the graphics software.

Another useful addition that can frequently be made to boxed graphics systems is the provision of additional or extended screen memory. A system, for example, with a resolution of 768 × 576 can be provided with a second equivalent area of screen memory on which a second independent image can be generated. While only one image can be seen at a time, the facility to switch between two displays can be useful and is equivalent to having two separate pages to work on. Alternatively, the total screen memory can be treated as one large page, with a resolution of 768 across by 1152 high, containing one continuous image, and, although the total image cannot be seen at once, the screen provides a window, 768 × 576, which can be moved up and down across the image. Such a system would be described as having a 'virtual' resolution of 768 × 1152, with a 'displayable' resolution of 768 × 576.

Changing colours is simply a matter of modifying the RGB values in the Look-up Table, and all pixels featuring that particular colour number will be changed instantly, within the next scan of screen memory. This makes it very easy to create images that use areas of specific colours, as required in most forms of textile design, and modify these colours individually.

3.1   24-Bit Systems

The 8-bit system uses one byte of memory for each pixel. If, however, the screen memory is expanded to three times its size, so that each pixel can be allocated THREE bytes, these bytes can now be used to represent the red, green, and blue values directly. This means there is no longer any need to go via 256 colour numbers to a Look-up Table to establish the colour. Instead EACH pixel in screen memory contains its own colour data within the full range of 256 values for each of the red, green, and blue, so that each pixel can be ANY colour out of the 16 million palette. Such systems are referred to as 24-bit systems, as there are three bytes per pixel in screen memory.

As mentioned above, 24-bit systems are used mainly for video work, particularly when frame-grabbing from a video camera is required in full colour. It should be kept in mind, however, that such systems no longer provide the facility to make global changes to a colour throughout a design. Each pixel has its own individual colour data, and changing the colour of a pixel will not affect any other pixel.

4. GRAPHICS SOFTWARE

Software is the generic term for the programs that can be run on any computer system, whether it is word-processing software, database software, software for stock control or for invoicing, or software to display graphics images on a colour monitor.

Any computer-graphics system can only be considered to be as good as the software it has to run on it. A computer without software is like a car without petrol – it will not go very far. The system may be capable of displaying millions of colours, but, if there is no software that allows the designer to create the type of image he wants, then it is of little use.

Regrettably, there is not much compatibility in computer-graphics systems. Each graphics system uses its own in-built graphics codes, and a program written to run on one system is unlikely to run on any other. This incompatibility lies in the individual graphics system, and there is the further complication that each graphics system will probably run on a limited range of host computers. Programs can be structured in such a way that they can be modified to work on a variety of graphics systems, but this decision rests with the writers of the software, and the tendency is to limit such portability to a handful of well-established systems.

Any new graphics system to be launched on the market needs to have some software to make it usable, and a general-purpose painting system is the commonest answer. Paint systems generally use a pen and tablet (or possibly a 'mouse') to permit free-hand sketching on the screen, with a full set of accompanying menus to select a range of functions. What must be remembered is that these paint systems are 'general-purpose', and are not aimed specifically at the needs of any particular area of design. The printed-fabric designer may be irritated to find there is no half-drop facility, or in-built colour separation; the carpet designer will find there is no facility to vary the pitch of his design, since all pixels are probably square. The programs are aimed down the centre of the market place.

The same really holds true of dedicated software, though to a lower degree. A program for woven-fabric design, although aimed at this specific market, must still aim to provide facilities that satisfy the majority of users, and the manufacturer whose working methods are at odds with the rest of the world will be unlikely to find software to suit him. Even in situations where the software is 95% right, to get the final 5% just the way YOU want it will probably mean a special commission. But software does not evolve by itself. It is only by getting feedback from users that the best software can be developed, and the longer an industry takes to grasp the nettle of new technology, the longer it will be before the definitive software is written.

Most areas of textile design are now catered for to some extent with dedicated software, offering design functions, various degrees of simulation of the fabric (good in weaving, poor in knitting), and usually some form of data extraction or direct machine linkage. The primary advantage of using this technology to simulate fabric designs is in reducing the amount of fabric sampling that has to be done. Design ideas can be seen, discussed, modified, built upon, all at no cost. Changes can be made instantly, and the result examined immediately, eliminating the need to wait while fresh samples are manufactured. Designers can be more adventurous, as even the wildest ideas cost nothing to simulate on the monitor, and they MAY work. Buyers can study ideas for fabrics before any fabrics are created, and, if samples are requested from these ideas, then at least these samples are ones in which an interest has been expressed. The demand for designers to move into the world of electronic design will almost certainly come from the fabric buyers, who will demand the speed of design made possible by these systems and will not be prepared to wait three or four weeks while a trial sample is manufactured, particularly if competitors can offer a service of instant design manipulation.

5. HARD COPY

A design or fabric simulation created on a monitor can generally be reproduced on paper by two alternative methods - by means of a colour printer or by photography. An important aspect of either method is the question of colour fidelity - how closely does the print match the screen original?

The technology of colour printing from a computer display is still fairly new, and even the newest colour printers - hot from Japan - cannot yet match the number of colours produced by the graphics system on the monitor. In the past twelve months, printer capability has extended from about 125 colours to several thousand colours ... but still nowhere near to the 16 million of the monitor or even the two or three million distinguishable by human eye. Ink-jet and thermal printers both build up the colour image by means of fine dots of cyan, magenta, and yellow (and sometimes black) in much the same way as a photograph is reproduced in a magazine, generally with about 200-300 dots per inch. Variation in colour is obtained by varying the pattern of dots in relation to the amount of red, green, and blue in the screen image. The actual colours obtained are governed by the program that does the interpretation (the 'printer driver'), and cannot be guaranteed in any way to give accurate representation of the screen image.

In the case of woven-fabric simulation, the situation is further complicated by the desire to reproduce each individual thread in its own accurate colour. In simulating a fine fabric of say 70-80 threads/in. (30 threads/cm), the graphics display will use only one pixel to represent the thickness of each thread. When this is being reproduced by a printer of, say, 240 dots/in., this gives only three dots in each direction to reproduce the colour of a single interlacing of the thread, a clearly impossible task. Instead, the printer attempts to get an average colour over several pixels, by using a technique known as dithering and, whereas this may be acceptable in certain designs, there will be many designs in which it is not acceptable.

The approach currently in vogue among printer manufacturers is to ignore the screen colour. Match colours or yarns to the shades produced by the printer, and judge designs on the basis of the paper print rather than the screen appearance. This sounds reasonable in theory, provided that the designer is prepared to tie himself to the printer palette, but in practice it means waiting about three minutes for each printout before making any judgement on how the design is progressing, which is not very practical.

The number of colours a printer will produce is largely

governed by how much money one is prepared to pay for it. Currently (February 1987) a printer costing about £4000 ($6000) will give up to 1000 colours. By going up to £20 000, the number of colours increases to 100 000. The scene will obviously change dramatically over the next two years, but what should be remembered is that printers are entirely independent of the program that generates the design on the monitor. The printer is a peripheral device, which can be upgraded as required quite independently of the design software.

At present the best hard copies (in terms of colour fidelity) are obtained photographically, by using either standard photographic materials or instant photography. A number of camera systems are available which permit photographs to be taken directly from the graphics system, without interfering with the use of the system. A separate very-high-resolution monochrome monitor, with a flat face, is also fed the RGB signals from the display controller, and a multiple exposure is taken on colour film through red, green, and blue filters, to re-create the colours of the original. Calibration of the relative RGB exposures gives an added facility for accurate colour rendering. Needless to say, such photographic copies are individually more expensive to produce than paper printouts from a colour printer.

On the economics of hard copy, it is well worth assessing whether the cost of the photographic equipment or the colour printer is almost as high as (or even higher than) a duplicate graphics system. In such a case, it may make more sense simply to duplicate the computer-graphics system in the main showroom, or even transport the design-office system at appropriate times of the year.

Designs can, of course, be transmitted from one system to another (assuming they are compatible), or even sent by mail.

6. FRONTIERS

The present 'state of the art', as far as micro-based medium-priced graphics systems are concerned, provides screen resolution of up to 1280 pixels, with virtually unlimited screen colour. Even assuming that the human eye distinguishes only 2 million of the potential screen colours, and the best in printer technology currently produces 100 000 colours, this still represents a twenty-to-one compression between screen colour and hard copy. This situation is further complicated by the fact that there is little consistency between the colours displayed on different monitors, even when the RGB specification of the colour is the same. A mid-grey generated from 128 red, 128 green, and 128 blue is likely to appear as distinctly different shades of grey on different monitors, so what is the basis for assessing the accuracy of the printout?

The design limitations imposed by the *resolution* of a system can be seen at both ends of the scale.

(*a*) Designs involving large areas (e.g., carpets, garments) can only display the total design by scaling it down to a fraction of its true size; otherwise the designer must be satisfied with studying screen-sized areas of the design

Table I

Decimal	Binary	Decimal	Binary	Decimal	Binary
0	0				
1	1	9	1001	17	10001
2	10	10	1010	31	11111
3	11	11	1011	32	100000
4	100	12	1100	63	111111
5	101	13	1101	64	1000000
6	110	14	1110	127	1111111
7	111	15	1111	128	10000000
8	1000	16	10000	255	11111111

Table II

Screen-memory Mapping - Alternative for 60K Bytes

Screen Memory	Bits per Pixel	Colours per Pixel	Resolution
60 000	8 (One Byte)	256	300 × 200
60 000	4 (Half a Byte)	16	400 × 300
60 000	1	2	800 × 600

187

at life-size.

(b) Designs involving very fine detail can only be resolved
to the finest limits of pixel density. With 1280 resolution on a monitor of 13-in. width, pixel density is 100
per inch, so 1/100 in. is the finest subdivision possible
in any aspect of the design - hardly enough, for example,
to represent minor variations in the thickness of a fine
worsted yarn.

Increased resolution in today's computer-graphics systems is
not simply a matter of allocating larger areas of screen memory.
There are two major problems. Larger areas of memory still require to be scanned and processed to the screen display in 1/25
second, so processing speeds require to be increased considerably
before any major increase in resolution can be obtained. But,
even if the larger memory can be scanned in time, the screen display is now being asked to handle greater pixel density, and this
imposes new demands on the design of colour monitors.

These considerations suggest that the present state of the art
will not be dramatically improved until three major design problems have been solved, and a quantum leap - or even a change of
direction - occurs in each of these areas:

(a) faster processing of large areas of screen memory:

(b) a dramatic change in monitor design, to give consistency
and stability of colour, at much higher resolution (the
monitor is a device inherited from television technology
... and we can ask if it is the right device for displaying
computer graphics; perhaps some lateral thinking is needed
here);

(c) much finer control of colour in printer output, to give a
fineness of colour-tuning that matches that of the human
eye, and also at very fine resolution.

When these three frontiers have been broken - and they will be,
eventually - computer graphics will move forward into areas that
are at present no more than dreams.

Scottish College of Textiles,
Galashiels,
Scotland.

188

Introducing Electronic Colour to the Design Studio

R.B. Norman

Abstract

A strategy for introducing the computer as a creative tool into
the design-studio environment is proposed. The use of computer-
graphic capabilities is a suggested adjunct to the basic studio.
Computer usage will focus on colour as an element of design, developing colour studies in support of studio objectives.

Techniques of colour-drawing on the computer are discussed,
and computer modelling of colour systems is recommended as an
introduction to colour theory. The effect of colour in the perception of buildings is explored and illustrates how colour selection can effect a building's line, form, and spatial quality.

Through these techniques, a student develops an appreciation
of colour behaviour, reinforces his knowledge of basic design,
and is introduced to graphic computing in a visually provocative
manner. The proposal recognizes the importance of both colour and
graphic computers to the changing studio environment.

1. DESIGN EDUCATION

Design education begins in that kindergarten of design ideas
known as the basic design studio. This approach to education as
it has developed in the American schools comes largely from the
teachings of the German Bauhaus in the 1930s. Elements of design
are explored visually and intellectually, with an emphasis on
the techniques of synthesis. Students work through a list of elements (line, form, space, texture, and colour) and experience the
particular qualities of each element and its contribution to the
design process. This basic studio would seem a logical entry
point for the most visually stimulating of all new mediums - the
colour-graphic computer.

Designers are familiar with this studio. Most of them have
worked their way through the exercises that produce a form of
art, though more importantly develop an intellectual understanding of the design process. They have done line drawings, built
demonstrations of space and of mass with cardboard and glue, and
created fields of texture and patterns. They have, with paint
pots and scissors, modelled the world of colour.

Is it now time to fill this studio with computer terminals in

189

order to have these experiences 'on line'? It is an accepted fact
that synthesis, putting things together, is a good computer task.
In the studio, it is logical to ask: should it begin here?

2. COLOUR DESIGN BY COMPUTER

Drawing on a mainframe computer is not really different from
drawing on a piece of graph paper, although, with the present
state of the art, it is a little more cumbersome. Once we understand a numbering system, we can quickly learn to draw a line
from any point A to any point B and can enter the information to
do so on a computer. Comparing the results to Japanese brush
strokes, or to the sketches by Leonardo da Vinci that are found
in the standard design texts, can lead quickly to disappointment.

Frustrations result when the line we draw on the computer has
only one width; if we draw a diagonal there are those horrible
'jaggies'. This may be called a new art form, the nature of the
material, but, for the aspiring designer in the basic studio, the
drawing of lines on a computer holds little promise. A variety of
pens, pencils, and crayons can produce results that are far more
joyous to the eye and stimulating to the mind. When dealing with
line work, there is little in the computer's unique and intrinsic
qualities to enrich the basic design experience.

Attacking the problems of illustrating form or space on the
computer becomes more complex and requires a degree of abstrac-
tion probably beyond the novice designer, or at least technically
overcomplicated for the elementary situation. Given a lump of
clay, he can make a shape, or he can make two shapes to see the
space between them. He can build shapes and spaces with cardboard
models. What can the computer add to this experience? The computer is a technical marvel that illustrates designs, even lets us
walk through them, and, as a student advances in architecture,
this can be a tremendous asset. At the basic level, one must ask
what can the machine do that is not more easily achieved by hand?

The manipulation of design elements, line and shape, is, in
fact, a challenge for all designers. To form these on the computer is not difficult, nor is it particularly meaningful. When
the assignment is to model colour, the usefulness of the computer
drastically changes.

Colour is the joy of the computer. On the screen, we create
an area of colour, and it is at once alive, vibrant, and, more
importantly, flexible. If it is too dark, we can make it lighter;
if it is too green, we can increase the blue. With most design
elements in the basic course, a computer would be restrictive to
the designer's creative efforts. Only in considering colour is he
liberated from the restrictions of traditional techniques.

With the computer-drawing process we define points, lines, and
finally polygons. For a simple design sketch, we can do this with
a pencil, more simply and probably with a better line quality. On
a computer, we give a 'fill' command. Suddenly the screen is
flooded with colour, rich and pure, colour that fills the shape.
Duplicate that experience without the machine if you will! Of the
basic design elements (line, shape, space, texture, and colour)

only the manipulation of colour is made easier by today's computer.

The individual who works with colour carries in his mind a model of the colours and their relationships. It may be the rudimentary three-point colour wheel, though more likely it is one of the more sophisticated models that defines colour in terms of its three intrinsic qualities: hue, lightness, and saturation. By these three terms, one can precisely define any colour. They are terms that give meaning to colour choices.

I recall taking a first course in oil painting. There I was, blank canvass in front of me and ten tubes of paint on the palette. Ten tubes! Whatever could I do with them? Put a little cadmium red in one corner and some ultramarine blue in another? It takes considerable experience to achieve on canvas a harmonious whole from the endless hues, values, and saturations that those ten tubes can produce.

On the computer, we cannot restrict our palette, and good colour systems offer millions of colours from which to pick. To us them, we need both a good colour model and a method of making our colour selections from it.

3. COLOUR MODELS

There has always been a rainbow in the sky with which to colour our dreams and illuminate our imagination. With the control of colour that computing provides, it is imperative to understand that rainbow so that we, and not our machines, are in charge of the colour in our environment.

Aristotle believed that the eye emitted rays that reach out and bring back the colours. Aguilonius, in the seventeenth century, pictured the spectrum of colour as a beautiful continuity from albus, the white of day, to niger, the black of night. Rubeus, the red of the rising and setting sun, dominated over viridis, the green of the fields, in the centre of the colour world. This is the same animal/vegetable, red/green, colour harmony pictured by the Mayan civilizations a thousand years before, a rudimentary colour-ordering that would today respond to a little boy's emotional inquiry into the nature of red. As a system of colour, it is not a useful means of conveying colour information.

Isaac Newton identified seven colours in the visible spectrum: violet, indigo, blue, green, yellow, orange, and red, the colours of the rainbow. By intuition, he connected red with violet to produce a continuity between two colours that in nature are strangers. In so doing, the colours of the prism were symbolically bent into a circle. The result was a wheel of colour and the origin of a system of colour classification.

From the colour wheel, a three-dimensional colour solid has gradually evolved in order to recognize the full dimensions of colour. In 1915, Albert Munsell published his colour solid, the first colour model of interest to both the scientist and the artist. Munsell reasoned that colour varies in three ways: hue, lightness, and saturation. Hue is a continuous function, which

191

can be represented in a circle. Lightness, a linear function, varied from white through the greys to black. This grey scale became the axis of his colour solid, with white at the north pole and black at the south. The circle of hues forms the equator. Saturation, which Munsell called chroma, is arrayed in the space between.

The Munsell solid explains many colour perceptions. The model is a complete guide to the world of colour and did, in fact, become its atlas for many years. The perimeter of the Munsell solid is open-ended in order to accommodate the yet-to-be-discovered colours, a fact that contributed substantially to its success as a method of colour classification. Computer technology has extended the original Munsell colours by some 40% outward.

When we direct our attention to colouring images on the surface of a picture tube, then colour definition becomes more demanding. Images must be electronically stored, translated to another screen, or even converted to a printed medium. Comparison with a standard Munsell chip of paint is no longer an adequate means of describing the colour.

A more measurable colour model for the electronic industry has been provided by the CIE Standard Chromaticity Diagram, a world standard for colour measurement and the colour basis of both television and computer colour terminals. It is a model based on the measurement of light and the study of how we see colour.

There are efforts to use the chromaticity diagram as a colour solid and as the basis for colour selection. By including the dimension of lightness or luminosity, the diagram does, in reality, become a colour solid. Some companies claim considerable success with the use of this colour model, for it provides positive, measurable control of colour. Each variation defined by the computer is colorimetrically accurate and can be matched to samples that are measurable by using a spectrophotometer.

What the CIE colour model gains in accuracy and scientific predictability, it loses in visual imagery. If we are selecting colour based on a Munsell model, hue or saturation may be changed without modifying other values. Using a CIE model is not very logical for a designer. Its use will either force changes that are not pictured or conversely require him to steer an amoebic path through the mountain of colour.

Efforts to find an ideal colour model continue. Frans Gerritsen has recently proposed a colour solid that is both responsive to computer colour generation and indicative of logical colour relationships. The Gerritsen solid is based on the familiar black/white pole of the Munsell solid and on a perimeter of saturated hues. But Gerritsen uses six primary colours, the red, green, and blue additive primaries and their complements, cyan, magenta, and yellow. The model is an object of beauty, a geometric construction that can be committed to memory and recalled as an object from which to make colour selections. It could satisfy the needs of art, though it lacks a scientific justification.

Several computer manufacturers provide alternative models for

colour selection. One example is a simplification of a colour
solid into a pair of cones with a common perimeter of saturated
hues. Colour specification is by digital values representing hue,
lightness, and saturation. These are good terms, since they correspond to the way we see, though the model is oversimplified.
Believing in the accuracy of these systems can produce many mis-
taken colours.

There is a need for a reasonable colour standard that is both
scientifically exacting and adequately pictorial. One system that
responds to both needs does not exist. If we could find a perfect
system, it would probably have two characteristics.

(1) It would be colorimetrically accurate. Any colour generated on a monitor would have a numerical value that could
be shared with a client, a patron, or a manufacturer. The
Commission Internationale d'Eclairage has established substantial standards that should make this possible.

(2) It would be visually descriptive of colour phenomena.
Given the three co-ordinates of hue, lightness, and saturation, their qualities should be geometrically perceiv-
able. Each colour variable should be visual and control-
lable on a model that could be committed to memory. The
model that Frans Gerritsen has proposed comes very close
to meeting this standard.

4. COLOUR-MIXING

Mixing colours on the computer can be an exciting experience.
Colours are selected from the computer's colour vocabulary and
used to fill simple geometric shapes. Selecting two colours side
by side, we can see what mixing the colours does or how the mixture reacts with the other colours we have chosen. If we do not
like the results, we can select other colours. With a computer,
it is possible to build a palette of colours for the composition
at hand and at any point simply to switch from that palette to
another in order to compare the results.

The computer procedure is simple, easily learned, and visually
informative. For the individual whose motivation is visual, as
opposed to scientific, satisfaction is immediate. One sees and
manipulates colour combinations with ease. As a student develops
skills in exploring colour on the computer, he learns that, by
his colour selection, he controls the colour, texture, and pattern of the evolving design.

The result of this process is threefold. Firstly, through hands-
on experience, he becomes familiar with colour-mixing and the
properties of colour. Secondly, he strengthens his knowledge of
basic design through applying the principles of basic design to
colour composition. Thirdly, through this design experience, he
is initiated into the principles of graphic computing. For those
people in the design studios whose visual acuity seems to dominate their scientific curiosity, colour can be a simple and stimulating introduction to computing.

5. COLOUR AND ARCHITECTURE

As architects, we have used computers in the basic design studio to apply the principles of colour composition to the coloration of buildings. A design student is expected to enquire as to how colour contributes to architecture. Our explorations of colour phenomena on the computer have begun to suggest several ways that colour selection influences the visual effect of buildings.

Line, created with colour, affects the perception of a building. This is evident with a curtain-wall construction, where the choice of horizontal or vertical expression is controlled by the strength (colour) of a line. Cityscapes are full of examples: some buildings appear horizontal whereas others by their choice of colour emphasize a vertical direction. The perception of a colour is entirely dependent on the choice of adjacent colours. By defining soft and hard colour boundaries, colour can be used to shift the emphasis of a building from horizontal to vertical.

Form, created with colour, is quickly grasped and modified by using the computer. Today's architects are using colour to suggest mass in buildings by modifying the appearance of the surface. A building can be textured with colour just as H.H. Richardson textured his works with stone. Cesare Pelli's new addition to the Museum of Modern Art does this by using a progression from a high saturation of blue to a neutral grey on the exterior panels to achieve a texturing of the surface and a definition of the mass. Colour becomes a surrogate texture. These effects are neither accidental nor capricious, they develop from a good utilization of colour edges and the way in which they affect our perception of the adjacent colours. By making appropriate colour selections, the surface can be modelled and given emphasis appropriate to the over-all design concept.

Space, created with colour, offers probably the greatest challenge to the architect/colourist. The perception of space is dependent on the coloration of the surrounding surfaces. Perspective can be created with colour alone, causing some elements to be frontal, others to assume background positions. This is understood in art and has long been used to support mechanical perspective in painting. The modern movement often explored this principle as a pure phenomenon, manipulating objects in space by means of colour alone.

One can conclude that, through colour study, the computer provides a basic design experience of considerable dimension. Line, form and mass, space and texture, the entire basic design vocabulary comes into use. The computer provides a means for the manipulation of these elements and encourages the exploration of their potential. We have not yet realized the paperless design studio; at this point in time, it is probably an absurd notion. But adjunct to the traditional curriculum, as a means of understanding colour and its relation to design and to the environment, computers need to be a part of the scene.

College of Architecture,
Lee Hall,
Clemson, S.C.,
U.S.A.

Attitudes Towards Voluntary/ Mandatory Flammability Regulations

A Survey Analysis of Attitudes Towards Voluntary/Mandatory
Flammability Regulations by the Upholstered-Furniture
Manufacturers in North Carolina, U.S.A., and its Implications for
Design

B.G.M. Oakland and A.C. Stonebraker

Abstract

This paper examines the issue of mandatory versus voluntary upholstered-furniture flammability regulations, a survey of attitudes, costs, and practices of upholstered-furniture manufacturers
in North Carolina, and the effects of the implementation of flammability regulations on product design. In discussing the flammability issue in the United States, three points are to be considered: (i) the government's position, as articulated by the Consumer Product Safety Commission; (ii) the upholstered-furniture
industry's position as articulated by the Upholstered Furniture
Action Council; and (iii) the consumer's point of view.

The objectives of this survey were: (*a*) to investigate flammability issues as perceived by the population of furniture manufacturers in North Carolina; (*b*) to establish a profile of the upholstered-furniture manufacturers in North Carolina; and (*c*) to examine effects of flammability regulation on upholstery design. On
the basis of a pilot study, a major mailing was made to all upholstered-furniture manufacturers in North Carolina. Follow-up procedures were used, and a non-respondent survey was made. Data from
respondents and non-respondents were compared to validate the results. The results are based on data reported by 88 upholstered-
furniture manufacturing firms in North Carolina.

1. INTRODUCTION

In 1974, the Consumer Product Safety Commission (CPSC) issued a
set of proposed mandatory flammability regulations that addressed
the problem of smoulder-resistant upholstered furniture. Research
indicated that cigarettes and other smoking materials were the
major source of ignition in upholstered-furniture fires. The proposed CPSC regulations were based on a system of fabric classifi-
cations and construction that passed a cigarette-ignition test.

In discussing the flammability issue in the United States,
there are three viewpoints to consider: the consumers', the government's as articulated by the CPSC, and the upholstered-furniture
industry's as articulated by the Upholstered Furniture Action
Council (UFAC). The government viewpoint has been clearly defined
via its proposed standards. However, data collected from the upholstered-furniture industry and consumers are sparse. It is therefore difficult to make any concrete statements about their respec-

195

tive stands on the issues of flammability.

1.1 Review of Literature

Furniture that is safe from cigarette ignition may be desirable
at first glance, but serious drawbacks exist. The cost of smoulder-
resistant furniture may be substantially higher than that of non-
smoulder-resistant furniture. Several government sources (1,2)
estimate that the CPSC regulations would impose a cost increase
of between $6.83 and $10.30 per piece of smoulder-resistant upholstered furniture. The furniture industry concurs with the CPSC's
higher estimate of a 13-27% increase. 'For example, a sofa currently retailing at $499.00 might have to retail at $599.00 if the
CPSC mandatory regulations are implemented' (3). Voluntary compliance is estimated at less than 2% by UFAC.

The effectiveness of the regulations in reducing loss of life
and property is also a matter of debate. According to Helzer *et
al.* (1), the U.S. Department of Commerce estimates that enforce-
ments of government regulations would decrease the number of
deaths by 80% and lower the number of injuries by 79%. The government also speculates that the decrease in property damage would be
approximately 68%. Consumers must decide whether the increase in
the cost of smoulder-resistant furniture is in line with the safety
benefits derived from the regulations.

Alternatives to the proposed CPSC mandatory regulations include
the following: (*a*) the voluntary manufacture of smoulder-resistant
furniture by the industry; (*b*) the use of smoke detectors; (*c*) the
production of self-extinguishing cigarettes; and (*d*) increased
consumer education.

The industry's viewpoint is valuable and critical to the economics of the state of North Carolina. In response to the CPSC
proposed regulations, the upholstered-furniture industry coalesced
to form the Upholstered Furniture Action Council (UFAC) in 1972.
This council worked to circumvent the intrusion of government regulations. Its goals were to develop a programme of voluntary industry compliance, enforcement, and consumer education to render
upholstered furniture safer in a cost-effective manner. By July
1981, UFAC was already enjoying 84% compliance (4) and had successfully prevented the implementation of CPSC regulations. It is
suggested that it has also prevented the demise of small furniture
manufacturers.

In November 1972, the Department of Commerce published a 'finding of possible need' in the Federal Register, declaring that it
may be necessary to issue regulations for the flammability of upholstered furniture (5). After this proposal, the Consumer Product
Safety Commission (CPSC) was formed as the federal independent
agency whose mission was to govern the development and enforcement
of safety standards for consumer goods. This commission was given
the responsibility of the creation of appropriate upholstered-
furniture flammability standards. The National Bureau of Standards
(NBS) Center for Fire Research (CFR) was approached to lend technical assistance to the CPSC. Subsequently, PFF-6-76, the Proposed
Standard for the Flammability (Cigarette Resistance) of Upholstered
Furniture,was created.

This proposed standard set forth a cigarette-ignition test
method and requirements for passing the test, as well as a fabric-
classification method for upholstery fabrics and other components
of upholstered furniture. Its objective was to reduce the number
of upholstered-furniture fires that occur in the United States
owing to careless smoking (6).

In order to quantify the problem of home fires, the CPSC and
the NBS commissioned the Bureau of the Census to conduct the
'National Household Fire Survey' in 1974. According to this survey,
in 10% of residential fires, 'fabric items were identified as the
first to ignite' (6); in only 2% of the residential fires was upholstered furniture the first item to ignite. In 1979, the NBS
prepared a report entitled 'Decision Analysis of Strategies for
Reducing Upholstered Furniture Fire Losses'. This study compared
the results of no action against fires with the increased use of
smoke detectors and with implementation of the proposed PFF-6-76.

It was found that PFF-6-76 was preferred 'for reducing total
societal cost plus loss' in the long run of 30 years. However,
the smoke-detector alternative achieved loss reduction at a more
efficient rate than did the proposed standard (1).

A 1977 article in *Retailing Home Furnishings* discussed an endorsement of smoke detectors by the CPSC. The Commission formed a
panel to study smoke detectors. It found that, if more consumers
had the devices installed in their homes and were better educated
as to the hazards of cigarette ignition of upholstered furniture,
the proposed standard would not be necessary.

Meanwhile, the furniture industry was predicting its own demise
and fearing that the introduction of PFF-6-76 would economically
crush the hundreds of small upholstery operations and fabric manufacturers (7). In the words of the CPSC, 'a very expensive safety
standard which induces consumers to substantially decrease their
purchases will impose costs which are not included in the cost'
(8).

Murphy (9) developed a list of costs directly borne by the consumer that were 'due to the use of flame-resistant chemicals and
processes in upholstery fabrics'. The ones not encompassed by the
DOC list above include: (*a*) health hazards due to the potentially
toxic chemicals, (*b*) environmental hazards due to non-biodegradable
chemical wastes, (*c*) potential decrease in wear-life of fabrics due
to flame-retardant treatments, (*d*) reduction in consumer choice,
and (*e*) loss of life due to continued use of non-flame-resistant
upholstery fabrics, such as older furniture used longer to save
money and reupholstery fabrics not covered by flammability standards. According to Oxford (10), who considered the issue of reupholstery, it is an important issue, but personal property of consumers is not something that is easily controlled. None of the
above-mentioned studies considers the economic feasibility of the
state-of-the-art flammability precautions.

Currently, the upholstered-furniture industry, under the administration of the Upholstered Furniture Action Council (UFAC), has
been using a set of voluntary guidelines developed to render upholstered furniture more smoulder-resistant.

The Upholstered Furniture Action Council's voluntary plan encompasses four major areas. These are: fabric classification, construction criteria, a labelling plan, and compliance verification. The fabric-classification system and construction criteria are the components that provide for the increased safety of upholstered furniture. The labelling plan is a first step towards consumer education and increased consumer awareness of the problem of furniture flammability. The compliance procedures not only encourage manufacturer participation but are also the vehicle by which UFAC is accountable to the industry, the government, and the consumer.

The United States Fire Administration has published statistics that report that one-third of all fire deaths are caused by cigarettes (11). Currently fifteen patents exist for self-extinguishing cigarettes (9). The technology therefore exists that could virtually eliminate the problem of smouldering cigarettes on upholstered furniture.

The tobacco industry has succeeded in having Congress pass a law that 'prohibits the [Consumer Product Safety] Commission from studying cigarettes as a potential hazardous product'. CPSC Commissioner Stuart M. Statler (11) said: 'Because of Congress's explicit prohibition, we're forced to approach the problem of these deaths through the back door'. He was referring to the decision of the CPSC to concentrate on the secondary source, the upholstered-furniture industry, which will decidedly give it considerably less resistance.

The UFAC voluntary programme is a compromise to upgrade flammability standards in an economically satisfactory manner. It has been highly successful in meeting its goals and fulfilling its obligations to the CPSC. In 1981, UFAC projected that 95% of the upholstered furniture produced in the U.S.A. in 1984 would meet UFAC criteria and would carry the UFAC hangtag for consumer information (UFAC, 1981). It is hoped that this will bring an end to the threat of impending PFF-6-76.

This study was designed to gain insight into the attitudes of the upholstered-furniture industry regarding the upholstered-furniture flammability issue. The attitudes and practices of the industry are important to the issue of furniture safety. The perception of the flammability issue can help us to assess the existing voluntary-action programme, the effects of mandatory regulations, and the effects on furniture design in the market place. Many studies have been made of the upholstered-furniture-flammability issue. None of these studies has surveyed the manufacturers or their perception of the issues and alternatives in the flammability problem. This study was undertaken to identify the issues and attitudes of the population of upholstered-furniture manufacturers in the state of North Carolina by means of questionnaires and follow-up procedures. The data were gathered over a three-month period in the Spring of 1983.

Table I

Profile of Upholstered-furniture Manufacturers in North Carolina by Number of Employees

Number of Employees	1983[1] f	%	1985-86[2] f	%
1-19	13	15	27	14
20-49	17	19	37	20
50-99	19	22	30	16
100-249	37	42	53	28
250-499	0	0	31	16
500-999	0	0	6	3
1000-2499	0	0	3	2
No response	2	0	3	2
Total	88	98[3]	190	101[3]

[1] Survey of North Carolina upholstered-furniture manufacturers.
[2] 1985-86 Directory of North Carolina Manufacturing Firms.
[3] Owing to rounding-off of percentrages, the total is under or over 100.
f = Frequency of incidences (similarly in Tables II, III, V and VI).

Table II

Profile of Responding Upholstered-furniture Manufacturers in North Carolina by Gross Sales and Number of Employees (n = 88)

Gross Sales Categories by $Millions	f	%	Number of Employees	f	%
Below 1M	12	14	1-20	13	15
1-5M	23	26	21-75	27	31
6-10M	14	16	76-150	18	20
Over 10M	25	28	151 and over	28	32
No response	14	16	No response	2	2
Total	88	100	Total	88	100

Table III

Profile of Fibre, Fabric Styles, and Upholstery
Components Reported by Upholstered-furniture
Manufacturers in North Carolina (n = 88)

Fibre, Fabric Styles, and Upholstery Components	f	%
Fibre		
Approximately what percentages of the fabrics in your line are:		
Blends		32
Synthetic-fibre (100%)		27
100% Cotton		25
100% Rayon and bast fibres (100%)		10
No response	4	5
Total		99
Fabric Styles		
Prints		47
Jacquards		37
Flat goods		26
Velvets		17
Tweeds		13
Quilts		9
Vinyls		2
Fabric supplied by customers		14
No response	4	5
Upholstered Components		
Urethane foam		100
Polyester-fibre batting		88
Barrier material		63
Treated cotton batting		57
Untreated cotton batting		26
No response	4	5
Custom Furniture		21

Table IV

Perceived Estimate of Cost Increases Due to the Effects
of the Implementation of the Mandatory Flammability
Regulations by the Upholstered-furniture Manufacturers
of North Carolina (n = 88)

Cost Increases	%
Product-testing	187
Record-keeping	50
Materials	14
Production	11
Administration	10

Table V

Perceived Estimate of Annual Cost Increase Incurred
Owing to Compliance with Voluntary Flammability
Standards by the Upholstered-furniture Manufacturers
in North Carolina (n = 88)

Estimated Cost Increases	f	%
1-5	41	47
6-10	21	24
11-25	11	13
26 and over	5	6
No increase	1	1
No response	9	10
Total	88	101[1]

[1] Owing to rounding-off of percentages, the total is
over 100.

Table VI

Ranking of Issues by Level of Importance for Mandatory Flammability Regulation by Furniture Manufacturers in North Carolina (n = 88)

Flammability Issues	f	%
Increase in production costs	73	83
Increase in material costs	73	83
Reduction in consumer choice	64	73
Increase in testing cost	68	77
Increase in record-keeping costs	66	75
Increase in administrative costs	66	75
Increase in deaths due to upholstered-furniture fires	54	61
Decrease in property damage due to upholstered-furniture fires	54	61
Unemployment payments	50	57

Table VII

Attitudes of the Respondents towards Voluntary Mandatory
Flammability Regulations by Upholstered-furniture
Manufacturers in North Carolina (n = 88)

Respondent Attitudes	Responses by Percentages			
	Agree	No Opinion	Disagree	No Response
1. It is the upholstered-furniture industry's duty to make furniture less hazardous	59	14	26	1
2. The Upholstered Furniture Action Council (UFAC) voluntary standards decrease the number of deaths caused by furniture fires enough to make the cost worth while	42	32	25	1
3. Mandatory Consumer Product Safety Commission (CPSC) standatds would decrease the number of deaths caused by furniture fires enough to make the cost increase in furniture worth while	6	1	3	1
4. The proposed Consumer Product Safety Commission (SPSC) standards protect only a small percentage of the population	66	27	6	1
5. The cigarette industry should handle the flammability problem by manufacturing self-extinguishing cigarettes	65	23	11	1
6. Smoke detectors are cheaper and just as effective a solution to the problem of furniture flammability as government regulations would be	56	4	19	1
7. The Upholstered Furniture Action Council (UFAC) programme of voluntary standards retains a greater degree of consumer choice than would the mandatory standard	80	17	2	1
8. Flammability regulations raise the cost of upholstered furniture for the consumer	97	2	0	1
9. The implementation of flammability standards reduces the amount of consumer choice of style, comfort, and fabric	80	9	10	1

2. MARKET SURVEY OF ATTITUDES, COSTS, AND PRACTICE OF UPHOLSTERED-
FURNITURE MANUFACTURERS IN NORTH CAROLINA

2.1 Survey Methodology

Face-to-face preliminary interviews were conducted to determine
basic items considered critical to the issue of flammability regulations by the upholstered-furniture industry. Based on the data
collected in face-to-face interviews, a survey instrument was developed to collect information in the following categories: (a)
demographic profile of the upholstered-furniture manufacturers in
North Carolina, (b) product lines, (c) testing practices, and (d)
attitudes towards mandatory/voluntary flammability regulations.
A pilot study was made of UFAC voluntary-compliance firms to test
the instrument.

A list of 303 upholstered-furniture manufacturers in North
Carolina was supplied by the Upholstered Furniture Action Council.
The list included members and non-members of UFAC. In addition,
three other sources were used to check firms listed in North Carolina: (i) The Thomas Register of American Manufacturers and Thomas
Register Catalogue File (1983), (ii) MacRae's Blue Book (1983),
and (iii) the Directory of North Carolina Manufacturing Firms. If
the firm were absent from two of the three sources, and its telephone was non-functional, it was deemed out-of-business. Of the
303 firms originally listed, 85 were eliminated from the study
for various reasons, including: (a) they had moved out of state,
(b) they no longer manufactured upholstered furniture, (c) they
were out of business, (d) they were unable to have mail forwarded
or (e) they could not be reached by telephone. The population of
upholstered-furniture manufacturers in North Carolina was determined to be 218.

After the original mail survey, a follow-up procedure was devised to contact the non-respondents. Each firm from whom a response was not received was telephoned to: (a) determine if the
questionnaire had been received by that firm, (b) describe the
study in brief, and (c) encourage those firms that had not responded to do so. If the firm did not receive a copy of the survey, or had misplaced it, it was immediately sent another copy unless it specifically indicated that it did not intend to respond.
Of the firms contacted during the follow-up, only ten indicated
that they did not wish to respond to the questionnaire.

The follow-up telephone interviews were unstructured and conducted by one interviewer, which thus minimized interviewer bias.
This allowed the interviewer to be flexible and assess each non-
respondent's case individually. Completed surveys received as a
result of the follow-up interviews were added to the final data-
base. Upon completion of follow-up procedures, the response rate
increased from 23.9% to 40.4%, an increase in response rate to the
questionnaire of 16.5%. The total sample size was 218, and the
number of respondents was 88.

After the above follow-up procedures, a non-response survey
was designed. Interviewers were located through the county Co-
operative Extension Office nearest those firms selected in the
sample. Each interviewer was given a packet with specific instructions on interview techniques. A 10% random sample of the 130 non-

responding firms yielded a sample size of thirteen for the non-respondent survey. Of the thirteen firms chosen for this follow-up, nine granted interviews, or 69.2% of the non-respondents. Two of the remaining firms could not be reached by telephone; the other two were unwilling to grant interviews. Of the nine firms participating in the survey of non-respondents, the average gross sales were $1-5M, and the average number of employees was 34.

2.2 Results

The profile of the upholstered-furniture manufacturers in North Carolina, by gross sales and number of employees, is shown in Table I.

The upholstered-furniture manufacturer listed blends, synthetic fibres, cottons, and rayon and/or bast fibres in order of importance and usage for exterior fabrics. Fabric styles, in order of importance, were reported as print, jacquards, flat goods, velvets, tweeds, quilts, and vinyls. The manufacturers were asked to indicate the composition of upholstery components used. The use of urethane foam was reported by all of the manufacturers. Polyester batting, which is recommended by the UFAC voluntary flammability regulations, was used by 87.5%. Barrier materials, such as polyester fibre and/or polyester-fibre/cotton mixtures, were reported by 61.5% of the manufacturers. The use of treated cotton (57.4%) and untreated cotton (26.2%) was reported in 1983. Currently, a blend of polyester-fibre/cotton is used to replace untreated cotton, and it performs equally well, as a barrier, as treated cotton.

Flammability tests were conducted in-house by 6% of the firms, and outside testing was reported by 29.6% of the manufacturers. Approximately 85% of the UFAC manufacturers indicated their dependence on suppliers to pre-test materials to meet the requirements of voluntary flammability standards. Some 30% of the upholstery manufacturers reported utilization of outside testing laboratories. This was predicted to increase from 30 to 75% if mandatory regulations were passed. No flammability testing was reported by 10% of the manufacturers.

Some 61% of the North Carolina upholstered-furniture manufacturers reported marketing in California. Manufacturers who do contract work operate on specifications rather than voluntary standards. California requires a high level of specifications in flammability regulations, and 19% of the manufacturers surveyed reported contracting to particular specifications, such as hospitals, hotels, and other institutions. Manufacturers who do contract work operate on specifications rather than voluntary standards.

The upholstered-furniture manufacturers reported their perceptions of the effect of mandatory flammability regulations on operational-cost increases. The respondents indicated projected cost increases in certain categories as shown in Table IV.

The perceived estimate of the annual cost increase due to compliance with voluntary flammability standards was 5% or less by 47% of the respondents, as shown in Table V. These figures may vary from those reported by the industry. UFAC has reported a cost increase of 13-27% for the mandatory regulations proposed by CPSC

205

and 2% for the voluntary regulations recommended by UFAC.

The ranking of issues by level of importance for mandatory flammability regulations by furniture manufacturers is shown by percentage of responses in Table VI.

Respondents' attitudes towards voluntary/mandatory regulations were examined. The majority agree that it is the furniture industry's duty to make upholstered furniture less hazardous. Some 42% agree that the UFAC voluntary standards will reduce the number of deaths, which would make the cost worth while, but only 6% consider that the CPSC mandatory standards would justify the cost increase. The majority agree that flammability standards protect only a small percentage of the population.

The majority of the respondents agree that smoke detectors are a cheaper, effective solution to furniture fires and that the cigarette industry should handle the flammability problem by manufacturing and marketing a self-extinguishing cigarette.

Of the respondents, as many as 97% believe that flammability regulations raise the cost of upholstered furniture for the consumer and that the implementation of flammability standards reduces the choice of style, comfort, and fabric of upholstered furniture. The fear has, in fact, not been justified with the UFAC voluntary standards, and this will be addressed in the discussion of the effects of flammability regulations on upholstered-furniture design.

3. EFFECTS OF MANDATORY VERSUS VOLUNTARY FLAMMABILITY REGULATIONS ON UPHOLSTERED-FURNITURE DESIGN

Upholstered furniture, at its best, is a three-dimensional art form, and smouldering cigarettes have been the most common cause of upholstered-furniture fires. Upholstered furniture is required to be 'smoulder-resistant' to a burning cigarette to meet either voluntary or mandatory regulations. The cumulative build-up of heat between the exterior fabric, padding, and urethane foam has been responsible for the spontaneous combustion resulting in fires.

The flammability regulations proposed by the Consumer Product Safety Commission would eliminate cotton, linen, and rayon exterior fabrics and limit consumer choice in design, while raising the cost and possibly eliminating small manufacturers. The government regulations would reduce the range of fabric choices and furniture silhouettes at a substantial increase in cost.

The manufacturers surveyed were asked to respond to open-ended questions as to the advantages/disadvantages of flammability regulations. The responses included limitations of fabrics, due to flammability requirements, reduced flexibility in furniture construction, and the mechanical barrier (fibre) breaking down with use, all detracting from the appearance of the furniture. Design restrictions were reported as one of the disadvantages of flammability regulations. Manufacturers consistently referred to the importance of the supplier in the issue of upholstered-furniture flammability. Manufacturers were asked to suggest viable solutions to the problem of upholstered-furniture flammability and responded as follows: (i) self-extinguishing cigarettes, (ii) development of flame-resistant urethane foam, at a very competitive price, that will not ignite and produce dangerous gases, and (iii) making mandatory the use of a vertical-wall barrier. The data are shown in Table VII. Mandatory regulations would require that an upholstered unit be tested to evaluate the functionality of components.

The voluntary requirements developed and recommended by the Upholstered Furniture Action Council (UFAC) include design modifications for a safer product with maximum design freedom. Upholstered furniture has been designed to reduce the cumulative build-up of heat that results in spontaneous combustion. A heat-conducting weltcord, with an aluminium core, has been designed to be used as the cord around the cushions to reduce the heat build-up by conducting it away. The 100% untreated cotton batting has been replaced with either a cotton/polyester-fibre or polyester-fibre batting that serves as a mechanical barrier between the exterior fabric and the urethane-foam cushions. In addition, the foam cushions are enclosed in a non-woven-fabric envelope, which acts as an additional barrier between the exterior fabric and the urethane foam. Flame-retardant urethane foams have been recommended by the upholstered-furniture manufacturers.

The voluntary regulations leave the upholstered-furniture manufacturers free to shape layers of fabrics and padding into pleasing furniture silhouettes at a reasonable cost. The heat-conducting weltcord, the mechanical space produced by a flame-resistant batting (polyester-fibre, polyester-fibre/cotton, or treated cotton), and the non-woven interior fabric reduce cumulative heat between the outer fabric and the urethane foam, which thus reduces upholstered-furniture fires and increases product safety.

The UFAC voluntary compliance of upholstered-furniture flammability requirements is currently used as a model of industry versus government control in the United States. Product safety has been improved, while there is great diversity in the design, and the design is relatively free of constraints.

REFERENCES

(1) A. Helzer, B. Buchbender and F. Offensend. NBS Technical Note No. 1101, 1979, p.23.

(2) P. Beck. Commentary on study of the economic impact of a proposed cigarette-ignition standard for upholstered furniture; commentary on possible economic impacts (unpublished work), Batelle, Columbus Laboratories, 1975.

(3) Upholstered Furniture Action Council. Furniture Flammability: Reducing the Hazard, 1982.

(4) Upholstered Furniture Action Council. Semi-annual Report to the Consumer Product Safety Commission (31 July, 1981).

(5) Upholstered furniture: Notice of finding that flammability, or other regulation may be needed and institution of proceedings, Federal Register, 1972, 37, 25239-25240.

(6) J. Loftus. Back-up report for the proposed standard for the
     flammability of upholstered furniture, PFF 6-76 (NBSIR 78-14
     78), U.S. Government Printing Office, Washington D.C.

(7) *Text. World*, 1979, <u>129</u>, 23.

(8) U.S. Consumer Product Safety Commission. Comments of the
     Council on Wage and Price Stability before the Consumer
     Product Safety Commission. (Lawnmower safety standard/cost-
     benefit), Washington D.C. 1975.

(9) B. Murphy. Cost-benefit analysis and consumer acceptance of
     product safety: Smoulder-resistance of upholstery textiles.
     Paper presented at Interdisciplinary Consumer Research
     AHEA-ACR Mini-workshop, New Orleans LA, 1978, p.9.

(10) N. Oxford. Evaluation of the performance level of reuphol-
     stery cover fabric with respect to cigarette ignition resis-
     tance (MS Thesis), University of North Carolina at Greens-
     boro, Greensboro NC, 1981.

(11) 'Self-extinguishing cigarette sought', *Greensboro Record*,
     1983, 14 Feb.

Department of Clothing & Textiles,
University of North Carolina at Greensboro,
Greensboro,
N.C.,
U.S.A.

Unika Vaev U.S.A.:
A Case Study in Furnishing-Fabric Marketing

S. Pearson

The contract-fabric industry in the U.S.A. has, in the past ten
years, become one of the fastest-growing, most profitable, and
most competitive segments of the office-furnishings business.
This small portion of the textile industry was born only 30 years
ago, when a handful of firms began to buy from mills fabrics designed to be compatible with the new 'modern' office furniture.
These new textile firms not only developed exclusive collections
but also inventoried those fabrics and provided samples to all
architectural and interior-design firms.

Most of the fabrics developed for office use were solid-colour
textured weaves in coarse wool or the 'new' miracle fibre, nylon.
The desire for long-wearing characteristics superseded any emphasis on creative design and marketing. A few industry design leaders, such as Jack Lenor Larsen and Boris Kroll, created collections that included complex weaves and unique designs and colours,
but, for the most part, there were few contract-fabric firms that
had such unique identities. With minimal competition, there was
little reason to create new products. During the early years of
this industry, colour trends had long life spans. The brilliant
solid primary colours on the 1960s lingered for fifteen years,
and the quiet earth-tone shades prevailed for ten years throughout the 1970s.

About fifteen years ago, however, the contract-furniture industry began to expand in areas of product design and marketing,
and it was the fabric industry that generated the greatest excitement. Furniture companies with fabric divisions, such as
Knoll International, saw the high profits achieved in that specialized area; the individual entrepreneurs, as well as other
furniture companies, decided to enter the fabric marketplace.
Suddenly, contract fabrics were 'hot', and the more textile companies and divisions that were introduced, the more competitive
the marketplace became.

Architects, searching for new colours and fabrics to use with
their post-modern buildings, turned to a new range of pastel colours. Pink, mauve, and celadon replaced rust and gold earth tones.
By the early 1980s, colour trends were changing so swiftly that,
after only five years, the post-modern palette was out of favour,
and bright jewel-like tones were in vogue. Competition among fabric firms reached new heights as each company tried to create a
new idea of design or colour direction to capture the architect's

imagination. The more innovative a fabric collection became, the more demand was placed upon that same firm to be even more creative. It became increasingly apparent that the contract-fabric business had become a fashion business.

How then, among all the competition and fast-moving pace, can a fabric company firmly established in the 1960s and dormant in the 1970s, leap forward to the 1980s and become an industry leader within five years of its rebirth?

Unika Vaev U.S.A. was one of the most highly respected fabric sources in the early 1960s. Its collection reflected the most important trends of the day. The Danish-styled bright-coloured woollen fabrics were admired for their quality, design excellence, and fine value. A single mill in Denmark wove the entire collection, and it therefore had an easily distinguished look. But, because all the fabric came from one source, the 'look' was limited to styles woven from one kind of yarn system. The contract-fabric industry had begun to be a fashion industry, and the specifiers demanded new colours and patterns. The American market had changed its style preferences, but the Unika Vaev collection, with its strong Danish influence, did not adapt. Consequently, sales diminished year after year. Six years ago, the decision was made by its new owners to once again make a commitment to design, quality, and service, and a new Unika Vaev U.S.A. was introduced to the marketplace. Within five years, it saw a fiftyfold increase in sales and an average of 75% growth per year, with 20% net profits. By examining the reasons for the new Unika Vaev's success, one can adapt to any industry the basic principles followed there and create similar success.

The new management of Unika Vaev soon recognized that the contract-fabric industry had become essentially a design-and-marketing business. While it was believed that contract textiles had become much more fashion-oriented and new fresh designs were more exciting than the old, the contract-fabric industry is also the most conservative of all textile businesses. Fabrics designed today must look good for between ten and twenty years, for that can be the life span of an executive's office furnishings or the offices of a corporate headquarters.

In developing the collection from scratch, Unika Vaev kept two ideals in mind: continuity and creativity. Basic classic weaves, such as mohair velvets and broadcloths, were added to the collection in extensive colour ranges that were neither trendy nor boring. Post-modern pastels were included in the new colour lines, but the colours were clean enough to complement darker and brighter colour values.

New colours were selected for the collection that were based on current trends in interiors and fashion, but many 'new' colour combinations grew out of research in historical textile-study collections. Many hues were added because they 'felt' right, not because of sales statistics, and often the most experimental of these became the most popular. Unika Vaev quickly developed a reputation for having colours and patterns that were fresh and different, but at the same time conservative enough to have lasting appeal.

Designers claimed they had fun working with the textile collection, since they were able to put their own colour ideas into their projects. Any combination of pastels, brights, or midtones was possible. The concept was introduced that this was a timeless, colour-co-ordinated collection, which would enhance, not overpower, the architect's own preferences of colour-and-design combinations. Each new fabric line had its own 'personality', defined primarily by the specific value of brightness of the colours. But every new collection could also be used with any previous introduction, so older fabrics never looked out of date. In fact, many of this year's best-selling items were created in the first year of the collection.

The collection began with 'basics' but found its success in creating new products that offered the specifier exactly the textile he was seeking. The idea of creating unique products came from the name itself: 'Unika Vaev', a Danish name, translates as 'Unique Weave'. Underlying all design ideas was that theme, and, as the marketplace filled with copycats, the issue of integrity and original design became a primary focus. If a fabric being developed was found by a coincidence to be similar to that offered by a competitor, the project would be dropped.

It was quickly found that the more common the design, the less successful the fabric would be. Some mistakes were made, but only because Unika Vaev's own market-research results were ignored. It was also kept in mind that one beautiful fabric introduction is better than six mediocre ones. The collection was therefore kept relatively small, with only 600 individual colours and fabrics, but it encompassed a broad range of weaves, yarns, colours, and designs.

The attention to detail of design was the common link among all fabrics. A simple two-colour balanced twill could have been an acceptable design, but a more exciting fabric was woven with a shiny nylon warp and a two-colour weft in a broken twill, producing a richer, more interesting surface.

Another basic but important principle followed was 'know what your customers want before they know it'. At an early stage, direct market research was used to determine trends and get feedback on forthcoming designs. By actually visiting potential clients and listening to their comments regarding new developments, Unika Vaev was able to determine whether a particular design or colour range would be successful. This was the key in creating fabrics that were introduced just at the right time.

The success of the Unika Vaev collection allowed exploration in an entirely new area for contract textiles. The rise in popularity of post-modern architecture made patterned fabrics, classic and otherwise, more appealing to architects. Furniture designed by renowned turn-of-the-century architects, such as Hoffmann and Macintosh, was already in high demand. It was natural that there would be interest in fabric designs by those same architects. In 1984, Unika Vaev introduced the 'Archives Collection' the first contract-textile collection that faithfully reproduced the textile patterns of William Morris and of Eliel Saarinen and the architects of the Wiener Werkstatte.

The fabrics designed in turn-of-the-century Vienna were, by their classic nature, appropriate for the most modern interior of the 1980s. Even the William Morris 'Crown Imperial' designed in 1876 met with widespread acceptance as designers sought architecturally defined structure in pattern. The most recent 'Archives' addition is 'Cranbrook', designed by Eliel Saarinen in 1929. Whereas Unika Vaev maintained these fabrics might not be appropriate for every installation, the immediate popularity the fabrics enjoyed was amazing. One unique installation was the use of 'Paradise', a Hoffmann pattern, on banquette seating in a Howard Johnson Motor Inn in Indiana. The Wiener Werkstatte had found a home in middle America.

While much of the success of the collection comes from the classic, yet fashion-oriented, designs and colours, Unika Vaev also focussed on quality and value. It surprised many specifiers that an upholstery fabric could take up to two years to develop, but much of that time was spent in experimenting with subtle weave changes to achieve both interesting designs and the most wear-resistant fabric possible. Although no textile firm can guarantee a fabric's longevity, Unika Vaev developed stringent testing procedures so that there was less risk of fabric failure.

Quality was also important in determining the company's advertising campaign. Even though Unika Vaev was a tiny firm, Massimo Vignelli, a world-renowned graphic designer, was hired to create a new Unika Vaev image. He came up with a classic yet fresh approach, which mirrored the Unika Vaev philosophy of textile design. Unika Vaev believed that its customers were some of the most visually sophisticated in the world, and it could not afford to compromise in the packaging of its product. The award-winning advertisements were a simple and direct approach to fabric advertising that greatly appealed to the specifiers and created a consistent image of quality and design compatible with the fabric collection itself.

Another area of concern was value. Because of the high level of quality of the yarns and weaves, Unika Vaev fabrics' quality could not be the least expensive in the marketplace. Nor should they be the most costly. Mark-ups were kept moderate but certainly afforded a sufficient profit to ensure adequate research and development for new product introductions. Bidding wars against competitors for similar products were discouraged. Likewise, a new product was never bought from a source simply because it was less expensive. Unika Vaev sold the finest quality and service to its customers and expected nothing less from its mill sources.

The success of Unika Vaev has been seen in the influence it has had in the market, particularly in the direction of colour and design. It is now regarded as one of the most innovative contract-fabric collections in the industry.

If Unika Vaev's success could be achieved by any U.S. fabric firm, it is also true that any mill that wants to sell to American firms could claim such success by adopting some of the principles followed by Unika Vaev U.S.A.

First, know the customer and what his needs are. Mill designers should not create in a vacuum but should visit potential customers in America, and they must then create original designs for that market. The sure way to success is to offer the customer that special design he was looking for but could not describe. Potential customers such as Unika Vaev want to see new ideas just as architect and designer clients want to look at the most recent designs from any textile firm. Showing a new product is the best way to start a dialogue between buyer and mill. The more ideas, the better it is.

Do not copy. Customers who want original ideas will develop lasting relationships with mills that exhibit high standards of integrity. If a mill knowingly shows and sells knock-offs, it eventually will suffer the consequences.

Be patient. The U.S. market is still growing and open to all, but the customer wants to see proof of commitment. A mill must follow through with excellent service before and after the fabric is sold. Nothing spoils a relationship faster than poor service or quality control or both. All U.S. fabric firms have to deal with demanding clients every day, so those demands will be passed on to the mill.

Just as there is always room in the U.S.A. for another contract-fabric firm, there will also be room for another mill source. Innovative designs, quality products, and outstanding customer service will always be in demand. If the basic rules are followed, success will be sure to follow.

Unika Vaev U.S.A.,
New York,
N.Y.,
U.S.A.

Creativity and the Market

A. Ratti

Abstract

Textile business has to face increasing difficulties because of
the global merging of markets. These difficulties are even worse
for firms operating in fields of high value, such as silk. This
is due to the fact that the competitive setting has changed because new firms, who competitively entered the market, have
brought in contrasting patterns of behaviour, and they do not
share the logic of profit to which we have been traditionally ac-
customed in the West.

The silk industry is among the first to confront the Western
world with the request to consider new and adequate approaches in
order to face these emerging competitive agents, who are so different from us and so little known to us.

These circumstances have to be faced responsibly, and the Western entrepreneur has to redefine his formula of competitive advantage through a vast view of reality, beyond the mere concern
for the aesthetic quality of his products.

1. BUSINESS CREATIVITY

It is no longer possible to conceive creativity in relation to
the product alone because of the challenge of competition and the
vastness and complexity of the world market. Business creativity
means being in a position to exert a lasting superiority, which
can be adopted within the market arena and which can be maintained
over a long period of time.

The formula for lasting superiority can be defined within the
areas of:

(1) technology - the product - the market;

(2) types of behaviour, i.e., the nature of advantages; and

(3) main structural resources to be implemented.

The main problems encountered by every firm becomes more critical in textile firms and most critical when they are oriented towards the clothing-fashion market.

The formula of lasting superiority is a theoretical practice

215

with no maximum permanent co-ordination of the following three
activities:

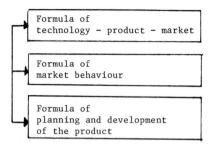

The superiority formula cannot last without adequate activity in
relation to the third point.

In order to achieve the greatest sales efficiency on the market, it is necessary to have the greatest efficiency in organization (a) at the different levels of hierarchy, and (b) among
the various operative functions.

2. THE MARKET

The market requires a global approach (the world). The two essential attributes are:

geographical extension in order to achieve a minimal industrial size; and

a clear view up to final consumption (styling from fabric).

A piece of clothing or an accessory can answer many needs, but
fashion plays a dominant role, as is shown in Fig. 4.

Italian per-capita consumption in various areas is shown in
Table I.

Clothing is the greatest medium of non-verbal communication
and, more than anything else, is heavily determined by fashion,
that is to say:

(a) aesthetic traits are extremely relevant; and
(b) changes occur at a rapid pace.

The need for:

(a) information on products and fashion, and
(b) establishing a difference in relation to competitors

becomes very keen.

Consequently, risks and difficulties multiply because of:

(a) long-term programming;
(b) fewer itemized purchases;
(c) delays as long as possible;
(d) purchases from different suppliers (more sources); and

216

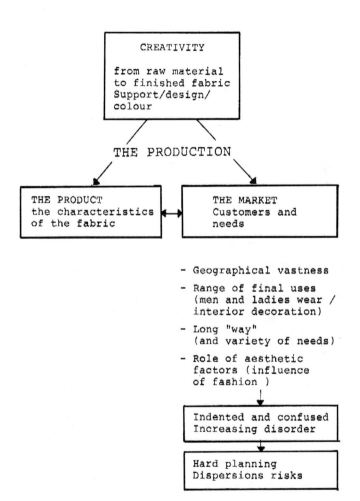

CREATIVITY

from raw material
to finished fabric
Support/design/
colour

THE PRODUCTION

THE PRODUCT
the characteristics
of the fabric

THE MARKET
Customers and
needs

- Geographical vastness
- Range of final uses
  (men and ladies wear /
  interior decoration)
- Long "way"
  (and variety of needs)
- Role of aesthetic
  factors (influence
  of fashion)

Indented and confused
Increasing disorder

Hard planning
Dispersions risks

Fig. 1

217

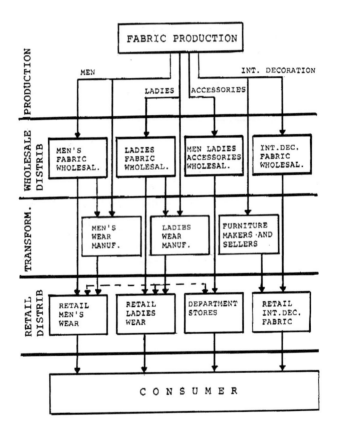

Fig. 2

218

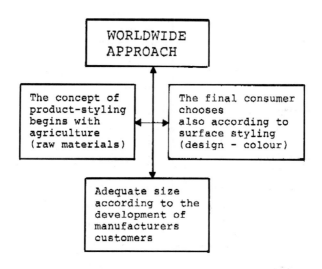

Fig. 3

Fig. 4

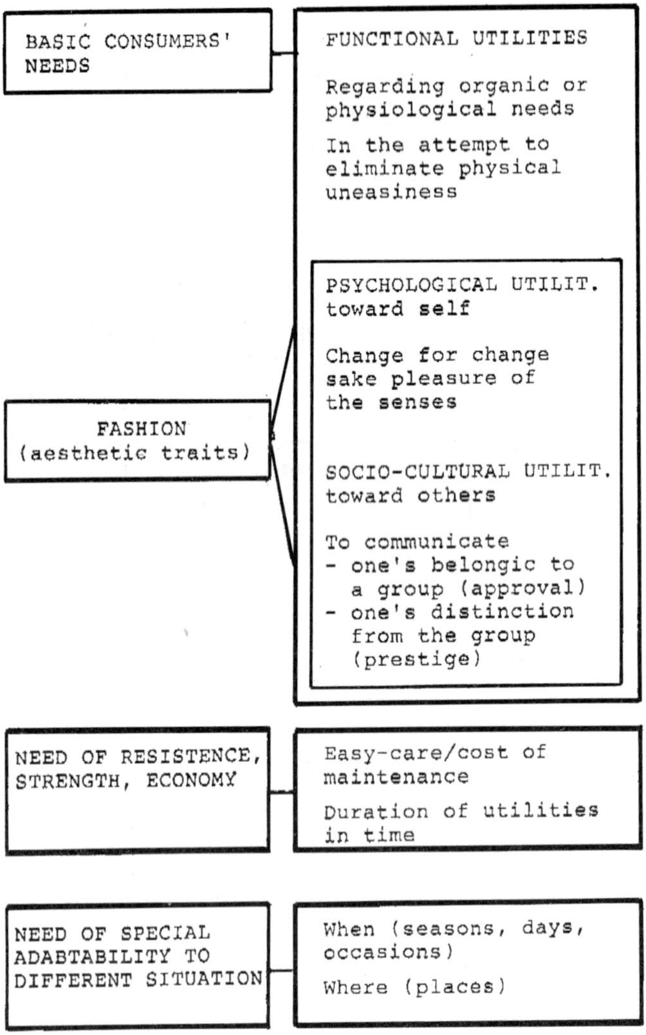

BASIC CONSUMERS' NEEDS	FUNCTIONAL UTILITIES Regarding organic or physiological needs In the attempt to eliminate physical uneasiness

FASHION
(aesthetic traits)
	PSYCHOLOGICAL UTILIT.
	toward self
	
	Change for change sake pleasure of the senses
	
	SOCIO-CULTURAL UTILIT.
	toward others
	
	To communicate
	- one's belongic to
	  a group (approval)
	- one's distinction
	  from the group
	  (prestige)

NEED OF RESISTENCE, STRENGTH, ECONOMY	Easy-care/cost of maintenance Duration of utilities in time
NEED OF SPECIAL ADABTABILITY TO DIFFERENT SITUATION	When (seasons, days, occasions) Where (places)

Fig. 5

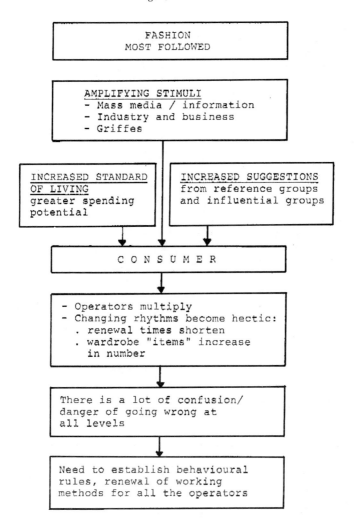

FASHION
MOST FOLLOWED

AMPLIFYING STIMULI
- Mass media / information
- Industry and business
- Griffes

INCREASED STANDARD
OF LIVING
greater spending
potential

INCREASED SUGGESTIONS
from reference groups
and influential groups

C O N S U M E R

- Operators multiply
- Changing rhythms become hectic:
  . renewal times shorten
  . wardrobe "items" increase
    in number

There is a lot of confusion/
danger of going wrong at
all levels

Need to establish behavioural
rules, renewal of working
methods for all the operators

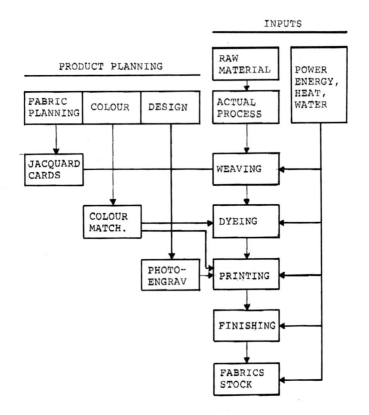

INPUTS

PRODUCT PLANNING

FABRIC PLANNING	COLOUR	DESIGN

RAW MATERIAL

POWER ENERGY, HEAT, WATER

ACTUAL PROCESS

JACQUARD CARDS

COLOUR MATCH.

PHOTO-ENGRAV

WEAVING

DYEING

PRINTING

FINISHING

FABRICS STOCK

Fig. 6

222

Fig. 7

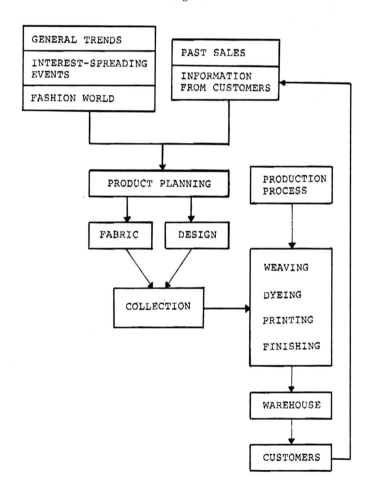

Table I
Italian Per-capita Consumption

	Percentage
Food	30
Housing/furnishing	14
Private transportation	10
Clothing	8
Education/culture	8
Health/personal care	5
Fuel/electricity	5
Public transport	3
Other	17
	100
	(390 000 billions Lire)

Sources: ISTAT 1986.

Table II

Markets/customers	– Double-entry information – Constant selection countries/customers
Process technology	– Flexibility – Automation and process management
Product	– Idea of global quality – Three-variable model in stylistic planning – Three levels of choice and programmed collection – Service-quality programme

Table III

Product-planning - Global Quality

1. The product	- The support
	- Styling (designs/colours)
	- Execution (no imper-
	fections)
	- Duration in time
2. The service	- Assortment (variety, choice)
	- Information
	- Pre-sale assistance
	(archives, strike-offs)
	- Logistic service
	(deliveries, batches)
3. The image	- Our credibility

All of these three points are elements of quality.

(*e*) more needs.

The stylistic strength of a product or collection, which is an important aspect of quality, is very difficult to measure in relation to competitors, and it is therefore very difficult to allow for it in terms of planning.

The search for a competitive superiority becomes hectic and must develop without an over-all evaluation of the entire front. Many moves can be either excessive or superfluous. Some are insufficient.

This affects

(*a*) the product, if the balance between intrinsic quality and aesthetic quality is lost;

(*b*) variety, if assortment is achieved with no specific reference; and

(*c*) the promotional and marketing supports, which are used massively in the belief that they will support sales.

A perverse spiral can be started, which will find an unprepared system. Navigation is by sight, with no instruments used.

3. PROCESS TECHNOLOGY

The essential traits of process technology do not change in relation to the changes in the combination of product and market. What is needed in process technology is therefore:

flexibility in production (adaptation to changes);

precision in execution (quality); and

a reduction of costs, towards the management system and automation of the process, rather than towards an increase of size.

At present, the system offers two contrasting solutions which are:

a drive towards an increase in *size*; and

a drive towards an increase in *flexibility*.

An outline of integrated planning (product-process system) is shown in Fig. 6.

4. CHALLENGES FOR THE FUTURE

The system of demand/needs is hard to interpret and becomes even harder, because of:

the world;
variety used;
the many steps before getting to the consumer; and
the influence of fashion.

The influence of fashion becomes even more dominant in the apparel industry. Competition is increasingly threatening. Within the silk field, competition rules have altered owing to:

the enrichment of fabric (increase of added value) that is
carried out by the producers of raw material; and

the socialist-state entrepreneurs, integrated from agriculture
to the finished fabric.

Moreover, clothing and tailoring centres change; factories are established where the cost of labour is lowest (Far East). Consequently, competition appears in the form of differences in cost
and price affecting many customers' choices. The balance of price
and quality shifts rapidly.

Technology today offers two contradictory solutions:

size; and
flexibility.

Together with external difficulties (setting), there are problems
ensuing from the adaptation of human and physical resources (con-
genital delays) to the rhythm of market and technological evolu-
tions.

Only business creativity conceived in its entirety establishes
the conditions for survival.

5. WHAT TO DO

Business creativity means:

(1) redefining the formula:

(*a*) level of differentiation (greater costs);
(*b*) level of the affordable cost position (greater
rigidity); and

(2) to guarantee greater future flexibility:

greater adaptability of the formula.

This is shown in Tables II and III.

Quality depends on three variables which are closely connected:

(1) process technology:
(*a*) weaving,
(*b*) dyeing,
(*c*) printing,
(*d*) finishing;

(2) product/structure:
(*a*) supports,
(*b*) designs,
(*c*) colouring;

(3) final customers:
(*a*) use (clothing/men's/ladies'/household),
(*b*) consumer's situation (high fashion/classical/etc.),
(*c*) basic traits of clothing (wearability).

Point (2) above is *styling* and point (3) is *fashion*.

Customers of apparel fabrics aspire to a maximum differentiation:

(1) fitted sales (maximum differentiation):
   (*a*) greatest creative assistance (use of archives, etc.);
   (*b*) setting up of equipment;
   (*c*) delivery service;

(2) collection-based sales (medium differentiation):
   (*a*) average creative assistance (colours as required);
   (*b*) use of available equipment;
   (*c*) shorter-term delivery;

(3) collection-based sale on available stock:
   (*a*) creative assistance in relation to collection;
   (*b*) prompt delivery.

The information system oriented towards the product is shown in Fig. 7.

Ratti Spa,
Como,
Italy.

Second-generation Marketing in the Textile Industry

A. Rigamonti

Abstract

Second-generation marketing comes about as a result of the increasing application of computers and computer programs in the
world of textiles. The principles involved are unchanged, but the
computer allows much more sophisticated and meaningful analyses
to be made of market data, competitivity, projections, and options
than could possibly be done manually.

This paper explores some of the potential and draws attention
to several specific and unique programs that have been developed
by Werner International.

The ultimate in marketing technique is far from being reached,
but recent developments in this field are as significant for the
1990s as the change-over from selling to marketing was in the
1950s.

1. INTRODUCTION

Today's world is a challenging one for the textile industry. The
development of new manufacturing technologies and new products has
been followed by the emergence of low-price manufacturing facilities outside the old industrialized countries and the dispersion
of the mass market in the developed world. Growth in textile demand worldwide, and especially in the richer countries, is expected to be low compared with the levels experienced in the 1950s
and 1960s. With hindsight, it is clear now that the 1970s were a
period of fundamental transition in the world economy, and especially for traditional industries like textiles.

The textile industry has responded to these changes by shifting
from a labour-intensive to a capital-intensive industry wherever
appropriate and possible and by developing a comprehensive set of
tariff or quota barriers designed to control the spread of world
trade in textiles and apparel.

Financial charges, maintenance and planning requirements, technological developments, the cost of energy and specialist materials, quality requirements, customer service, and the sheer size of
the investments needed, all combine to allow the developed world
to become a competitive base for *primary* textile operations again.
Nevertheless, many plants have been set up in the developing

229

countries, which, though marginally competitive on a commercial basis, are frequently subsidized by local governments to ensure that the investment is a source of hard-currency earnings. As a result, worldwide production capacity constantly exceeds demand.

The cost relationship illustrated in Table I shows a comparison of yarn costs in four European countries, one with very low labour costs, ageing machinery, but very high finance costs (Portugal), one with medium labour costs and a below-average performance in most respects (Spain), and two with high labour costs but up-to-date technology, one (Germany) with high efficiencies and the other (France) with only average efficiencies.

The final yarn-cost relationship between Portugal and West Germany is not appreciably different. Spain was brought into the competitive area by its peculiar export-support system, and France illustrates an unrealized competitive situation.

These figures relate to 1985 and there may have been changes since that time; certainly the DM has appreciated considerably, but the principle remains that, in a modern, high-tech, low-labour environment (in terms of numbers), primary textile manufacture in high-labour-cost areas is viable.

The situation in making-up is somewhat different. On the basis of current technology, it is not as capital-intensive as primary textile manufacture. The relatively unsophisticated technology, traditionally characteristic of this sector, is also easy to assimilate in a developing country.

The costing element is demonstrated by the figures in Table II, showing the cost of making a shirt in two EEC countries with high labour costs, Portugal with low labour costs, and two Far Eastern countries with very low labour costs. Clearly, labour cost in making-up is still very significant and does give advantage to low-labour-cost countries.

Making-up operations in these countries are frequently highly competitive compared with their counterparts in the developed countries. The problems of this sector relate to fashion and the logistics of distribution.

Fashion by itself does not create demand. It is wealth or purchasing power that creates demand. The amount of money spent on fashion depends on the availability of funds and not on the influence of fashion itself. It is fashion as well as quality that determines the choice of whether to purchase discretionary textiles from source A or source B. This role of fashion in determining demand in the apparel sector is especially important in those parts of the developing world that produce for export.

It is interesting to see the relationship between apparel expenditure in a given year and total textile-fibre consumption. In countries with up to 5 kg *per capita* consumption, i.e., the majority of the developing countries, fashion has a minimal impact, the bulk of the market being for basic or utility textiles. In the emerging countries, with up to 9 kg *per capita*, there is still a very large proportion of the demand for basic textiles, but discretionary textiles are starting to have some impact. In respect

Table I

*Costing Example: Cotton Yarn, Carded, Count Ne 24
on Cone in Current DM per kg (1985)*

	Portu-gal	Spain	West Germany	France
(1) Raw material	5.23	5.07	5.03	5.11
(2) Direct and indirect labour cost	0.46	0.99	1.42	1.71
(3) Energy cost	0.36	0.31	0.40	0.30
(4) Manufacturing expenses	0.49	0.60	0.75	0.70
(5) Depreciation cost	0.28	0.40	0.48	0.38
(6) Total manufacturing cost	6.82	7.37	8.08	8.20
(7) Financial cost	1.12	0.60	0.28	0.49
(8) Selling and administrative expenses	0.36	0.47	0.40	0.59
(9) Total cost (6+7+8)	8.30	8.44	8.76	9.28

Source: Werner International, 1985.

Table II

Costing Example: Cotton Shirt in DM per Shirt

	UK	West Germany	Portu-gal	South Korea	Hong Kong
Raw material	9.34	9.19	8.53	7.48	7.78
Direct and indirect labour cost	3.21	4.36	1.43	1.05	0.80
Energy cost	0.11	0.12	0.10	0.15	0.15
Manufacturing expenses	0.91	1.15	0.98	0.55	0.63
Depreciation cost	0.40	0.35	0.30	0.26	0.22
Total manufacturing cost	13.97	15.17	11.34	9.49	9.58
Financial cost	0.66	0.50	1.85	1.12	0.73
Selling and admini-strative expenses	0.99	1.35	1.44	0.77	0.62
Total cost	15.62	17.02	14.63	11.38	10.90

Source: Werner International.

Table III

Strategic Marketing

Stage	Factor
I	Market knowledge - research Market projection Strategic positioning of the company
II	Review product range Review marketing policy
III	Detailed marketing plan

Source: Werner International.

Table IV

Preparation for Strategic-marketing Plan

Stage	Item	Responsibility
1	Analysis of environmental factors	Joint
	Analysis of market and products	Joint
	Projection of market and products	Werner programme *
	Analysis of strengths/weaknesses: manufacturing selling distribution design/image	Werner programme *
	Comparison with competitors	
2	Appraisal of current marketing practice	Joint
	Definition of marketing policy	Company board of directors
3	Quantification of draft marketing plan	Marketing management
	Alternative scenarios	Werner programme *
	Finalization of plan	Joint

* Second-generation marketing input.

Table V

Example of the System in Operation

SALES AND CONTRIBUTION SUMMARY
WERNER MODEL SPINNING COMPANY

Date 04-01-1987

PNo.	Ply	Count	$MrgCst	$Selprc	Dely/Wk Kg	$Sales	$Contrib	%
8 1143	1	20.0	2.9115	3.8000	4700	17860	4176	23
26 1234	1	14.0	2.9226	4.0500	10000	40500	11274	28
86 1342	1	9.0	3.4022	4.5000	17000	76500	18663	24
92 245	1	16.0	1.9457	3.5000	6500	22750	10103	44
96 142	1	22.0	4.2040	4.2500	1800	7650	83	1

Summaries & Totals

$Sales	$GenAd	$FixLab	$TotFix	$TotContb	$GrsP/L	%P/L	$Amort
165260	17813	4364	22177	44299	22122	13.4	8106

Programs (C)opyright Methods Workshop Ltd, 1986/87. System Designed and Marketed by Werner International.

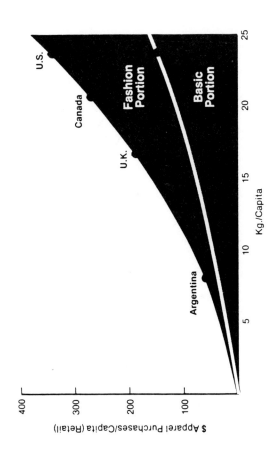

Fig. 1   Relation between apparel purchases *per capita* and total textile-
fibre consumption (in kg *per capita*), showing division between
basic apparel and fashion apparel.

Source : Werner International

235

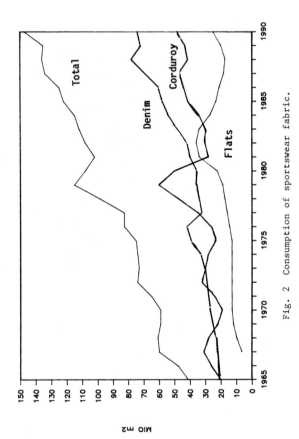

Fig. 2 Consumption of sportswear fabric.

Source : Werner International

236

"BASIC APPAREL SURVEY IN AUSTRALIA"

DISTANCE MATRIX

CLUSTERING CRITERION IS COMPLETE LINKAGE – (MAXIMUM DISTANCE)

DISTANCE

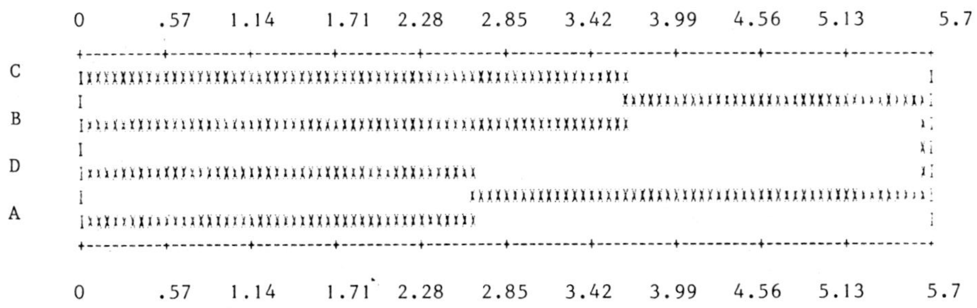

| 0 | .57 | 1.14 | 1.71 | 2.28 | 2.85 | 3.42 | 3.99 | 4.56 | 5.13 | 5.7 |

C
B
D
A

| 0 | .57 | 1.14 | 1.71 | 2.28 | 2.85 | 3.42 | 3.99 | 4.56 | 5.13 | 5.7 |

Fig. 3 Cluster analysis.

Source : Werner International

237

Key to Fig. 4

Companies

A - Client

B
C } Competitors
D

Factors

1 - Performance of rep/salesman

2 - Length of delivery times

3 - Handling of complaints

4 - Special orders

5 - Telephone service of sales dept.

6 - Special deliveries

7 - Sympathy

8 - Credibility

9 - Management

10 - Relative cost/benefit

11 - Quality/service worth price

12 - Manufacturer of low-cost products

13 - Durability of products

14 - Easy-care

15 - Handle of fabric

16 - Colour-fastness

17 - Quality in general

18 - Keeping of delivery dates

19 - Pre-sale presentation

20 - Frequency of contact

21 - Accept small orders

22 - Terms of payment

23 - Products suitability

24 - Impact of public relations

25 - Support in sales promotions

26 - Price policy

27 - Packing

28 - Repeatability piece to piece

29 - Known as manufacturer of quality

30 - Best support for sales

Fig. 4   Strategic-positioning correspondence plot.

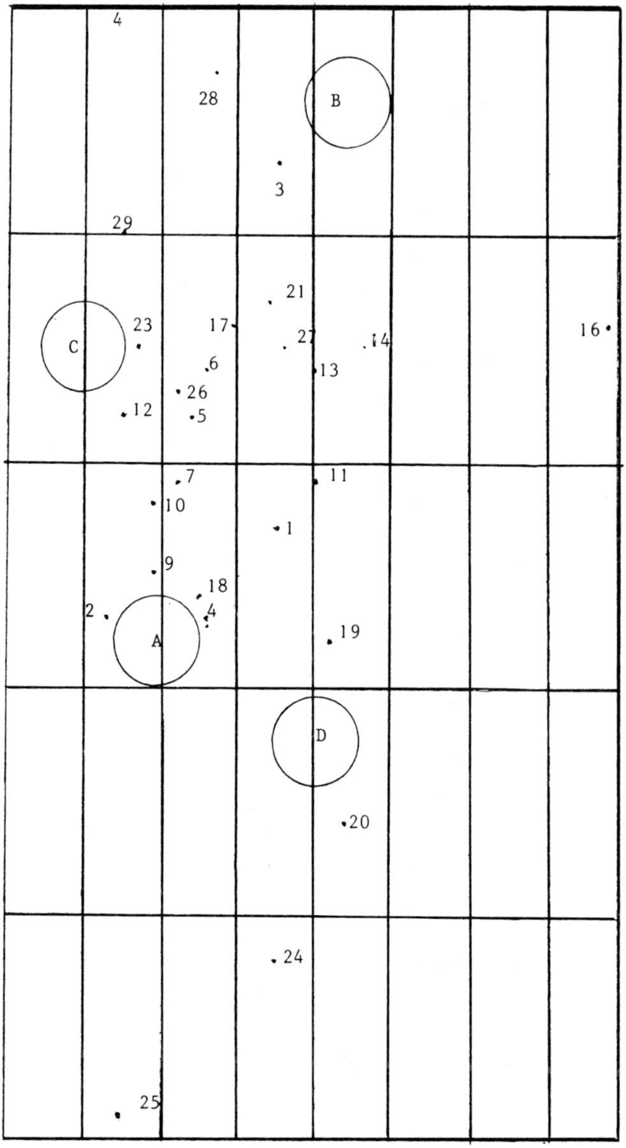

Source : Werner International

239

of countries with over 10 kg *per capita*, the major part of the consumption is for discretionary textiles, reaching in the U.S., by our definition, 60% of all apparel expenditure (Fig. 1).

Investigatory studies that we have made show that the fashion element of textile consumption becomes significant when a country's fibre consumption exceeds 10 kg *per capita*. Up to that point, textile consumption is mainly taken up by basics, although it has to be observed that some countries, for example, Brazil, like their basics to be fashionable. The point at issue really is the level of economic development at which textile consumption becomes more discretionary than sheer necessity.

Fashion, however, goes beyond apparel. It includes carpets, towels, sheets, upholstery, automotive fabrics, and similar products. To be able to penetrate the market for these types of discretionary textiles in the U.S.A. and Western Europe, it is not sufficient to have only the right price and quality; it is essential to have the right fashion image, too. The further away production facilities are from the market, the more difficult it is to keep up with changes in fashion.

With consumption growing slowly in the economically developed markets, attempts to launch new fashions are constantly made in efforts to increase market share. This in turn exacerbates the logistic and distribution problems of remote making-up sites.

In all market sectors, it is clear that greater marketing flexibility and capability will be needed in the future to maintain profitable trading activities. The textile community worldwide should be aware of the need for proper marketing policies as indispensable tools in the struggle for survival and profits.

Even today, plants are being built on the basis of cheap labour, low-interest loans, and special grants or tax concessions. Without a proper marketing strategy, these facilities can easily end up as 'white elephants'.

The present controls on the industry cannot last for ever. The market forces for change are too great, and, when combined with pressures for trade concessions in other industries, the existing arrangements, for example, the MFA, are unlikely to survive into the 1990s in recognizable form.

2. MARKETING PRINCIPLES

To consider the application of second-generation marketing, one has firstly to identify what is meant by first-generation marketing and even what is meant by marketing.

Marketing as an art or a science, and it is, in fact, a mixture of the two, has not changed in thousands of years. Joseph, in his coat of many colours (is this the first recorded example of colour weaving?) and with his granaries full of corn at the onset of a famine, was a marketing man *par excellence*.

It is a matter of providing what the customer wants at the right time; and at the right price, some would say, but price in fact is the most flexible element in the marketing mix.

Joseph was said to have had divine inspiration in respect of the projected corn market, but we cannot rely on that in the textile business. We have to have market research on which to base our projections: we have to have projections on which to base our marketing plan, and we have to have a precise idea of our position and that of our principal competitors in the market. We also have to know which of our products make the best return.

Marketing is a state of mind: some companies, especially entrepreneurial-type companies, have it naturally, but some companies even today have no real concept or practice of marketing.

They have manufacturing, of course, and they have selling, but they have little liaison between the two outside order-planning. What they do have is constant bickering between the two - 'not enough orders' says production, 'late and inaccurate deliveries' says sales.

Marketing-planning and all that it entails can improve on such a situation, and, for a company that is going to make an adequate return on its investment, a realistic marketing plan is a vital element of its management.

The formal process of business planning for most companies is a misunderstood, often-imprecise, and under-utilized management tool. Frequently, planning is either indistinguishable from the budgeting process, or else it is a form of aimless philosophical speculation with no tangible or specific results.

Even when planning is understood and taken seriously, it is often ineffective. In the modern world, the weaknesses of conventional strategic planning methods have become apparent because they are traditionally unconcerned with the implementation of the plans they create. This has become an increasingly important issue in recent years as the industrialized world moves into an era of slow growth.

Skilful planning is a prerequisite for success. The key to good planning is a thorough understanding of the markets in which one's company's products are sold. This planning must be supported by a comprehensive set of monitoring and control systems that help management to supervise the implementation of the plans.

Let us assume then that our first-generation marketing director was blessed with a board of directors who had produced a corporate and a strategic plan. Table III shows the outline of what came after that.

Planning demands firstly market knowledge and market projection and secondly strategic positioning of the company and its competitors.

This can be regarded as Stage 1, the foundation on which a strategic marketing plan is built, and it consists essentially in marketing ground work, i.e., knowing the size of the market, the direction in which it is moving, where the company is in the market, and where it is going in comparison with its competitors.

The second stage is to review the existing marketing and product policy and to define the objectives of the strategic marketing policy for the future. These two stages set the scene for action.

Once the stage has been set, management can begin devising and implementing detailed programmes that specify how the company will achieve its objectives in a variety of operational environments. These programmes are categorized in order of preference and include contingency plans to cope with changes in the operational environment. They take detailed account of the company's resources and allocate these resources within the various alternative marketing scenarios. The outcome of these deliberations is the marketing plan (Stage 3).

The detailed marketing plan, which is the blueprint of the company's commercial endeavour, will identify markets by area, volume, and value (unit price) and the marketing cost of the entire operation.

First-generation marketing-planning was really a paper chase. Every time a new idea cropped up or a projection was changed, a whole series of new calculations and new pieces of paper had to be produced.

In the earlier era of sustained growth, management's main task was to ensure that the company kept up the growth momentum. Today, the world is characterized by mature markets, and the challenge is to optimize a five-dimensional equation to maximize profitabilty. The five factors are sales, assets, human resources, raw materials, and primary energy.

Traditional planning methods, either single-cycle, such as budgeting, or two-cycle, which includes functional planning, embracing research and development to production, are no longer sufficient to ensure continued long-term viability. It is necessary to add a third cycle, strategic marketing, in order to have a coherent comprehensive approach to management problems.

The addition of this third cycle dramatically increases the number of strategic options considered by a company. In the present environment, it is more important than ever before that a company has the widest scale of options available to it and that it has plans to exercise these options when circumstances demand.

Here we enter into consideration of second-generation marketing. The principles are the same, but the tools and the potential for optimizing the company's resources are infinitely greater.

Second-generation marketing is done on the computer – an absolutely ideal tool for marketing – and one that widens the horizons and the options immeasurably.

There is no substitute for information assembly, and that still has to be done; market research and market feedback are the essential nuts and bolts of a marketing plan, and without them one just cannot make a meaningful plan.

The main objective is to understand the markets in which the company operates and in which it is considering operating. This understanding consists in identifying the position of the company *vis-à-vis* that of its competitors, the relationships between competitors in markets, and the perceptions of customers. This is the essence of competitive strategy.

Werner has developed several new tools, which help clients to produce the best possible marketing plan. These cover three aspects of the work involved.

On the basis of this need, Werner has devised a new systematical approach to the process of marketing-planning and to the implementation of plans. Based on the concept of a in-house network linking specific internal corporate resources, this new approach constantly emphasizes the process of making the strategy operational. It also recognizes that, in the future, strategic-marketing planners will have to change their view of the relative importance of external and internal factors. More emphasis will have to be laid on increasing internal flexibility and speed of reaction if profitability is to be sustained through periods of environmental turbulence.

3. PROJECTION OF MARKET AND PRODUCTS

In both first- and second-generation marketing, forecasts need to be made of likely developments in each market, projected product-life cycles are drawn up, market shares are defined, and trends in the development of these elements are documented.

The difference between first and second generation is that new forecasting techniques have been developed exclusively by Werner for the benefit of its clients.

Werner has developed new forecasting techniques and multidimensional strategic-positioning tools, which are uniquely well suited to pre-planning in the textile industry. These serve to complement the traditional technical skills, which allow the company to benefit from short-term benefits while the mechanisms are being developed that will put the long-range plans into effect.

For the purpose of outline forecasting, Werner's new model of world textile consumption and trade allows its staff to identify market opportunities and threats far ahead of those available via first-generation techniques. This model analyses the demand for textiles by main product families and shows how demand for them can be expected to develop over time. The model uses several different techniques to forecast demand and can be applied to individual products as well as families of textiles.

In relation to market forecasting, let us consider just one product, for example, denim. Denim has only one regular and rational outlet, sportswear, although in 1976 everything went denim crazy and it appeared in luggage and upholstery and in Levi Strauss's Brussels office as carpet even, but those outlets are market freaks. Denim is a sportswear fabric. But so are corduroy and certain flat cloths.

In considering the market for denim, it is therefore not sensible to do so in isolation. The market has always been shared with

corduroy and 'flats' in differing proportions over the years. A
rise in consumption of sportswear fabrics in general does not pre-
destine an equivalent rise in each of the participating fabrics.

This again is where second-generation computer-aided marketing
can provide so much better a forecast outline than could be gauged
previously. By plotting the development pattern of woven sportswear (say) for a number of years - and the more the better - a
pattern will emerge, as shown, for example in Fig. 2, which, in
conjunction with the macro-economic textile model, will enable a
very good market forecast to be made.

The beauty of assembling market information on a spread sheet
is that it can be added to or updated as better information is
assembled, without being painstakingly rewritten or recalculated
by hand, and the computer will draw the graph.

All the work to this point is routine/mechanical, but at this
stage, all the background information having been assembled, management has to decide on its targets, market share, current and
projected, market sector, and precise product range. This element
represents the first decision point of the marketing plan.

4. ANALYSIS OF STRENGTHS AND WEAKNESSES

Werner can also show its clients how to define their profile in
key markets, how to identify their strategic position in these
markets, how to locate the key variables in establishing and
changing that position, and how to devise the strategies and tac-
tics that will achieve their newly specified objectives.

This strategic positioning service is unique to Werner because
Werner alone has developed the software and interviewing techniques
that enable a consultant to provide a definitive, objective description of a market.

A detailed questionnaire is drawn up to cover four key areas
of the marketing mix:

    quality
    price
    performance
    design/image.

With from 30 to 36 specific questions put to a cross-section of
clients or potential clients, in respect of the company and its
competitors, answers are recorded against a numerical scale,
usually from 1 to 7, 1 being supremely excellent and 7 exceedingly
bad.

The results of the interviews, not fewer than 40, are synthe-
sized via the specially developed computer programs to give a
series of analyses. Two of these are illustrated by Fig. 3, cluster
analysis, and Fig. 4, correspondence analysis.

The objective of the cluster analysis is to identify the similarity between companies and at what stage this similarity develops.

All the companies analysed are shown in one illustration
(dendogram), and the distance from the left-hand side before companies become similar to one another indicates the degree of similarity. For example, if two companies came together very near the
left-hand edge, they would be very similar, and, if they did not
come together until almost reaching the right-hand edge of the
diagram (or not at all), they would be very dissimilar.

Cluster analysis illustrates how competitive suppliers to a
market are grouped in the eyes and minds of the customers making
up that market. At the same time, the strengths, weaknesses, and
characteristics of the companies are identified in Fig. 4, so that
it is readily apparent whether it is an advantage or not for a
similarity to exist with a given company.

This is a process that thinking, analytical marketing directors
have previously carried out in their heads (first-generation-mar-
keting assessment of competitivity), but this numerically-based
assessment covering very many aspects of company attitude and
achievement is much more accurate and not subject to individual
personal bias. One is obtaining the views of the clients and potential clients, and they are therefore not only more objective
but also more useful.

The strategic-positioning diagram, Fig. 4, illustrates how competitive suppliers are rated in terms of specific performance
issues. Each of the companies examined is positioned within the
grid on the results of a penetrating questionnaire to show their
competitive relationship to one another. Those with more plus factors are positioned towards the top right-hand corner of the grid.
At the same time, and on the same diagram, the degree of importance
of certain performance issues is shown, and, by virtue of being on
the same diagram, it demonstrates which companies excel at which
performance issue through the proximity of company to performance
issue.

These analyses, combined with multivariate and other statistical inputs, allow a comprehensive map to be drawn of the company's
position in that market and indicate which aspects of the company's
performance need attention.

This combination of quantitative market research, market forecasting, and strategic-positioning analysis is combined with environmental surveys to produce a comprehensive analysis of a company's situation, its strengths and weaknesses, opportunities and
threats, as perceived by both the company and its customers.

From this extensive and detailed analysis of the markets in
which the company operates and the environments that surround
these markets, the major foundation components of the company's
action programmes are derived. Note that these components can be
created for specific market segments, product groups, or even particular products.

The most recent addition to the marketing director's armoury
is contained within Werner's Texmix programme. This is pure second-
generation marketing and the most fantastic marketing tool to be
made available to date.

To work out the sales scenario with the best return was hitherto a cumbersome job of monumental proportions and was rarely done for this reason alone. But now, with this most recent addition to management assistance, the task becomes one that the computer can be left to work out alone, after feeding in the relevant modifications in product mix or proposed sales pattern.

Texmix has been prepared as a second-generation tool for general and technical mill management, but it is, in fact, even more of a sophisticated marketing and sales-planning tool in that it readily allows:

market simulation,
product-range upgrading
value assessment of the 'special-premium' order, and
product-mix optimization

by working out the contribution that can be made by any given product mix that the plant in question can make and therefore any given product mix that is planned to be sold.

During the course of preparing the sales plan, alternative sales and product-mix scenarios should be devised and compared with one another to provide the optimum sales plan.

Table V illustrates the printout that will be available from Texmix to indicate the vital parts of the sales/production programme, what suits the plant best, what return is gained from any given product mix, and hence the product mix that ensures the best return.

Taken the other way round, market constraints can be tested out on the programme and so guide the marketing team as to which products should be avoided (or more highly priced). It not only shows the most advantageous product mix but also demonstrates the pitfalls of following alternative mixes.

5. CONCLUSIONS

Strategic marketing is the most important single ingredient in business management.

Marketing is currently entering its second phase of development helped by the computer industry and specifically designed textile software programs.

Yet some companies are not yet into first-generation marketing, and many more that were not are no longer here today.

With ever-increasingly foolproof technology becoming available, the business elements most needing the human thought process are in planning and marketing - and they are the most neglected.

Until fairly recently, most new companies in developing countries were set up without adequate thought being given to marketing the resultant product, and such companies either went under, or became a drain on their country's resources, as a result of the subsidies they received in some form or another in order to keep them alive. The situation has improved in recent years, and the

international funding agencies do make a marketing review, of a
sort, in deciding whether their project is feasible.

Even in fully developed economies, and this includes the United
States of America, the paucity of effort devoted to strategic marketing by much of the textile industry is astonishing and frighten-
ing.

The opportunity exists to make the quantum leap - straight into
second-generation marketing.

We can but invite readers to think about it.

Werner International,
Brussels,
Belgium.

Fashion: The Way Forward

H. Robinson

1. INTRODUCTION

The way forward is not always as clear as we should like. To chart
it, one needs to look at the recent past to consider what influences will bear upon the future: lifestyle trends; new technology;
economic conditions. Getting this information into order allows
clear conclusions and decisions to be made, from which one can
plan one's way forward.

Together we shall explore some of these influences and the way
in which they may be incorporated into future planning for success.

2. DEFINITION OF FASHION

What is fashion? Not just clothes. Fashion designers known traditionally for their fabulous women's clothes, such as Karl
Lagerfeld, Yves St Laurent, Zandra Rhodes, Calvin Klein, and
Perry Ellis, have all branched into non-traditional areas and
brought them into the fashion arena.

In extending his own fashion boundaries beyond clothes, Ralph
Lauren has made us look again at the comfort and style of simple
things: a walk on the beach; a comfortable shoe; crisp blue and
white in a country cottage; the pleasure of family life. Fashion
has taken on a new meaning far from the crystal chandeliers of
the Avenue Montaigne - equally relevant in their own time and
place. In other words, the frontiers of fashion have been pushed
back.

3. THE IMPORTANCE OF STYLE

Fashion may be the wrong word nowadays; style means so much more.
If *style* is what is evaluated as opposed to fashion, the commercial opportunities are better pinpointed.

What is style? Who has it? The stars shine with it. Products
sell because of it, and all over the world there is a handful of
leaders of countries, companies, airlines, schools, banks, and
international consortia who dazzle us with style.

What *is* style? Can I buy it? Can I have it delivered to me?

249

Do you find it in a packet? Or is there a hat to match it? Does it cost much? The answer is 'no' to all these questions.

What is it? How *do* you get it? If you analyse the style of successful businesses, you will notice how *consistent* they are. They are profitable because they know who they are and what their market is. They care. Everything they do exploits their sureness.

Style fits well into company structure. It is a management tool and an aid to profitability.

The '7 S Framework' or the 'soft S's' appears in Chapter 1 of 'In Search of Excellence', by Thomas J. Peters and Robert H. Waterman, to whom I am indebted. It shows in a clear and simple way that style (which some people regard as an ephemeral and subjective art) is as much part of the administrative structure of a successful company as are good systems and excellent staff. This framework, as the authors point out in the book, 'reminds the world that "soft is hard". It has enabled us to say in effect, "all that stuff you have been dismissing for so long as the intractable, irrational, intuitive, informal organization *can* be managed. Clearly it has as much or more to do with the way things work (or don't) around your companies as the formal structures strategies do. Not only are you foolish to ignore style, but here is a way to think about it. Here are some tools for managing it. Here, really, is the way to develop a new skill."'

In establishing a company style, it is obviously necessary to identify the aim of the business. In discussing fashion (manufacturing and retailing), that means being clear about who you want to sell to (and never everybody, for that means nobody); what you want to sell; and what price levels would appeal to your target customers.

4. TWO COMPANY EXAMPLES

A few years ago, Hepworths – a dull menswear business in the U.K. – took on George Davis to launch a company aimed at the now-thirtyish products of the baby boom of the 1940s and 1950s. He was from a company that had sold directly to the customer through organized parties at home.

He launched Next in 1981 – closely targeted, colour-co-ordinated, stylish, and very competitively priced. All the shops and fixtures were designed to provide the right environment – exciting windows, easy co-ordination, helpful, knowledgeable staff, a calm atmosphere – very different from the noisy, dark, crowded boutiques of the 1960s – and most importantly, he sold tights, belts, bags, shoes, and hats in the same trends. Seventy shops of around 4500 ft^2 were opened in two weeks – not impossible, as was proved – and the sole promotion was a colour brochure inserted into *Vogue* plus massive PR coverage in magazines and newspapers.

Now, six years later, Next has 227 womenswear shops. Cosmetics, lingerie, shoes, and accessories all form part of the range, sometimes standing alone. Next for Men was launched in a similar way and now has over 170 shops that are just as successful: the look is very stylish, and the prices are fantastic. A couple of years

ago, the company launched made-to-measure suits - a new development that cleverly used up the old Hepworths' menswear factories'
idle capacity.

From being a low-growth company, selling dull menswear in dull
surroundings, Hepworths made £8.6m profit in 1983 and £27.7m
profit in 1986. This is amazing even if one considers the capital
invested in opening around 450 brand new shops on the High Street
and the required return.

Did they stop there? No. Three stand-alone shoe shops have
been opened, as well as shoes appearing in 227 womenswear shops.
In 22 outlets, a cafe and a flower shop are included. In Regent
Street, London, Next opened its first Home Shop and Chose for the
launch another top designer, Tricia Guild of Designers Guild, to
co-ordinate a range of furnishing including fabrics, wallpaper,
tiles, linens, towels, furniture, rugs, lamps, ceramics, and
glass. Next now has 40 Home Shops.

Alongside this, Next has also bought Grattan, a mail-order
company, so that it can capture every possible customer - as
Habitat, Laura Ashley, and Warehouse have done. The mail-order
catalogues fulfil two purposes: to provide mail order for customers who cannot or do not want to go shopping and to tempt in
customers who can and do.

George Davis, having done the kind of homework mentioned at
the beginning of this paper, saw the way forward clearly. His
success is demonstrated by his financial results and the reputation of Next as a fashion and retail revolution.

In the U.S.A. someone else who has done the same kind of homework is Leslie Wexner, of the now-famous The Limited. The figures
speak for themselves, profit before tax rising from $13.1m in
1980 to $145.3m in 1985. Wexner, as *Forbes Magazine* wrote recently,
'has refined the art of formula merchandising, overseas manufacturing, and rapid-response distribution to a high degree of polish.
Everything is sharply focussed on merchandise and pleasing the
customer'.

Leslie Wexner has turned his company (which consists of The
Limited, Limited Express, Victoria's Secret, Lane Bryant, Brylane
Mail Order, Sizes Unlimited, Mast Industries, Lerner, and Now
Henri Bendel) into a runaway success. But the high-profile, high-
flyer of his company is the The Limited. According (once more) to
Forbes Magazine, which analysed the major 1000 companies in the
U.S.A. it is the fastest-growing, most profitable, speciality-
apparel retailer that it surveyed. Its shares have appreciated
faster over the last five years than those of any of the other
companies analysed. In its Annual Report, The Limited's mission
is stated as follows:

'We will maintain and hopefully improve the values of our
business, the most important being:

to offer the absolute best customer shopping experience
anywhere - the best store - the best merchandise - the best
merchandise presentation - the best customer service - the
best "everything" that a customer sees and experiences;

to become the leading retailer of lifestyles fashion for
women in the United States;

to be known as a high-quality business with an unquestioned
reputation for integrity and respect for people;

to maintain a revolutionary, restless, bold, and daring
business spirit, noted for its breakthrough, cutting-edge
style;

to maintain a management style which is action-oriented,
always flexible, and never bureaucratic;

to be tough-minded, disciplined, demanding, self-critical,
yet supportive of each other and our team;

to never be satisfied and to maintain a bold, aggressive,
and creative vision of the future.

And lastly we want The Limited to be a magic place to work –
a place where there are no limits to individual accomplish-
ment, no limits to our respect for every individual associate,
no limits on having fun while we work, and a place where individual and group dreams can come true.'

What a fantastic credo!

Wexner commissioned Kenzo, the master of colourful modern
clothes for today's lifestyles, to design a special range for The
Limited. Situated in the front of the stores, magically merchan-
dised to glow through the windows, this range initially set the
pace for the other merchandise and positioned The Limited clearly
as a fashion leader for the mass market, from coast to coast, in
the U.S.A. Now Wexner has added Krizia to The Limited with a
special range called Krizia Moods, as well as developing two major own-brand labels, Forenza and Outback Red. This single-mind-
edness and discipline of the approach to visual merchandising
create a single identity from which the strength of the corporate
image springs.

Other stores around the world are facing the challenge of the
competitive 1980s and successfully turning fashion 'know-how'
into profit:

Bloomingdale's, Macy's and Sak's Fifth Avenue, in the U.S.A.;
Galeries Lafayette and Au Printemps in France;
Harvey Nichols and Harrods in the U.K., and many more.

Now, however, new challenges appear for groups like those of
Davis and Wexner. How they solve the problems success and growth
bring will determine their future.

Firstly, as a base becomes larger, it is difficult for it to
grow at the same or a higher rate, yet the valuation of its shares
is dependent on high rates of growth.

Secondly, as Martin Trust, President of Mast Industries, says,
'Great quality factories don't grow on trees'. Finding consistent
sources of supply for the increasing quantities of merchandise
needed to satisfy a fast-growing number of outlets is difficult.

Thirdly, it is easy for the dynamic that develops the initial
success to become diluted and diverted. The brilliant merchant who

originated the successful formula wants to retain the 'hand-on'
method of management so essential to success yet has his time increasingly taken with other matters inextricably tied up with
growth – property and finance, to name but two.

Big businesses seem to find it impossible to grow new ones in
the same way as the original success was developed. It is human
nature that, although the very top innovators and managers may
want and understand change, most middle-management personnel dis-
like and fear it. Karl Marx nearly said 'in success lie the seeds
of decay' – and maybe that is a much more succinct way of making
this point.

Change there will be, and it will come in our industry in two
ways. Firstly, youth, energy, and ideas *will* break out outside
large companies. Think of Sock Shop, valued at £27.5m, just being
taken to the Stock Market in Britain after only four years, with
43 shops, a turnover of £6m and profits of £773 000, which look
like doubling this year to £1.7m. Yet no one would lend Sophie
Mirman (still only 30) money to begin, and she and her husband
started by investing £2000 each – all they had. Secondly, large
companies with foresight will structure themselves so that there
is a genuine possibility of the same sort of thing happening
within them.

Whatever happens, it will not be the same as now. Not because
companies will make change for change's sake, but because the
public will change, and good designers and merchants will recognize the opportunity this affords them.

Now, I have identified some people, things, and businesses
with style and success. We have seen how, today, style is inextricably part of the shared value that must be identified as the
heart of the administrative structure in a successful business.

We have analysed the success of two high-flying businesses.
Now let us look at a different aspect: *style and capital investment* – odd bedfellows as they may appear.

The most successful European textile exporter is Italy. The
latest figures available are for 1984, when, of $27 billion worth
of textiles sold, one-third went to export, second only to shoes.
One-third of the money spent in the EEC in recent years on textiles and clothes was on Italian goods: a surprising statistic,
but true.

Italy has recognized that privately run companies, however
large, can be a recipe for success (and, in the U.K., privatiza-
tion of nationalized industries grows apace). These firms have
been quick to invest to capital-intensive automation – just as
Hong Kong began to do ten years ago. Italy's *private* textile firms
are able to invest heavily in automation. *State-run* firms are politically less able to reduce their workforce in order to take
advantage of investment in automation. They therefore tend not to
do it.

During the past ten years, the number of textile workers in
Italy has halved while production has risen. New technology has
made privately owned firms more efficient, flexible, and better

able to produce quality yarns, fabrics, and clothing than the giant state-owned ones.

Change *is* possible, even though, to quote Machiavelli in 1513:

'There is nothing more difficult to plan, more doubtful of success, or more dangerous to manage than the creation of a new system .... For the initiator has the emnity of all who profit by the preservation of the old system and merely luke-warm defenders in those who would gain by the new one!'

In spite of this, as true today as it was then, some retailers and manufacturers have been brave enough to concentrate on changing systems to improve profitability. Benetton in Italy and Liz Claiborn in the U.S.A. are good examples of how this pays off.

Now we must invest in consumers. They are becoming more discerning and respond very positively when they are offered good design at affordable prices. The best retailers and manufacturers are achieving market-share increases because they have concentrated on their customers and their aspirations.

The great baby boom of the 1950s produced the vast numbers of free-spending teenagers of the 1960s with money in their pockets and their own attitude towards clothes, music, food and shopping. Dark, crammed, noisy boutiques were places their mothers hated, but where *they* felt at home. The effect on the fashion world and its opportunities was electrifying. Fortunes were made and lost.

These ageing swingers are now thirtyish, and the falling birth-rate has meant that these same people are still the great fashion opportunity in their new guise. Age groups are not the only consideration or statistic, however, that affect us. Geography, education, occupations, income, lifestyle, all influence spending patterns. Implicit in the evaluation of lifestyle is the understanding of financial values and how they differ. What is important and worth spending a lot on to an outdoor-living, sports-loving family would be quite different from what is important to a single, young, ambitious executive, to whom appearance is all-important.

The number of people employed in manufacturing is declining. Finance and leisure sectors are increasing their numbers of employees. The large, mass-production, low-wages era of the 1940s and 1950s has changed, and higher incomes have meant a change in lifestyle for many. In the U.K., the top 20% of earners account for 30% of total spending, much of it on consumer-durables and lifestyle products. In the U.S.A., the top 15% account for nearly 40%. This must mean that, for success, we need to trade up.

In the U.K. ten million women form about 40% of the labour force – many of them part-time, with a similar proportion in the U.S.A. These days, in both the U.K. and the U.S.A., 50% of women return to work within four years of having children and do not downgrade their incomes when they return. The myth of the little woman sitting at home waiting for her husband's charity has finally exploded. Maybe the numbers quoted for England and America are straws in the wind. Figures alone are not enough: we must understand attitudes, interests, and preferences. We must also communicate that understanding and reflect it in all our marketing.

Recognizing and updating information of this kind are the ways to make statistics work for you. They enable you:

(1) to do research;

(2) to identify a market or markets;

(3) to forecast;

(4) to design;

(5) to buy not just items, but to range the assortment; to co-ordinate and merchandise it;

(6) to promote, display, and SELL;

(7) to repeat, adapt, or change; and

(8) to stay close to the market.

As Lew Young, Editor-in-Chief of *Business Week*, wrote:

'Probably the most important management fundamental that is being ignored today is staying close to the customer to satisfy his needs and anticipate his wants. In too many companies, the customer has become a nuisance whose unpredictable behaviour damages carefully-made strategic plans, whose activities mess up computer operations, and who stubbornly insists that purchased products should work.'

The days when the world of couture dictated have ended. In those days, the mass-production of the 'Look' began a season or even a year later. But fashion is now instantaneous, which makes its market-place even more dangerous.

The world is smaller as communications encircle it. Higher aspirations fuel raised standards. Women are more sure of themselves, are confident, know their rights. They spend their *own* money, not just husbands' earnings. Women are more active, more health-conscious – over-all, more in control of their own destinies.

Dangerous this speeding up of the fashion-trend process may be. Dangerous is this new breed of demanding, decisive women, buying not only for themselves, but for their husbands, children, and home, too.

What everything adds up to is that 'getting it right' *consistently* is essential to the continued success of any business in our expanded fashion world. Capable of great loyalty, women are at the same time quick to recognize an 'off' season in a favoured brand name. A second 'off' season will lose them completely – and it is always harder to woo back a disillusioned customer than to woo a new one. All this is as true for the 'trade' customer as for the consumer.

'Getting it right' consistently results in improved profits from higher stockturn, less mark-down employed, and therefore less room for mistakes. When mistakes happen, as they will, control systems should ensure they are instantly recognized, measured, and dealt with.

From all this, it is clear that flair alone cannot survive, important though it is. In the end, the 'boring' bits, i.e.:

planning,

timetables,

administration,

financial control, and

merchandising,

are what turns flair into profits.

The fashion industry's future depends upon recognizing this. Too many colleges are turning out talented but ill-disciplined fashion-design students, to whom this checklist seems irrelevant and who feel it should be left to boring number-crunching people, who will never take a risk or understand creativity.

The Royal College of Art in London two years ago found a new life, direction, and success under Jocelyn Stevens. As Rector of the Royal College of Art, on whose Council I sit, Jocelyn Stevens is fulfilling his role as Chief Executive with powerful business and political connections rather than as an academic in an ivory tower.

English *Vogue* published some comments by his students about him and the College. There were many, of which I shall quote just a few. Some are funny, some perspicacious, and some are still living in their own ivory towers.

'The administration is miles better. You know there is someone strong-willed in charge, someone who will get things done. That's good.'

'It would be crippling if, every time you put pen to paper, you had to think, "Is this going to sell?" And I'm afraid that's what will happen.'

'It's good to have a bastard at the helm, someone in charge you can hate.'

'If you *are* an artist, you will be an artist. Nobody can stop you. This man is attracting a lot of publicity to the College, which is good. He is attracting industry, which is better. There will be bursaries and grants from the industries. It's a very clever way to keep the college open when others are being closed down.'

It is the responsibility of all to change many of the attitudes and curricula of Design Colleges. Readers of this paper should ask themselves: 'When did *I* last involve students in *my* business? What formal contacts do *I* have with colleges?'

To consider now the transitions from old to new, the changes in demographics, culture, and lifestyle discussed in this paper mean that, quite apart from the *natural* swings in fashion and merchandise, changes in shopping environments, services, and habits will be substantial between now and the end of the decade. Some of them around the world are out-of-town and edge-of-town developments; the revitalizing of city centres; high-rising rents, taxes, and staff and energy costs; changing demands in shopping hours; lower boredom thresholds; higher expectations; clear knowledge of consumer rights; the move from money to plastics to electronics; these are all elements about which we should be thinking.

The 'live now, pay later' attitude means that what customers decide is whether or not they can afford the *monthly payment*, not the final price. Up to now, this approach to credit has tended to be in 'heavy'-goods departments – electrical, television, suites of furniture, fitted kitchens, carpets. Increasingly, now, wide-awake retailers see it as a powerful tool to trade up and sell on in clothing areas. Not for nothing did Marks & Spencer launch their own credit card to be used in a massively successful business selling mainly soft goods and food, and Sears in Britain have seen their card-holders increase by 43% since 1985.

People's perception of what they expect to find in stores is changing, for example, estate agents, building societies, banks, opticians, telephone shops, dispensing chemists, to name but a few. These services pull in the whole family for one-stop shopping, so the fashion offering for men, women, and children needs to be stylish, up to the minute, and presented in a way to tempt extra, unplanned purchases that become irresistible. These purchases may be unplanned by the customer, but not by the manufacturers or the stores.

While merchandise is being improved, the environment in which it is sold must keep up, and here are a few of the world's pacesetters. There is a danger now that, in the U.K. at least, design is *the* fashionable word and is thought to be all that is necessary to cure most manufacturing and retailing ills – an end in itself. It is, of course, one of a number of management tools and, as far as store interiors are concerned, should provide a background to shopping that enhances merchandise but never takes from it and flatters customers.

The last piece of the jigsaw is promotion in store as well as in the great wide world: ticketing that is in keeping with the style of the business, showing a clear message; display that allows customers to buy ideas as well as merchandise; effective advertising, in which there is no substitute for top-class photographs, artwork, and graphics, which help to make stylish advertising that can tell people a lot about the kind of company you are.

In retail, however beautiful the store, however good the merchandise, the attitude of the staff is perhaps the most important ingredient in the mix. They *are* one's company. Their training in service, in product knowledge, and in attitude is crucial. The same goes for the salesforce in a manufacturing company. Anyone who has seen a presentation of a collection in the U.S.A. cannot fail to have been impressed by the enthusiasm and the professionalism of the salesperson – the ultimate sales clincher.

Service and all its aspects are today crucial. 'We try harder', declare the Avis team and *in saying it they do*. 'How may I help you?' ask all Trust House Forte telephone operators and, in the question itself, *help is given*. Company-wide attitudes that are unambiguous are irresistible.

What can all this mean?

It must be recognized that fashion is no longer just about clothes. The horizons are much wider, the rewards commensurately far greater. Understanding that the *world's* fashion markets can provide rich pickings is essential.

Governments must be persuaded of this and, where they are un-supportive, shown that fashion has become, for other countries, a huge export earner, right up in the top league. They must be lobbied to provide financial aid by tax relief or by direct fund-ing for capital investment in new technology and for promotion abroad. To achieve this, you will need to be clear and confident about your own role in the way forward, to set up research sys-tems that allow you to recognize and react to demographic changes and their influence on the lifestyles and expectations of your market segment, and to create critical path analysis so that the right thing happens at the right time.

Remember The Limited's ambitious aims that seemed so impossibly high and yet were achieved. Remember, too, what they said in their mission statement about making The Limited a magic place to work. What comes first, magic then success, or success then magic?

Pepsi Cola President, Andy Pearson, says:

'Perhaps the most subtle challenge facing us in the decade of the eighties is to ensure that Pepsi Cola remains an ex-citing place to work.'

Chuck Knight of Emerson, a large successful company, says, 'You can't accomplish anything unless you have some fun', and David Ogilvy, of advertising fame, urged his organization: 'Try to make working at Ogilvy and Mather *fun*. When people aren't having any fun, they seldom produce good advertising. Kill grim-ness with laughter. Maintain an atmosphere of informality. En-courage exuberance. Get rid of sad dogs that spread gloom.'

Magic and fun are the secret ingredients of success.

Enjoy the way forward.

International Retail,
  Fashion, and Design Consultant,
London S.W.6,
England.

258

Major Trends in the Industrial-Fabric World

F. Scardino

1. INTRODUCTION

Over the past three decades, the industrial-fabric world has been witnessing a materials revolution that has resulted in improved product performance and a greatly expanded market. Woven cotton fabrics once dominated the industrial market. For the most part, cotton has been replaced by superior-performing man-made fibres, and woven-fabric technology has been successfully challenged by non-woven- and knitted-fabric technologies in several industrial markets, such as coatable scrims, filters, etc.

One important outcome of this materials revolution has been the development of new applications and new markets for industrial fabrics, such as geotextiles, architectural, composite, etc. New applications and new markets offer new business opportunities for manufacturers of industrial fabrics. The most exciting new markets for industrial fabrics from a potential growth/value-added/profitability point of view involve the high-tech or high-performance applications.

Another important outcome of this materials revolution has been the opportunity to process, finish, and fabricate industrial end-products in new and different ways. For many years, new materials for industrial-fabric products were usually processed in a traditional manner on conventional equipment and manufacturing systems. Today, industrial-fabric suppliers and end-product manufacturers are beginning to take greater advantage of the unique properties and behaviour of the newer materials (especially the thermoplastic materials) in processing, in finishing/coating/laminating, and in fabrication techniques.

The forecast of what will most likely happen in the industrial-textile world during the next fifteen years is based upon current trends in industrial fibres, yarns, fabrics, finishing, and end-product fabrication.

2. MAJOR TRENDS IN THE INDUSTRIAL-FABRIC WORLD

The major trends in industrial-fabric products have been ... from natural fibres to man-made fibres ... from spun yarns to continuous filament yarns ... from exclusively woven fabrics to non-woven, woven, and knitted fabrics ... from natural finishes to man-made finishes ... and from cut-and-sewn systems toward moulding and

259

threadless seams. These trends have resulted in greater productivity, improved product durability and performance, expansion of traditional markets, and the development of new applications and markets (such as architectural, composite, geotextile, medical, etc.). Such benefits could not have been possible without the utilization of the new materials and the new material forms.

Current and projected fibre consumptions in major U.S. textile markets are given in Table I. The figures for apparel, furnishings, carpets, and other categories include a substantial poundage in industrial-fabric applications, which should be added to the industrial and tyre-cord categories. Accordingly, it is estimated that industrial-fabric products now account for 20-25% of the total fibre consumption, depending upon the method of classification. It is estimated that industrial-fabric products will account for 25-29% of the total U.S. market by the year 2000.

2.1 Fibre Trends

The fibre trends in industrial fabrics, excluding tyre cord, are shown in Table II. At one time the leading industrial fibre, cotton still accounts for a significant share of the market. Nylon, which once enjoyed a much larger share of the market, now accounts for less than 10%. Because of high versatility and outstanding performance relative to cost, polyester fibre and glass share a major portion of the industrial market in different products/applications.

New fibre variants for special end-uses or processing behaviour will continue to invade the industrial-fabric market. High-modulus fibres will dominate the textile-composite market and high-temperature fibres will continue to dominate the speciality industrial-textile markets. The Japanese and Europeans will most likely continue to lead the way in the development of new fibre variants and exotic fibres for speciality applications.

It is quite unlikely that either polyester fibre or glass will be overtaken on a total-volume basis by other fibres in industrial-fabric applications based upon cost/performance/availability/versatility/etc. However, new highly oriented fibres, such as the Spectra series, should make a major impact in the industrial market.

2.2 Yarn Trends

The most significant new industrial-yarn trend will be the increased use of partially oriented yarns in draw-warping operations. Partially oriented yarns can be purchased for substantially less than fully oriented yarns and can be custom-drawn for specific tensile properties. Draw-warping of partially oriented yarns is particularly suitable for preparing warps for weaving and warp-knitting processes.

Partially oriented yarns can also be used in woven and knitted fabrics to provide for new fabric properties and behaviour. For example, woven fabrics made from partially oriented yarns can be engineered for greater extensibility, tear-resistance, and toughness. Woven fabrics made from partially oriented yarns can also be designed for improved mouldability, 3-D draw-moulding, 3-D draw-finishing, 3-D draw-wrapping, etc.

Any thermoplastic melt-spun fibre can be made available as a partially oriented yarn. Most of the applications for partially oriented yarns will involve polyester fibre more so than other fibres. Furthermore, most of the applications for partially oriented yarns will involve woven, warp-knitted, weft-inserted warp-knitted, and multiaxial stitched-through fabrics.

2.3 Fabric Trends

The current and projected shares of the industrial market by fabric construction, excluding tyre cord, are shown in Table III. Woven fabrics, which were the exclusive construction, now account for less than half of the industrial-fabric market and are projected to account for 38% by 1993. Non-woven fabrics have over half of the total industrial-fabric market and are projected to account for 56% by 1993. Knitted fabrics, while now accounting for only 2% of the market, are projected by conservative estimates to account for 6% by 1993, representing the greatest rate of growth. It is of interest to explore the reasons behind the no-growth projection for woven fabrics, the projected dominance of non-woven fabrics, and the superior projected growth rate for knitted fabrics.

2.3.1 Woven Fabrics

Many advances have occurred in weaving technology ... shuttleless looms ... improved productivity ... faster and wider looms ... and even 3-D shaped weaving. Woven fabrics provide the highest cover in the thinnest, lightest and most flexible fabrics, and can be finished on any equipment. With a rich tradition and a tremendous production capacity, woven fabrics will maintain a substantial share of the industrial-fabric market especially where variable directional behaviour in mechanical properties, yarn crimp, etc., do not adversely affect product performance.

2.3.2 Non-woven Fabrics

Non-woven fabrics consist of a large family of widely varying constructions ... spunbonded ... resin-bonded ... needle-felted ... spunlaced ... blown-film, etc., rather than just one construction. Made directly from polymer, filament, or staple fibre, non-woven constructions exhibit the greatest range of structural innovations and properties. New structures mean new opportunities/applications/markets, and it appears that non-woven fabrics will continue to dominate the industrial-fabric market because of the constant introduction of new structures and variations.

Examples of recent, interesting additions to the non-woven family are Enkamat, Evolution 3, Corweb. Enkamat, a 3-D spunbonded structure made by Enka for geotextile applications, is quite stable, resilient, and voluminous. Evolution 3, a shelter fabric made by Kimberly Clark, is an assemblage of fibre webs and blown film exhibiting dimensional stability, water-repellency, and breathability. Corweb, a 3-D fibrous structure made by the Mastech Division of

Table I

Fibre Consumption in Major Markets

(billion pounds)

	1983	1988	1993	2000
Apparel	4.4	4.2	3.8	3.2
Furnishings	1.6	1.7	2.0	2.2
Carpeting	2.0	2.1	2.4	2.6
Industrial	1.9	2.0	2.2	2.5
Tyre cord	0.6	0.7	0.8	0.9
Other	1.7	2.0	2.2	2.3
Totals	12.2	12.7	13.4	13.7

Table II

Fibre Trends in Industrial Fabrics
(Excluding Tyre Cord)

1900	1940	1980

cotton	13%
rayon	10%
glass	26%
nylon	8%
polyester fibre	26%
polyolefin fibres	14%
others	3%

Table III

The Industrial-fabric Market
(Excluding Tyre Cord)

(million pounds)

	1983	1988	1993	2000
Woven fabrics	824	735	841	710
Non-woven fabrics	1036	1198	1262	1560
Knitted fabrics	44	81	131	230
Totals	1904	2014	2234	2500

C.H. Masland & Sons, provides a multitude of vertical fibres, folds, and channels, through a web-corrugating process.

2.3.3 Knitted Fabrics

Knitting technologies offer the widest range of engineered fabric behaviour. For example, simple weft- and warp-knitted fabrics provide considerable extensibility in all directions and are therefore quite suitable for deep-draw moulding. Weft- and warp-knitted fabrics can be designed for specific directional extensibility and, through the use of laid-in (non-knitting) yarn systems, can be designed for stability in one direction and conformability in the other directions. With laid-in yarn systems in biaxial directions, special weft- and warp-knitted constructions of maximum stability are quite possible.

Whereas warp-knitted fabrics offer the possibility of greater fabric width and greater productivity, weft-knitted fabrics offer a choice of tubular or flat fabrics. A very special form of weft-knitting, electronic full-fashioned presser-foot flat-knitting, can also be used to produce fabric panels or pieces of specific size and shape, minimizing cutting waste and hand lay-up operations. The major disadvantages of knitted fabrics for certain applications are fabric thickness (from 3 to 5 yarn diameters) and high yarn consumption relative to fabric cover.

2.3.4 Weft-inserted Warp-knitted Fabrics

Weft-inserted warp-knitting technology is well suited for a variety of industrial-fabric applications because of the flexibility in designing for performance requirements and because of the unusual preservation of high-modulus yarn properties. Specifically, weft-inserted warp systems offer higher yarn-to-fabric tensile-translation efficiencies, greater in-plane shear-resistance, and better handling in open constructions than comparable woven fabrics. Special model weft-inserted warp-knitting machines are available from Karl Mayer and LIBA for handling heavy-industrial and high-modulus yarns.

One of the most practical constructions for industrial applications is a two-bar weft-inserted warp-knitted fabric with a biaxial yarn arrangement stitched together in a simple tricot motion. The laid-in yarns are perfectly linear, and each system is in its own plane. This simple construction is far superior to comparable woven constructions from a cost/performance point of view for a variety of coated-fabric and laminated-scrim applications.

Malimo stitchbonded fabrics can be quite similar in appearance and performance to two-bar weft-inserted warp-knitted fabrics. Stitchbonded fabrics with nearly biaxial laid-in systems offer acceptable stability with slight conformability. However, stitchbonded fabrics are not as consistent in structure and often cause considerable damage to weft-yarn strength during stitching. A new machine with true parallel weft insertion for the production of industrial fabrics is being developed by Textima.

Multiaxial stitch-through fabric can be made by stitching together two or more layers of yarn or fabric. The stitching process provides through-the-thickness strength and integrity. Stitching can be performed efficiently and with high productivity on any suitable multineedle process capable of through-the-thickness penetration, including sewing machines, Mali machines, warp-knitting stitch-through machines, etc. The major advantages of multiaxial stitched-through fabric are high density, control of yarn orientation in each layer, and the integration of the yarn/fabric layers by stitching. The major disadvantage is the impaling and localized dislocation of yarn during stitching, which leads to reduced strength and to poor structural consistency.

The companies currently involved in multiaxial stitch-through technology are Knytex, a division of Proform, in Sequin, Texas; Hi-Tech Composites, a subsidiary of Hexcel, in Reno, Nevada; and Bean Fiberglass Company in Jaffrey, New Hampshire; each of these has devised its own unique multiaxial-orientation system. Commercial stitch-through machines without bias-orientation capability are available from LIBA, Karl Mayer, and Textima. LIBA is also currently marketing a machine called Copcentra-Multiaxial, which coordinates multiaxial orientation with stitching through on a weft-insertion warp-knitting type of machine. Multiaxial stitch-through fabrics are available in several plies of yarn systems oriented in the warp, weft, and bias directions. Light non-woven webs can be added as a ply, if desired, and fabric widths of from four to eight feet are possible.

All the laid-in yarns are linear, are in a specific plane, and are continuous between fabric edges. Obviously, multiaxial stitch-through fabrics can be engineered for specific directional properties. Currently, most fabrics are composed of high-modulus laid-in tow/yarn systems with a fine polyester-fibre stitching-yarn system. Fabric constructions of the various ply orientations can be made up to approximately 1/4-in. thickness. Multiaxial stitch-through fabric weights vary according to construction but are often in the range between 12 and 48 oz/yd^2.

Multiaxial warp-knitted fabric technology has been developed recently by the Karl Mayer Textile Machine Company in West Germany. The process is officially known as multiaxial magazine weft insertion and informally referred to as the bias machine. As an alternative to multiaxial stitch-through technology, the Mayer bias machine precisely *knits* rather than *punches* the stitching yarn through the various layers of laid-in yarns. Consequently, no yarns are impaled, and the texture is quite uniform throughout the fabric, leading to higher translation efficiencies. The major design limitation of the Mayer bias machine is a maximum of four yarn layers (0°, 90°, +45°, -45°) plus a fibre web, if desired.

2.4 Finishing and Fabrication Trends

Traditionally, industrial fabrics have been finished/dyed/printed/coated/laminated in flat form and cut/plied/seamed into end-products. The trend in the fabrication of end-products is away from hand-cutting/conveying/seaming and strongly towards mechanized assembly or automated systems to avoid high production costs associated with hand operations and cutting waste. Where possible, seamless-moulding systems are preferred for speed, reduced cost, higher product performance, and consistent quality.

Obviously, an interrelationship exists between fabric construction, fabric finishing, and end-product manufacturing techniques. The trend in industrial-product manufacturing is towards a more integrated rather than sequential approach. Major changes in end-product fabrication technology cannot come about without major changes in fabric constructions and in fabric-finishing techniques.

By the year 2000, the amount of fabric backcoating and pre-impregnation should increase substantially. More unusual combinations of scrim fabrics and films should be expected. Solution-dyed fibres, end-product dyeing, and jet-spray dyeing/printing/coloration techniques are expected to have a greater impact in the industrial-fabric world.

2.5 Industry Trends in America

Industrial-fabric products associated with routine manufacturing/large markets/retail-outlet distribution will continue to come under heavy competition from foreign and domestic producers. Companies mainly involved in the apparel and home-furnishing business will shift towards the industrial-fabric world, which is perceived as more profitable, more stable, and less vulnerable to foreign competition. Many companies not at present involved at all with industrial fabrics will try to shift into the industrial-fabric business for the same reasons.

Manufacturers of industrial-fabric products must stay on top of the new materials and processing techniques to survive. End-product manufacturers must also view customer service as another prime requirement for survival. The best strategy for end-product manufacturers is involvement in several products and markets rather than just a few.

Beyond strategy for survival, end-product manufacturers should concentrate on opportunity. The emphasis should be on value-added product-manufacturing rather than on volume production alone. Speciality and high-tech products provide the greatest opportunity for high-profit and value-added manufacturing.

2.6 Trends in Western Europe

The largest-producing and largest-consuming countries in Western Europe for industrial-textile products are Germany, Britain, Italy, and France. Germany is by far the leading country in industrial-textile manufacturing and consumption. The Western European market, while not as large as the North American market, has greater diversity in industrial-textile products.

The largest industrial-textile markets in Western Europe are for medical/hygienic, packaging, transportation, ropes and nets, and geotextile products. The Western European industrial market is expected to grow by 10% in the next five years. Accordingly, by 1990, the size of the industrial-textile market in Western Europe is projected to be two-thirds of the American market and twice the size of the Japanese market.

Non-woven constructions dominate the industrial-fabric market in Western Europe, much as they do in the United States. Woven constructions appear to be more prominent in the Western European market than in the American market. However, Western Europe trails the United States in the utilization of innovative knitted constructions in the industrial market.

Polyester fibre is the leading industrial fibre in both Western Europe and North America. But high-tenacity nylon and rayon are far more important in the Western European market than in that of America. Polyester and polypropylene fibres are dominant in the dry-laid and spunbonded non-woven markets, and viscose and polyester fibre are dominant in wet-laid non-woven fabrics in Western Europe. In the rapidly growing geotextile market, polyester and polypropylene fibres are the major fibres. The European market for high-modulus fibres (glass, carbon, aramid, etc.) is expanding rapidly but is still much smaller than the American market.

From a business point of view, there are several differences between the industrial-fabric worlds in Western Europe and the United States. Industrial-fabric suppliers in Western Europe are generally more willing to specialize, customize, and deal with smaller markets. Developing longer associations with a few valued customers seems to be the preferred way of doing business.

In general, Europeans demand a high level of craftsmanship in all manufactured products. Accordingly, industrial-fabric suppliers regard consistent high quality as a top priority. Industrial-fabric users also make great efforts to integrate fabric quality and product design in manufacturing processes.

Fabric aesthetics appear to be of greater concern to European fabricators of industrial-textile products than to American fabricators. For example, coating is generally preferred over laminating because of certain visual and tactile fabric-surface impressions associated with laminate products. Moreover, the large cellular impressions associated with open-woven or weft-inserted warp-knitted fabrics are particularly avoided. Finer textures and smoother-surfaced fabrics are preferred in coated or uncoated products. In general, a more traditional approach in fabric manufacturing and finishing is quite apparent.

With regard to the exploitation of technological innovations and new marketing opportunities, Western Europe trails the United States even in those innovations originating in Europe. New concepts are much more likely to be embraced and adapted in the United States, even if not yet fully developed or commercially practicable. In geotextile applications, however, Western Europeans are very innovative because they need to solve a variety of critical problems.

Industrial knitted fabrics are a good example of the quicker exploitation of technological innovations in the United States. The impact of weft-inserted warp-knitted fabrics on the coated- and laminated-fabric market has been far greater in America than in Europe. Multiaxial warp-knitting technology will also be more quickly utilized in the United States according to current indications.

Imports have not had as dramatic an impact on industrial-textile products as they have had on apparel and home-furnishing products on either continent. For several years, however, imported industrial fabrics and finished products have been more noticeable, and they are increasing at a rapid rate. It is expected that more partnerships will be formed between European and American industrial-textile counterparts to take better advantage of available opportunities on both continents.

Philadelphia College of Textiles and Science,
Philadelphia,
Pa.,
U.S.A.

Timing: The Key to Success

D.R. Shah

Abstract

According to the Collins English Dictionary, the word 'timing' can be defined as:

'the process or art of regulating actions or remarks in relation to others to produce the best effects - as in theatre, music, and sport'.

To that list should be added fashion. For, to make it clear from the start, even though the textile world is going round in ever-decreasing circles offering earlier and earlier information in return for later and later orders, and even though the industry can boast a whole new dictionary of high-tech terms and acronyms like QRS (quick-response systems) and JIT (just in time), this paper - 'Timing: the Key to Success' - is not about 'speed'. It is about getting textiles and fashion to the streets at the precise moment that the consumer is susceptible and ready for that design message. It may involve speed. It could involve technology. It certainly calls for design. But, above all, it means good market intelligence and understanding the consumer.

1. THE SITUATION TODAY

Was it less than ten years ago when we all lived in the golden age of seasonal fashion? Things could not be more different now. The market has fragmented into myriad speciality clothing areas. The retailer screams and everyone runs. Today's clothing manufacturer is expected to supply early, yet complete window fillers at volume prices. Later, he is expected to come up with the big fashion themes on spec even if there are no concrete orders. Simultaneously, new fashion trends missed at the traditional ordering time should, of course be offered in 'instant' programmes.

In spite of all this, the customer still expects his supplier to deliver near-perfect merchandise on time. Merchandise that is not right is equivalent to breaking the contract. So is merchandise delivered hours late. The name of the game is to concentrate sales and profits on oneself and leave the risks and all the costs to one's supplier. And so the effect dominoes back, down the pipeline.

At the root of all these problems is the impossible dream that

269

would allow retailers the chance to defer purchasing decisions
until the last possible moment and minimize 'mark-downs', which
would benefit manufacturers through improved customer relations
and value-added prices built round service and speed.

2. TURNING THE DREAM INTO A REALITY

Many efforts have been made to turn that dream into a reality.

2.1 Mid-season

This is the principle of an industry that buys and sells less but
on a more regular basis. It is now quite common for fabric companies to offer principal ranges at Première Vision but follow
them up with smaller additions at Interstoff, etc. The drawback
with that is that it could lead to still more uncertainty. And
that, in turn, leads to later ordering, creating havoc with production schedules as everybody waits for the latest thing. The
same is true at the retail level. Six-week stock-turns are now
commonplace to minimize the effects of freak weather and to tempt
customers back on a regular basis. On the other hand, that calls
for better planning. It also means learning to spot an immediate
from a long-term seller, handling fabrics on a cross-seasonal
basis, and being more flexible on colour.

2.2 Prontamoda

So long a heinous word, this has now developed into a permanent
sector of its own and one that is not just dedicated to 'spewing'
out ideas before the next man gets his hands on them. It is, however, still very limited. Le Sentier in Paris may be able to work
on eight-day turn-rounds from fabric-design concept to finished
garment, but quantity is very limited. So is quality. Even if you
scoop the market and live off the creativity of others, you still
have to take big risks. As soon as you see it, you have to buy it
(300 metres per colour for an order of 1000 metres plus is the
fabric minimum in Italy today; if one of those dies on you, then
you are out on the street).

2.3 Exclusivity

The growing concept is to show shell collections and then develop
them with customers. The drawback, however, is that most people
want to see everything from everybody else first before commit-
ting themselves. It also means expanding design departments. Worst
of all, exclusivity is becoming the norm, not the exception. Companies are virtually giving it away for nothing. In Italy, one can
buy print-screen rights for 250 000 lira - plus the cost of the
design. Three years ago, exclusivity came at 900 metres for the
very best, 1200 metres for general print, and 2000 metres for
polyester fibre. Divide by two and you will be much closer to today's rate.

2.4 Flexibility

Now this is a word that is being thrown around a lot. What it means is readiness to change, and the less weight you have to carry, the fitter you are. But, even though it may seem that the converter has the upper hand, switching at will from story to story as the market demands, there are times when producer-based companies are in the stronger position. As a converter, you can get 500 metres of base cloth and sample away madly. But you still have to block bulk capacity of 20 000 metres six months ahead. Being a converter is being a speculator. Take prints on jacquards. Everyone had them in Como two years ago, but who could deliver them?

Also having your own plant, as Ratti's profits show, can be quite a good thing. It allows you to keep your ideas under wraps, control your own investment levels, build up relations with clients, introduce high-speed lines at will, and plan production to deal with rushes, etc. Above all, it allows you to experiment thoroughly with technology and design development.

2.5 Technology

Enough has been said and will be said about CAD and CAM in this conference and elsewhere. Technology is a reality and an expensive reality. Weave design by computer is a fact of today. Tomorrow, we shall have electronic home-shopping systems. (J.C. Penny starts experimenting with its Telaction in Chicago in June; 125 000 households will be involved and all you need are a push-button telephone, cable television, and a credit card.) So is 3-D designing on computer. One Michigan company, Computer Design Inc., offers CAD turnkey systems capable of actually showing how the garment would look on a mannequin or figure right down to the detail of how various fabrics would hang and drape. Laser engraving of print screens is reducing production time to 12 minutes according to Holland's Stork Company. A year ago, the same process took 30 minutes. Soon, better computer-chip capacity will bring it down to 5-10 minutes. The future is mindblowing. But, as with all technology, it is not what you have but what you do with it that counts.

2.6 Quick-response Systems

QRS, according to Rod Gunston and Peter Harding (Kurt Salmon Associates) is a mode of operation in which a manufacturing or service industry strives to provide products or services to its customers in the precise quantities and varieties and within the time frames that those customers require. The objective is to do this on a continuous basis with minimum lead times and risk, while maintaining maximum competitiveness and flexibility. Achieving this requires top performance at all the following levels:

    accurate interpretation of market trends;
    design of a desirable range at competitive prices;
    product development, materials-sourcing, and organizing/plan-
        ning for manufacture;
    manufacturing and delivering on schedule; and

managing and organizing systems to provide flexibility and
cover if one gets it wrong.

Getting it right does produce results. Prices are better, and
so are customer relations. However, any idea that QRS will keep
imports out is misplaced. It is wrong to think that those in
less-developed countries do not have access to modern technology.

The important thing about QRS and all the above systems is
that they do not make the slightest difference if you have not
got the product right in the first place, and vice versa with
the whole question of timing and rapid response, of total irrele-
vance to those companies that can read the market perfectly. After
all, if the product is right in the first place, why should any
manufacturer or retailer have to respond to demand in mid-season?

3. DESIGN

Getting the product right starts with design and trend information. Now, as the trade has become increasingly obsessed with
timing, so has its thirst for knowledge and its phobia about being 'scooped' by the man down the road. The result of all this is
a boom in the forecasting/consultancy business.

But who are these fashion 'gods' who sit incognito and plan
the clothes we are going to wear two years in advance? At the
risk of shattering a few myths, there is absolutely nothing mythi-
cal about the way fashion trends and prognoses are made up. It is
a logical process of decision-making, cleverly promoted and chan-
nelled into industry. There is an expression in journalism that
'if you hear it three times, then it must be true'. Well, exactly
the same thing is true of fashion prediction. Nothing passes
through the fashion trade as fast as a hot trend, except perhaps
a piece of really juicy gossip and a bankruptcy or two.

3.1 Cyclical Factors

Where the initial inspiration for tendencies comes from is another question. Some of it is cyclical, though this is definitely
less true than it used to be. Just ask corduroy manufacturers how
long they have been waiting for a comeback.

3.2 Socio-political Factors

Part of it is socio-political. The late 1960s and 1970s were the
colour purple thanks to Hendrix, heavy metal, and RIT dye in almost every American washing machine. Terrorism in the 1970s triggered off military colours and uniform looks. London's punks and
street fashion opened up a new dimension in colour clashes.

3.3 Sex

Morality is another big factor. Now, after such a period of unisex sportswear as we had at the beginning of the 1980s with the
military look, colonialism, indigo denim, etc., it was only

natural that feminism should sweep the stakes. But there are different kinds of feminism. The most obvious way to go was sexy -
bodyline or provocative in see-through, nudity, etc. However, the
current mood in Europe at the moment is definitely anti-sex,
largely owing to the mass hysteria and blatant publicity campaigns
against the sexually transmitted disease, AIDS.

That does not mean feminism is not here. It is a different kind
of feminism. It is the *haute couture* style à *la* Chanel, Hermès,
etc., or based on heroines like Kelly, Katherine Hepburn, etc.
Both are definitely 'woman' but with hidden sensuality, not blatant sexuality. Furthermore, the styling is based on eternal
shapes like the swirl skirt, the clean blouse, coupled to eternal
accessories like the shoulder bag and flat shoes. These things
are eternal not because they are classic but because they are
practical. And that is what fashion is about today. Not extravagance, or overstatements, but clarity and simplicity done in a
feminine way.

3.4 Street

Street, in general, has played its part. London was the epicentre
of this. A trip to the capital for fashion victims was almost as
important as a trip down the gangways of Première Vision. All
that is gone now as classicism and dressing up have taken over
from the 'extraordinary', but the impact of street direct or
through Gaultier was absolutely critical, and it will return.

3.5 Culture

Exhibitions have an influence, but the degree of impact is questionable. Vienna 1900 inspired many print designers, but it did
not inspire many dressmakers. Films are something else. There is
no need to mention 'Out of Africa', which incidentally caught
everybody by surprise. 'Room With a View' has had quite an impact
on the summer of 1988. If you have not caught it yet, do not
worry. You can still see 'The Name of the Rose', which we believe
will have a major influence on the winter of 1988-89 and for the
more adventurous there is Bertolucci's new epic on the last of
China's emperors.

3.6 The Designers

Of course, the biggest influence of all is provided by the designers. No matter what you say, they are at the root of all
things. It was they who gave us short skirts, tight skirts, full
skirts, puffed skirts, pleated skirts, wrap-around skirts, bus-
tled skirts, pants skirts ....

Black-and-white was 'mumsy' until Montana tried it. Pastels
were 'icky' until Mugler put them into skiwear. Black was for
funerals and the mafia until Comme des Garcons came along. Who
gave us minimal for summer 1988, all those beach stripes, table-
cloth checks, and clinical-clean designs?

Of course, it all sounds so easy. The question is that some-

body has to research and rationalize all this information. And
that somebody happens to be a group of pretty hard-nosed, rather
intelligent people (mostly women) who either run and work for
trend services or put their resources and brains behind exhibitions like Première Vision. They are individuals, but they often
work in groups. They co-ordinate their fashion accordingly and
then have the muscle and influence to pass on these ideas in a
pure or more personalized format to their own clients, magazines,
etc. And this, in my opinion, is what makes Paris the styling
centre rather than individualistic Italy.

Over the last few years, the whole concept of trends has
really come under question. Since everybody uses them, there is
a growing hue and cry that trend predictions are self-defeating,
i.e., if everyone says pink, then you had better do black.

Nor is the situation helped by the fact that access to this
kind of information is becoming easier and earlier, largely owing
to the growing influence of yarn fairs and service reports. It is
not uncommon to pick up a good consumer magazine (*Marie Claire
Bis* or *Vogue UK*) and see before your eyes the very ideas that you,
as a fabric company, have not even started upon. It is not so
much the garments that tell the story in these fashion features
but rather the stylist and clever accessorizing. But, whoever it
is, the result is the same: scooped again.

Now that trends are available over such a wide time span, it
is becoming even more difficult to predict when any particular
theme will hit the market ... and when it will leave. Black-and-
white has been with us for three years. Deco never happened, nor
did brown denim.

As a magazine, we still refer to seasons but in fashion catalogues try to cover three of them at one go. We believe that seasons *per se* are out. So is radical change. Ideas roll and develop
gradually from moment to moment. The only thing that we work along
is woman types - natural, chic, junior, city - working themes according to their tastes.

The other big problem is that there is no such thing as international fashion, no matter how hard companies try to prove the
contrary. Britain did chintz three seasons before the Italians
ever thought about it. Try and sell this summer's Bardot story to
a formica-and-fifties-weary Britain and see what happens. Fashion
may travel at designer level, but it does not when you move down
to volume areas.

As a result, more and more companies are going their own way,
developing and selling their own image and beliefs in the way it
was done fifteen years ago, in the way that some of Italy's most
creative Comaschi have always done it. The only problem with this
approach is that it is limited to the best or companies that have
the kind of market leadership in which buyers are willing to accept what they say without question.

Building an image can be a hard business. Again, I take the
example of Ratti. The whole 'Ratti and Paisley' concept with the
New York exhibition now, to be followed by shows in Tokyo this
autumn and in Paris and Milan next year, will cost a lot -

274

financially and in time. So will the Ratti Foundation. However, the concept as a homogeneous theme with paisley's historical interest, its development as a specialist area, and its challenge to creativity is one that cannot fail to capture the imagination. Certainly, no one after this will ever fail to equate the paisleys with Ratti.

For the rest of us, nobody has come up with an equally practical way of presenting collections and directions. Besides, whoever, whatever, and wherever we are, we all need to start somewhere. And starting somewhere is something we, ITBD, know well. We produce International Colour Authority. The team of professionals that puts that card together meets 20-22 months ahead of the season. Most people would say it is impossible to predict colour so far in advance. True, changes take place. The market evolves, but still I think we have a 70-80% success rate, the point being that everyone takes it because it is the first, the starting point from which to evolve more individualistic lines.

4. THE CONSUMER

Pre-season design flair as a substitute for quick response depends not only on design ability and professional management but also on consumer-watching. Nobody would ever say that Max Mara and all its spin-off lines like Pianoforte, Penny Black, and Sportmax deserve the acclaim given to Gaultier and Alafa in recent years, but they sell consistently well. Why? Because they are well priced. Because they are exactly what the consumer in that income bracket wants. Max Mara is fast becoming the Marks and Spencer for 'yuppies' and 'dinkies'.

The consumer is the boss these days. Gone are the days when the retailer told the public what to buy, and the manufacturer told the retailer, and so on down the line. The consumer take-over has been a gradual take-over. But the transition really came to notice in the summer of 1985. That was when the fashion industry tried to bring back colour and dramatic fashion statements. The public said no. What it wanted was 'new-classical', 'eternal', 'quality', 'heroine' - call it what you want - dressing. The public won.

What the consumer was saying is that we are not going to be dictated to and that fashion, and with it the whole fashion system has lost its appeal.

If you had not noticed, we are in a period of 'go get'. Life is hard, life is aggressive. You have to work twice as hard and twice as long to stay where you are. The gap between the 'haves' and the 'have nots' is growing, not narrowing. Those who have it want to show it - but not in a vulgar '*nouveau-riche*' manner.

The American magazine, *GQ* summed this up best in an article entitled 'The New Luxury', from which the following is a quotation.

'Luxury itself remains the same, after all a John Lobb custom shoe is luxurious no matter who wears it. What has changed is lifestyle. The leisure class is out of a job. Most of us are

275

working so hard that today's most precious commodity is the
time to enjoy the spoils. Hell, we deserve a little luxury ...'

I think that the company that has best captured this mentality
is Ralph Lauren. A trip round his Paris shop at La Madeleine is
a lesson in lifestyle retailing. Above all, he realized that what
the new salaried buyers want is a luxury that has been tried and
tested, not a revolutionary gamble.

It may be of interest to recall what else was in *GQ*'s list of
what luxury is:

'Dancing until dawn ... a hairstylist and a manicurist who
make office calls ... handmade silver cutlery for everyday
use ... a hand-finished navy cashmere blazer from Savile Row's
Gieves & Hawkes ... linen sheets by Frette ... writing a letter
on Smythson stationery with a Mont Blanc pen ... Poggio al Sole
extra-virgin oil ... Hermès leather luggage ... cashmere sweaters ... an Indonesian cruise with a stay at the Mandarin in
Hong Kong and the Oriental in Bangkok ... engraved Christmas
cards ... and finally the time to read Proust cover to cover.'

The lesson in that list is that clothing is only a fraction of
the story. Gone are the days when it was enough to wear mink and
Dior to make your image statement. Lifestyle living and dressing
today encompass a battery of accessories and expensive habits.
Being a 'dinkie' or 'yuppie' not only calls for the monthly visit
to Armani and Josephs, it also means having a Filofax, Mont Blanc
fountain pen, a compact-disc player, the Zippo lighter, a perfectly equipped kitchen and wine cellar, and a season ticket to La
Scala. Lifestyle is total, clothes are only the part.

5. CLOTHING PRIORITIES

In a recent survey carried out by Mintel, the U.K. market consul-
tants, it was quite clear that clothing is low in the British consumer's list of priorities. When asked where people were most
likely to spend their money if income suddenly increased 25%,
40% said on travel and holidays, 21% on leisure activities, 39%
on the home, 25% on more investment, 21% on a better car, but
only a meagre 13% on more clothes. (Interestingly it was the
lower socio-economic groups that went for clothing.) The same
was true in the reverse situation. If incomes were cut, then 33%
would cut back on holidays, 24% on the home, and a very big 24%
on clothing. In sum, it is clear that clothing is a market area
more sensitive to recession than expansion. Nor is that situation
helped by changing socio-economic attitudes among today's young
women. They are all into individualism. They are all into independence. They want to leave home earlier and live their own
lives rather than wait with their parents for the right man to
come along and they will spend all that extra income on clothes
to entice him. This is all very good for the Milan property market, but all very bad for the Milan clothing market.

6. THE MANIPULATOR

It is not the intention of this paper to cause depression. But

it is quite obvious that, unless public attitudes are changed,
then the future for clothing is a pretty stagnant one.

The effort needed to change those attitudes will call for many
disciplines. Design speaks for itself, but it is no longer enough
on its own. It needs to be integrated into a marketing mentality.
What is becoming increasingly clear is not what you say but how
and when you say it. That means that companies are going to have
to start engaging a new talent - 'The Promoter' or 'The Manipulator'. That does not mean pure sales, image, and advertising: it
means a person who has his finger on the consumer pulse, who can
take a product and dress it up in the right way and then persuade
the buyer that it is a vital part of whatever lifestyle story is
current at the time.

6.1 The Manipulator and Advertising

Apart from Ralph Lauren, the laurels for consumer-handling in
recent years have to go to Levi's. I would like to quote extensively from a presentation made by John Hart, Managing Director
of Levi Strauss (UK), and Nigel Bogle, Managing Director of
Bartle, Bogle & Hegarty, made at a Mintel conference held in
London recently and entitled 'Consumer Lifestyles - Evolution or
Revolution?'

The campaign that won everyone's hearts was the Levi's 501
story; when Bartle, Bogle & Hegarty took up the campaign, they
arrived as outsiders at the following opinions about the state of
the fashion market.

'That the arrival of punk and post-punk street meant that
everybody was into his own thing. That was good news for the
individualist, bad news for the mass-market clothing business.

'Despite economic stagnation and tragically huge unemploy-
ment amongst young people, the mood of the moment was: flaunt
it, whether you had it or not.

'Where was the money? A lot was going on clothes that said
a very firm goodbye to Boy George, punk, and the rest. All of
a sudden, the clothing code was smart and classy. 'Badges'
made your statement: Lacoste, or Fred Perry - the Pringle
sweater, the Nikes, perhaps the Tacchini tracksuit. Bass Wee-
juns started selling classic U.S. loafers and you accessorized
the look with a pair of Raybans and a Zippo lighter.

'Heritage, authenticity, and integrity were back in fashion.
It was smart to look smart, cool to be 'squeaky clean'. Hair
was short, but not too short. And the common thread was products whose form was defined by their function.

'All this was good news for 501s. What garment was more
classic, authentic, stuffed full of functional heritage?

'The problem was, 501s were a well-kept secret. Only the
leading edge knew. And denim was definitely not part of this
new 'squeaky-clean' look.

'The job was to expose this secret, in the right way, at
what seemed to be the right time. The challenge was: could
advertising actually start a mass fashion trend?'

Before starting the campaign, the agency investigated several
roots. Contemporary, urban east-side U.S. cut little ice with
young people in the U.K., who felt they led the States today in
most aspects of music, fashion, and lifestyle. And films did not
address the important attributes of heritage, authenticity, and
integrity that make 501s unique. If contemporary America did not
appeal, neither did nineteenth century America. They checked out
the original heritage of 501s, and they checked out every aspect
of the Wild West. Again, not right. Too much heritage, not enough
style.

In the end, it was the late 1950s, early 1960s. To people like
myself, that is a real period. But Levi's discovered that it
still held magic for people not born until ten years later. There
is a kind of latent and passive recognition that America fought
the big youth-culture battles then. That was when it all started.
America led the field and was admired for liberating young people.
It led in films, heroes of the young, and music. Critically, that
period mirrors today so closely. James Dean died on September
30th, 1955. But that picture could have been taken yesterday.

That time was when Levi's and 501s established the credential
they have again today as the first, the authentic, and definitive
jeans. So, they made the first two films screened immediately
after Christmas 1985. Their effect was instaneous. Sales took off
immediately. Journalists wrote about them. Even other advertisers
copied them. Nick Kamen became famous. He made records. He was
lucky. The rest is history.

7. RETARGETING

Retargeting and relaunching your image form one way of stimulating the market. The other is to carve out new market areas. Consumer-watching is again the key element behind this. Consider the
age question.

8. THE AGE QUESTION

Since the War, fashion has been the domain of the young. From
the invention of the teenager in the U.S.A. in the late 1950s,
through the 'Swinging Sixties' and into the 'Liberated Seventies',
the teenage young market was the one almost everyone wanted to
exploit. Only in the 1980s has there been widespread recognition
that an equally profitable area could be those well over 25 and
even 30. I believe that this is what this decade will be best
remembered for, the decade when retailers traded up to supply
'investment dressing' for the older customer group, which demanded quality and value as well as styles. Now, as the 1990s approach, is it not time to prepare for another shift in emphasis?

The figures tell the inescapable story. In the U.S., by the
year 2000, there will be almost 3 million more women aged 25-44
than there were in 1985; there will be 8 million more aged

278

between 45 and 64. In the United Kingdom, the number of women in their forties will increase by 500 000; there will be another 400 000 aged over 50. In the Netherlands, the number of women between 40 and 60 will go up by about 420 000.

The demographic trends are just as strong among males too. In Italy, the years 1985-2000 will see about 300 000 more men in their forties, with an extra 200 000 reaching their fifties. The population of men aged over 40 in France will increase by about a million. In the U.S. the 25-40 male age group will swell by 3.5 million, the 45-64 segment by a huge 8.3 million.

These predictions are not wild guesses. Barring apocalyptic disaster, they will be actualities. But, apart from the bare figures, medium- and long-term planners must be aware that the ageing population in the Western world will have attitudes and aspirations that will mark them apart from equivalent earlier generations. Put simply, as consumers, they are, and will continue to be, educated, discerning, and demanding.

In a recent analysis of the future for shopping centres in Britain, the design consultancy Fitch & Co. identified at least two groups within the ageing population - the 'new old' (the over-60s) and the 'new middle-aged' (the over-40s).

Fitch pointed out that tomorrow's 60-year-olds will be fitter and more active than the 'old old', they will usually have enjoyed a better standard of living, have travelled more widely, and be more used to spending money on themselves, but they will also be used to getting what they want. Importantly, those who have had a prosperous or comfortable working life will probably have good pensions. They will often have paid for their own homes and so are likely to have a significant amount of disposable income. (It goes without saying that those who have been poor while in work will not improve their status when retired.)

Perhaps even more interesting for the clothing and textile industry are the 'new middle-aged'. These, says Fitch, have grown up in a youth-dominated world and are the consummate consumers. They have been used to having their own music, media, fashions, shops, and even holidays during their teens, twenties, and thirties. Is it really likely that someone's attitude is going to change just because he has celebrated his 45th birthday? We think not. The 1990s will be the decade when the stereotypical view of the over-40s will have to be redrawn.

9. READING THE MARKET

The list of possible demographic and social influences on fashion is enormous.

9.1 Women

To consider first women today, they, with new-found economic independence and hard-fought freedom from restrictive social conventions, are increasingly in charge of their own lives, and they want their images to reflect that. When women first started along the path to emancipation, their clothing reflected struggle. Pants, men's jackets, hats, the Annie Hall look were what the independent career woman wore. Now that she has arrived, she can afford to dress her own way to suit her own lifestyle. Wearing a printed dress today no longer conjures up the image of a 'weak, meek secretary'. Femininity will play an increasing role in 'career dressing'.

9.2 Men

In the meantime, no one can have failed to notice how much more attention men are paying to themselves and their clothing.

After a period of exuberant freedom - printed shirts, unisex, and amazing colours - the current image is neither overtly macho nor obviously effeminate. Late 1980s and early 1990s man will be neither Rambo nor wimp. He will look like a real man, even a gentleman. Contemporary classics are the line, i.e., clothing that is comfortable and relaxed, with sufficient elements of colour, novelty, and design innovation to distance it from the conventional.

One of the most obvious reasons for the male style revival is the resurgence of the work ethic and good old - or bad old, depending on one's political viewpoint - capitalist values.

In the increasingly success-oriented world of the late 1980s and early 1990s, 'dressing for success' at work is going to become increasingly essential for those who aspire to any degree of affluence. For those who are looking for work, a smart appearance must be an asset. As the English critic Thomas Fuller noted as long ago as 1632, 'good clothes open all doors'. But there is another, less obvious reason for men sprucing up their image. They are dressing not just for success at work but also for success with the 'new' women, which they are not finding too easy.

Today women do not actually need men for their survival, so they can afford to pick and choose - or reject - potential mates as men did for so long. Consequently, male image - the right image - now becomes as important for a man seeking a mate as it always was for a woman.

10. CONCLUSION

I see the textile industry polarizing or working into concentric circles but with very different diameters. At one end, there are the super-classic production systems, essentially off-shore, working on long-planned production schemes and tight price points from anywhere between Porto and Peking. In the middle, there are the wonder-companies of the 1980s. Here I mean Max Mara, Benetton, Escada, Mondi, etc., who manage to work on rolling but regular production concepts that produce continuous selling lines every six to eight weeks. Then you have the Catherine wheel of fashion with Prontamoda companies sparking off fashion ideas just like that and doing them in eight-day turn-round programmes from design to delivery.

Each is into its own thing and none of these sectors should be scared of the other. If Prontamoda is doing minimal blue and white spot dresses of polyester fibre today, the image leaders can still do it tomorrow on much better-quality fabrics with their own level of distribution. When 'Out of Africa' broke, Oxford Street tripped over itself in the haste to get it into the windows first. Its stores spoilt it for themselves rather than anyone else with cheap versions of a look that went on for another two years in much better, value-added versions that made other companies a lot of money.

However, there are things that unite all these sectors. There is the pressure to move up and up to escape cheap imports from new textile-producing countries. The clothing industry is a pyramid like anything else. Everybody is scrambling for the top, but there is not room for everyone.

What will separate the winners from the losers? The answer to that question is worth more than a million pounds, but certainly part of it is:

(a) investment in equipment and automation;
(b) service, whether through improved collaboration or setting up special lines for the 'quick-response system';
(c) having the means and ability to experiment under one's own roof;
(d) improving the intellect of staff so that they can understand the rapid design and marketing changes required in today's sophisticated market; and
(e) identifying where and how to apply technology and determining which is most important: quality, speed, or saving costs.

Finally, and above all, being able to spot and service consumer moods is the secret ingredient of 'timing – the key to success'.

To round off this paper, some predictions may be made about the future, all based on consumer-watching.

(1) We are now in a period of overdesign. It is just like the 1930s, when everything was 'designed', from tableware to typography. A war stopped all that. Hopefully that will not be true of the 1980s. What will happen is that design for design's sake (the Alessi coffee pot) will stop. We shall have design for function – the Zippo, the VW.

(2) Synthetic fibres are on the way back. There is a new generation that never went through the Crimplene-revulsion stage. Brought up on the natural-fibres boom, they find synthetic fibres a total novelty, especially the new synthetic fibres which are in a world of their own, far removed from the 167-dtex false-twist textured polyester-fibre yarns of the mid-1970s.

(3) Nostalgia is going to die out. Soon we are going to wake up and say: 'It's the 1990s. What am I doing wallowing around in fashion stories based on the 1930s, 40s, 50s, 60s?' Let us look forward and do something that is 2000. By that, I do not mean space suits, but just a total new

281

concept in styling to go with all the brilliant technical
advances being made in fibre and fabric type and performance.

(4) The future is exciting. But the consumer will still be
king. No revolution is ever going to change that.

ACKNOWLEDGEMENTS

Credits go to the following: Alan Charlesworth, Managing Director, Mintel Publications; John Banks, Chairman, Young & Rubican;
John Hart, Marketing Director, Levi Strauss (UK); Nigel Bogle,
Managing Director, Bartle, Bogle & Hegarty; Joanna Bowring, Associate Design Director, Courtaulds plc; Sign. Gentile, Managing
Director, Ratti; Dott. Emanuele Milani Capialbi, Relazione
Esterne, Ratti; Dr Gianni Brovia and Dr Adriano Benvenuto, Asso-
ciazone Italiana Industriali Abbigliamento; Rolf Vonrufs, Diret-
tore Commerciale, Leglertex SpA; Rod Gunston and Peter Harding,
Kurt Salmon Associates ('Quick Response: US and UK Experiences'
in *Textile Outlook*, March, 1987).

International Textiles,
Amsterdam,
The Netherlands.

Sourcing Fashion in World Markets

K. Stuart-Smith

1. INTRODUCTION

When our forebears were trading in bolts of cloth with overseas
partners many centuries ago, they could hardly have appreciated
that their business would develop to a global level of international export trade of an estimated US$106 bn by 1986. The growth
has not been regular; there have been a number of milestones over
the years that have stimulated export growth and opportunities.
These milestones include:

the industrial revolution some 200 years ago that started in
the United Kingdom and then moved to the United States of
America and Germany and subsequently into some other European
countries;

the opportunity for these original industrialized countries
to sell into their 'dependent' territories until they began
to develop a self-sufficiency or independence;

the emergence for the first time of a ready-made garment industry during the First World War, making military uniforms,
and the development of this clothing sector between the two
World Wars;

the development of the textile industry in Japan that took
place also between 1918 and 1939;

the industrialization of many countries since 1945 in which
textiles and clothing have had only second priority after food
production; Portugal, Hong Kong, Taiwan, and the Republic of
Korea are but four of the main countries that had only small
or no textile industries until the 1940s but which today are
among the world's major textile- and clothing-exporting
countries;

in 1987, even more countries have emerging textile and clothing industries whose objectives are initially for import substitution and secondarily to export and maximize foreign-cur-
rency earnings; and

the market competition between retailers and also between
manufacturers in the relative-higher-cost, mature-industry
countries that has facilitated import growth from lower-cost
source countries.

These key factors and other important aspects are considered
in the later part of this paper.

International trade in textiles and clothing is expected to develop further in volume and, especially, value terms in the coming years. Global-export-trade levels of US$120 bn by 1990 and US$130 bn or more by the mid 1990s are not inconceivable (Table I).

These global-trade levels are additional to the very large intra-nation sales by manufacturers into their domestic markets. This trade will also increase, especially in the southern countries, as their populations and economies develop.

To some degree, the rate of growth of the new textile industries and their ultimate levels of trade will be disciplined by international agreements and regulations such as the Multi-fibre Arrangement (MFA) and national protectionism (unilaterally imposed barriers or tariffs). It is not my intention to discuss these legislative aspects, as many learned papers have been published hitherto that cover these subjects in great detail. I should like to consider, though, the pragmatic aspects, both quantitative and qualitative, that condition the shape and structure of the international industry today, together with the expected changes over the next ten years that are likely to influence buyers' decisions in sourcing fashion.

2. DEMAND FACTORS

It is extremely difficult to quantify the world demand for textiles and clothing but a realistic guide is provided by the published data on fibre production (Table II).

Global demand for textiles and clothing will inevitably show continued growth as populations increase further and the standard of living, especially in many of the poorer countries, develops. It seems inevitable that the demand for synthetic fibres will replace cotton as the major fibre within a few years. At first glance, it is surprising that synthetic fibres, especially polyester fibre have found a ready market acceptance in the very hot countries, for example, India and Indonesia. There still remains a frustrated demand in these hot countries for both 100% polyester-fibre fabrics and blended staple-fibre fabrics containing polyester fibre because of their attractive lightweight qualities, bright colours, easy-care properties, and, especially, durability. One of the main factors reported for the decline in *per caput* textile consumption per year in India and Indonesia from some 16 m to 12 m is the reduced replacement level necessary with polyester fibre.

Within the global picture, demand changes have taken place in recent years. Some of these changes have been catalysed by the fibres themselves, some by the new manufacturing and processing technologies, and others by the skills of the fabric and garment designers, who have given the concept of fabric and colour co-ordination a totally new dimension. But the vehicle that has allowed many of these changes to take place is the change in lifestyle with the demand for less formal and more casual/leisure modes of dress. Who, only some fifteen years ago, would have considered bank tellers wearing trousers, sports jackets, and ties or jeans and open-neck shirts? In the Western world, some may

Table I

Global Exports of Textiles and Clothing:
1985-86*

Sector	Year				
	1975	1982	1986	1990	1995
Textiles	21	52	56	60	62
Clothing	8	41	50	60	68
Total	29	93	106	120	130

* US$ bn: 1990 and 1995 projections at constant
1986 value

Table II

World Fibre Production: 1950-86*

Fibre Type	Year					Percentage Increase 1950-86
	1950	1960	1970	1980	1986	
Natural fibres:						
cotton	4 647	10 113	11 784	14 039	16 789	261
wool	1 057	1 463	1 602	1 610	1 661	57
Man-made fibres:						
cellulosic	1 608	2 656	3 579	3 554	3 284	104
synthetic	69	702	4 818	10 673	13 113	18 904
All fibres	7 381	14 934	21 783	29 876	34 847	372

* Thousand tons

Source: CIRFS.
Note: Non-wool animal hairs and some vegetable fibres are not
included.

285

Table III

Installed World Capacity in Spinning (Cotton System):
1980 and 1985*

| Country Grouping | Spinning System and Year | | | |
| | Ring-spinning | | Open-end Rotor-spinning | |
	1980	1985	1980	1985
(1) Developed countries	347.0	350.0	8.2	10.0
(2) Developing countries	697.6	777.4	6.1	8.2
(3) Eastern Europe	231.5	232.6	25.8	} 46.75
(4) China	255.9	300.0	–	
Total	1559.0	1660.0	40.1	64.95

* Hundreds of thousands of spindles.

Source: ITMF.

Table IV

Installed World Capacity in Weaving:
1980 and 1985*

| Country Grouping | Loom Type and Year | | | |
| | Shuttle | | Shuttleless | |
	1980	1985	1980	1985
(1) Developed countries	602.8	470.8	99.2	155.4
(2) Developing countries	1024.3	1124.3	65.3	107.7
(3) Eastern Europe	487.1	304.9	95.3	121.1
(4) China	500.0	575.0	–	–
Total	2614.2	2475.0	259.8	384.3

* Thousands of looms.

Source: ITMF.
Note: Handlooms are not included in the data.

Table V

World Textile Export Trade: 1984 (%)

Source Country Grouping	Destination Country Grouping		
	Developed	Developing	Comecon
Developed	40*	15	3
Developing	22	10	2
Comecon	3	3	2

* Of which, intra-EEC trade accounted for 58% of intra-developed-country trade and 26% over-all.

Table VI

World Clothing Export Trade: 1984 (%)

Source Country Grouping	Destination Country Grouping		
	Developed	Developing	Comecon
Developed	35*	5	1
Developing	38	8	1
Comecon	5	2	5

* Of which intra-EEC trade amounted to 60% of trade between developed countries and 23% of all exports.

Note: The developing countries have the major share of world clothing export trade, especially in their trade to developed countries.

Table VII

Outline Profile of Strategic Options

Activity	Orientation	Requirements	Opportunities	Results
(1) Produce	Manufacturing	Order-takers	Basic products vulnerable	Low margins
(2) Sell	Manufacturing/ Marketing	Active selling	Basic products less vulnerable	Better results
(3) Upgrade	Marketing	Active marketing Design management Quality Delivery performance Credibility Interdependency with customers	Products focussed on target To work with the market Better control of business	Good potential
(4) Diversify	Marketing	As (3)	As (3) Stronger business base	Good potential

lament the declining demand for formal suits; in other countries, there are laments of a similar kind for the reducing demand for sarees, batik, and other kinds of national or traditional dress. In nearly all cases, the replacement is international, Western-style dress that is provided largely by ready-made clothing in most countries.

The major retailing stores in the main market countries have also made a significant contribution to the changing pattern of demand. Their need to compete against each other for market share and to impose their own 'handwriting' on products targeted on very specific market segments has been facilitated by the availability of highly designed, lower-unit-cost casual- or leisure-wear garments, where fashion demand can be generated at short notice by colour changes. In order to obtain the merchandise they want to optimize their sales and results, the major retailers have for thirty years or more been the driving force for sourcing out suppliers who could often reproduce the retail buyers' designs and who could certainly do so at their critical price points and requirements for quality consistency and delivery scheduling. Today, these same buyers and others find it less necessary to chase sources and give designs; many world suppliers are now bringing to the buyers some highly fashionable new ranges that are based on their own in-house design skills or on their skills in managing design.

Although there are many obvious differences between the product demands of the high-, medium-, and lower-cost countries, for example, colouring and design; quality levels; retailers' and manufacturers' brand labels; and especially the channels of distribution and the critical price points, yet there are also many areas of similarity that will probably become even more critical over the next ten years. These factors include:

an oversupply situation in all markets will allow buyers to be more selective in their choice of supply sources, which will develop into yet more market segmentation;

a further upgrading of product demand from both quality consistency and maintained delivery-scheduling;

a generally faster response time to changes within seasons;

smaller orders and shorter colour runs;

more flexibility in order-programming to respond to changes in the increasingly dynamic market;

a major design input from the fabric, garment, and household textiles in terms of design and product engineering to meet international or retailers' specifications;

the wider use of 'Western-style' garments and household textiles in countries in which their usage has been introduced in relatively recent times.

These comments on demand factors are based on our experiences in countries from the north and south in all five continents. They are the motivating forces for change to which many supply sources around the world have responded already and in which others are recognizing the necessity to change their strategic business plans if they are to be successful in the future.

3. SUPPLY FACTORS

Whereas global demand for textiles, apparel, and household textiles has grown rapidly since 1950, the world-supply capacity has expanded at an even greater rate, with the consequence of an oversupplied market at the macro-level.

Data are already available to show the increase in world capacity for spinning and weaving (Tables III and IV). Although the corresponding data for the processing sector have not been published, it has been our experience that the installed capacity is mixed with much obsolete equipment in many countries. Whereas many Western buyers are now looking in the lower-cost countries to buy processed fabrics rather than grey cloth and upgraded made-up products rather than basic products of variable quality, the pressure on the processing sector to modernize has been recognized and is being responded to. Even in the lower-cost countries, investments in the latest processing technologies are being made with the prime purpose of improving quality levels and consistency and not in order to reduce conversion costs by employing fewer people.

The distribution of production between the developed and developing countries and the changes since 1953 are shown in Fig. 1. Although the rate of change in the distribution patterns has slowed down since 1975, there is still a movement of production to the developing countries. But the distribution of clothing production that was 8% in 1953 in the developing countries reached 26% in 1985 and is indicative of the wide acceptance of ready-made clothing in these countries as well as their increasing export volume.

The distribution of employment between the developed and developing countries is shown in Fig. 2.

Before turning to the types of strategic business plans that many supply companies have adopted in order to be more in control of their own destinies, and to which many more other companies are looking to help them through the next decade, one should first look at the relative positions of exporting countries in terms of world export trade. In the world textile-export trade, intra-developed-country trade represented 40% of all exports in 1984, whereas trade from developing countries into developed countries stood at 22% (Table V).

As the distribution in machine capacity and output moves progressively in favour of developing rather than developed countries, it may be expected that export trade will shift rapidly to the lower-cost countries. There are circumstances that also favour developed countries that will continue to apply:

investments in the latest technologies in high-cost countries to maximize output speeds with automatic handling systems and minimum conversion costs from continuous operations;

a geographical proximity to the major markets that enables companies to respond quickly and with flexibility to the changing requirements of dynamic markets;

a close working relationship between buyer and supplier that

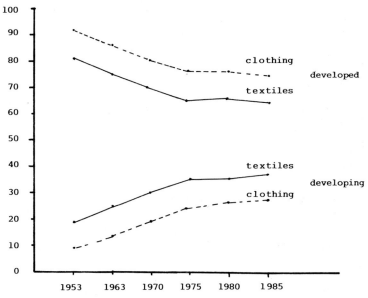

Fig. 1 Distribution of production between developed and developing countries

Fig. 2   Distribution of employment between
         developed and developing countries

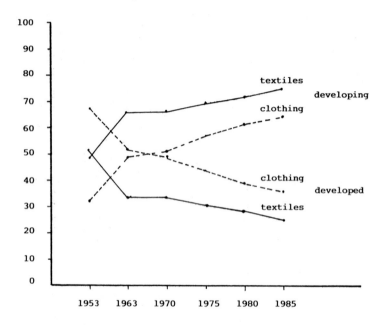

leads to a mutual interdependency for design, ranges, pricing, quality reliability, delivery scheduling, and short-term repeats; and, especially,

a marketing orientation that allows the manufacturer fully to serve the market needs.

But the critical price points in the different market segments remain, and the convenience of working with a local supplier - or in another developed country - carries only a relatively small premium.

Some high-cost countries, for example, Germany, Holland, and the United States particularly, have developed the outward processing business to a fine art, so that, for garment production, the garment manufacturers have retained control over the quality, price, and availability of the fabrics and accessories and have shipped cut panels with accessories into cut, make, and trim (CMT) factories established in lower-cost countries. Yugoslavia is a major such producer on behalf of Germany and Holland; North African countries are also important outward-processing producers, as are many countries around the Pacific basin for the United States and Canada. Garments produced by this method normally have separate quotas, and these are usually much higher than the direct-import quotas, where they apply. Some countries, for example, the United Kingdom and Ireland, do not permit these two sorts of quota arrangement so the outward-processing route hardly operates.

The direct-import route is probably the most important opportunity for changes in export patterns in the next ten years. Since nearly all country markets are oversupplied, all producers are looking to establish niche opportunities in their local markets and in the export markets. The opportunities for high-cost producers will be primarily in high-cost countries with the possibility of some sales into lower-cost countries, where there are opportunities to import without punitive tariff barriers to be overcome. The opportunities are much greater for lower-to-medium-cost countries to focus on specific opportunities in their own countries and on niche opportunities in other developing, and especially developed, countries.

Many producers of basic textile and clothing products in the lower-cost countries have recognized their decreasing competitiveness in these bottom segments of the markets. Traditionally, they may have been used to buyers coming to them with orders and designs for high-volume production. But, when the buyers stayed away for a season or more, these companies have always been most vulnerable. They could not sell their capacities in their local markets, but equally their export outlets were sealed. Many companies have recognized their weakness in this respect and are changing their corporate profiles by adopting strategic business plans to enable them to serve the markets either by selling under their own names, as licensees to international manufacturers, or with retailers' labels directly.

The determination with which many companies in the low- and medium-cost countries have adopted aggressive market orientations is indicative of their intentions of being successful. Investments in marketing and active selling, smaller batches and/or specialist machines and management systems, including design management, have enabled the businesses to be turned around, and they are in position (3) or (4) in Table VII.

Those companies that have remained as producers and act as order-takers supplying basic products are finding margins less and less attractive as new suppliers from lower-cost sources are competing against them. Such companies have a number (1) profile in Table VII.

4. THE FUTURE

As export trade continues to develop, as projected at the beginning of this paper, the balance will most likely be in favour of the low-to-medium-cost countries. Not only are many companies in these countries adopting strategic business plans to match those companies that are already successful, but their governments are also endeavouring to ensure that the environment is geared to helping exporters more than ever before. Some MFA quotas are only partly utilized from several source countries, and many products are not covered by quota limitations.

The increasing demands by buyers in developed countries for finished and made-up products from developing countries are indicative of the changes that can be expected in the future.

Gherzi Textil Organisation,
Zürich,
Switzerland.

Exports: Selected Countries: 1963 and 1983*

Exporting Country	1963			1983		
	Textiles	Clothing	Total	Textiles	Clothing	Total
Italy	530	340	870	4175	4560	8735
Germany (BRD)	530	150	680	5354	2640	7994
S. Korea	–	–	–	3300	4300	7600
Japan	900	200	1100	5541	400	5991
Hong Kong	110	240	350	767	4900	5667
France	630	200	830	2630	1900	4530
Belgium/ Luxemburg	510	100	610	2841	770	3611
United Kingdom	710	110	820	2000	1560	3560
USA	490	90	580	2261	990	3251
Netherlands	360	70	430	1665	700	2375
Canada	5	10	15			
Switzerland	240	40	250	1370		
Austria	110	40	150	1020		
Portugal	90	20	140		660	
Pakistan	90	–	90	930		
India	540	–	540	1140		
Taiwan	5	10	15	1750	3100	4850
China	–	–	–	2200	2450	4650
Romania	–	–	–		810	
Finland					660	
Yugoslavia					650	

* US$ mn.

Appendix 2
Imports: Selected Countries: 1963 and 1983*

Importing Country	1963			1983		
	Textiles	Clothing	Total	Textiles	Clothing	Total
Italy	150	30	180	2120	692	2812
Germany (BRD)	770	260	1030	4865	6910	11775
Japan				1610	1830	3440
Hong Kong	200	20	220	2970	1472	4442
France	190	70	260	2999	2650	5649
Belgium/ Luxemburg	230	70	300	1750	1560	3310
United Kingdom	410	180	590	3288	2660	5948
USA	680	390	1070	4344	9350	13694
Netherlands	370	150	520	1610	1947	3557
Canada	270	60	330	1130	1317	2447
USSR	300	520	820	2000	2750	4750
Australia	240			1110		
Sweden	220	90	310		1110	
S. Africa	200	20	220			
Switzerland	150	90	240	860	1420	2280
Austria	140			940	810	1750
Singapore		30		880		
Norway	4	50	54		680	

* US$ mn.

Industry and Stylists: Group GFT's Experience

L. Trossurelli

I believe that the theme of the relationship between industry and stylists is a very significant point of view in understanding some of the most crucial times through which some great firms in the textile sector have lived in these last ten years. During the passage of these years, there has been, in my opinion, an enormous change in the operative criteria and functioning of a firm like Group GFT.

I think I can say that the success of the collaboration with the stylists has been especially important for us because we have seen in it the chance for a radical revision of our internal working procedures and, in general, of our approach to the market.

To understand how much impact style has had on industrial structures, one has to go back to the type of thinking that reigned about ten years ago, in discussing the fate of this particular industry, which was described as 'mature'.

Everyone then thought that the textile/clothing sector would never have emerged from the crisis of the 1970s, especially since everybody believed that all textile and clothing production would be moved to the new developing countries, where labour costs were far lower. Actually, the logic of this idea was marred by a great fallacy. First, it assumed that the model of organization in the industry was incapable of change because it did not take into account the enormous discrepancy between supply and demand.

The thesis that said that the decline of the textile industry was inevitable in the rich industrial countries had the great fault of thinking exclusively about the soaring costs. It attached no importance to the great change in the tastes of the consumers and to the fact that mass production was no longer able to satisfy these more modern and culturally aware consumers of the great western nations. This new public was the biggest novelty to emerge from the crisis: it asked for a new, modern, more subjective type of style. The market, in other words, no longer passively accepted the usual products of our industry: on the contrary, it tended to change according to the tastes of a certain social environment, which demanded individuality and originality.

The market then became more and more a composite of requests, which showed differences in the style of living and consumerism, much less homogeneous than in the past. But the organization and

297

the strategy of mass production, which had kept up the development of the 1950s and 1960s market, now appeared inadequate to
meet a situation in which quality was becoming much more important than quantity.

We know now that it was this scenario to determine the transition from a 'product-oriented' strategy to a 'market-oriented'
one that was adopted by all the firms that successfully came out
of the crisis. But this solution looked then far less clear, and
the changing process that Group GFT decided upon, against all
pessimistic prognosis, was neither easy nor straightforward.
Group GFT had the great problem of offering a positive answer to
a new market situation without renouncing its enormous wealth of
experience and knowledge and its great 'know-how' in production,
commercial, and project terms. Furthermore, Group GFT felt it
should be possible to find the right market strategy for these
changed times, but, at the same time, one that was compatible
with the industrial vocation of the firm.

In the mid-1970s, Group GFT was still characterized by a
medium-price product, good quality, and a great deal of choice,
but very little imagination. Facis and Cori showed these characteristics most of all. With the crisis, our firm decided to go
for a middle-upper market, which wanted elegant clothing. In order
to do this, it became essential to develop a type of product full
of creativity, quality, and imagination. Choosing to work with
stylists, who had started then to appear on the fashion scene,
was the practical way to achieve our objectives. It has been
thanks to the work done with the stylists that Group GFT has
learned how to change its product lines continually to suit demand and thus has been able to supply requirements. In a sense,
the decision to work with stylists has been the new way for our
firm to keep abreast of the changes in the market; in fact, by
producing models created by the stylists, and accepting the enormous growth of styles offered, Group GFT has managed to corner
an ever-growing slice of the internal market. It has also made
the firm less bureaucratic and more flexible. From this point of
view, putting on the market the first clothing designed by stylists represented an element that broke away from the traditional
structural thinking of the firm. Up to that time, our firm, like
other clothing-manufacturing firms, had simply thought in terms
of quantity based on standard models.

Now, the reverse was asked of our firm; we were required to
produce original, elegant, imaginative garments. All this imposed
a deep change in the mentality of the operators in our firm, it
asked for a very wide revision of the criteria used in evaluating
the performance of the organizers in this firm. For example, this
new situation put a lot of pressure on the sector that had to produce new models. They kept on changing with each season and each
year. The distribution of designer clothes had to start, right
away, abroad. Most of all, the times between producing and distributing were becoming shorter and shorter. This meant that the organizing structures had to show an ability to cope with the
changed market, with this demand occurring almost at the same
time as the production.

From a political point of view, this collaboration with the
stylists meant that Group GFT had to find solutions to problems

298

among the workers in the various sectors. In the organizing areas, which were the most critical, because they took the biggest brunt of all the changes, we created task forces, which had the job of working side by side with the more traditional type of structure and thus made it easier to accept a new way of working.

In time, we were able to put together all our experience and professional know-how and thus help the firm achieve smoother working than in the past. But the change in the firm, because of the rapport with the stylists, was enormous at all levels.

Think of the repercussions in the sector researching the product, going from a few styles to very many, to styles that had to change season by season, year after year, styles that had to please the customer. Furthermore, this caused a greater application of computer technology in all manufacturing sectors in the firm, totally changing at times the process of planning and working methods. As one can see, the collaboration with the stylists is the easiest cause to locate of all the changes that have made Group GFT so different from the firm of ten years ago. Most of all, it has now become international.

As the number of stylists interested in working for us has grown, so also has our firm, whose market was essentially a home one but is now moving more and more to exports to the point that even today almost half of all its manufactured items go abroad. Even so, I still feel that the most important change has been in making the firm more flexible. Our partnership with the stylists has been, during these years, a strategy of flexibility.

Whoever wished to compare the Group GFT of today with the one of ten years ago would discover that it appears more as a constellation of various enterprises than one great unit. This striving for flexibility has made each sector as dynamic and imaginative as if Group GFT were a small enterprise. Managing one of our business units is rather like managing a small firm, and in each one the number of models manufactured is high, the degree of standardization has been lowered, and there is a very high level of flexibility in the workforce and the machinery.

I am forced to conclude that the direction we took when we decided to work with the stylists has led us towards a system of flexible specialization. The attention given to the market and to distribution, the great care taken in the advertising of our products, their quality inseparable from the firm's guarantee, are no longer secondary factors to our manufacturing but a fundamental part of our economic strategy.

In many ways, Group GFT came out of the great crisis of the 1970s because it recognized and made its own the new economic and cultural needs. I have long believed that the strength of 'Made in Italy' in the world is due to having been able to combine a very solid industrial experience and a new flexibility towards the market and the models demanded and also to continuous research in order to achieve the highest quality and creativity.

In other words, we have been able to use our know-how in production while adding new specializations that did not emanate from the manufacturing sector.

The most important thing is that all these different occupations and specializations can live in harmony in our restructured
firm, and all who work in Group GFT share their experience and
knowledge.

All I have described is not yet completely developed in our
own Group GFT: the changing process is still going on. Still, I
do feel that entering into partnership with stylists has given
us a wider horizon. I am not implying that we have become a model
for other firms, but we certainly have reached a greater equilib-
rium between supply and demand. The same goes for our rapport with
the stylists. At the beginning, Group GFT simply had licence-con-
tracts with the stylists; now we tend more and more to be partners
with them. This method is far more beneficial to both parties. Our
use of the trade-mark 'guffes' has made us partners on a 50% basis
with VCI, whose task is to control the name of Valentino in U.S.A.
and Canada.

The strengthening of our partnership with the stylists must be
seen not only as a stronger bond of the stylists with group GFT, but
also as a possibility to stabilize a name and make it less dependent and vulnerable to the fashion creators' personal problems.
In other words, it means 'industrializing' the phenomenon of
'stilismo'. All this means we must develop, even more, our reports on marketing, distribution, and the financial side.

To summarize, I am inclined to conclude that the most vital
thing the industry has gained from its partnership with the stylists has been this new ability to cope with problems that did
not belong to the textile and clothing industry. From the shock
of the 1970s, the firms that managed to restructure and renew
themselves have gained a new insight into the external world.
After all, these talents of creativity and imagination possessed
by the stylists had always been considered unimportant by our particular industry. Not any longer! We have found out that creativity and efficiency can go hand in hand, that to be original is
certainly not an obstacle to the firms making money. At the same
time, learning to appreciate creativity and originality has made
the textile/clothing industry more aware of the social values of
the public's taste and of the change in people's way of thinking.
Thanks to all this, these firms have been able to attract new
young talent, something that did not happen in the past.

I believe, though, that the advantage of the partnership between industry and stylists will have been mutual.

The world of fashion has, in fact, left the narrow confines
of the past because it has learnt to work side by side with the
logical organization of the industry. It has also enabled the
designers to be assured of the distribution and marketing of
their labels. In the last analysis, the fortune of 'Made in Italy'
is the result of this partnership. It now enjoys a 'double image',
one due to the imagination of the stylists and the other to the
efficiency of the industry in Italy: not only in Italy, of course,
but I believe we were the first. The same experience of Group GFT,
which now has partnerships with foreign designers, shows how
'Made in Italy' is more a method than a national peculiarity.
That is why I firmly believe that our industrial sector should

reinforce even more, in the future, the integration between creativity and industry.

GFT Spa,
Turin,
Italy.

Managing Design

L. van Praag

Of all industries, the textile industry should be the last in need of being convinced about the importance of design. The problem for any industry is to find ways of manufacturing a product that looks and works well and meets or creates a need, as well as being sought after by the right-sized market and being able to be produced and put on the market at the right price - a price that earns a good profit. This is not a new problem. How does an organization use design to find the solution to a problem and turn it into a commercially viable product that meets consumers' needs? The difficulties of finding a new product that has the right-sized market and is more desirable than its competitors constituted a problem with which the British wrestled in the middle of the nineteenth century, when the competitiveness of other European manufacturing nations was biting British trade. In 1851, the British Government sponsored a Great Exhibition at the Crystal Palace, near London, which showed how British industry was beginning to fight back; it was also the moment when Henry Cole masterminded the formation and system of central and provincial art schools in Britain to provide designers for industry. Henry Cole strongly believed that harnessing what were thought of as 'artistic skills' for the design of manufactured products would solve the problems of product development and improvement.

Without describing the historical development of art and design education in the U.K., it has to be said that some 140 years of formal art and design education in my country have not yet produced a sufficiently informed climate of opinion that values design *per se* or knows well enough how to use designers as an integral part of product strategy. However, there is the start of a hopeful new movement. It is not helpful to assign blame for these failures, which are also apparent in several other countries, but it may be productive to try to detail the relationship between the need for a positive climate of opinion about the nature and value of design and knowing how to use it; knowing how to use it is the subject of this paper. It must be self-evident that, if there is a common recognition of what constitutes good design, then this must assist the building up of a *cultural* acceptance that the application of design is an economic necessity.

A propos culture, in his seminal work 'English Culture and the Decline of the Industrial Spirit', Martin J. Wiener sets out to demonstrate how the British middle classes were, from the beginning, absorbed into a 'quasi-aristocratic élite, which nurtured

303

both the rustic and nostalgic myth of an "English" way of life
and the transfer of interest and energies away from the creation
of wealth.' This, he claims, has led to a pattern of industrial
behaviour suspicious of change, reluctant to innovate, and ener-
getic only in maintaining the status quo. But according to the
magazine *The Economist*, this phenomenon is not unique to Britain.
Quoting from Fred Hirsch in 'The Social Limits to Growth', it
asks whether economic growth will bring satisfaction once people
have reached a certain affluence (a second car, perhaps, but
surely not a third; Bali for a holiday, but not if its beaches
are crowded with other tourists, all staying in skyscraper hotels).
But economic growth will be driven by man the inquisitive rather
than man the acquisitive. 'People will want to find new ways',
writes *The Economist*, 'of doing old things', and much of this
inquisitiveness will show up in G.N.P. figures. Designers are
surely among the most inquisitive people, and this characteristic
is capable of being managed for the greater economic wellbeing of
the world economy.

There is no need to apologize for labouring the wider cultural
issues before coming to discuss design management specifically,
for what I am seeking to underline is that design-management
strategies are directly related to general cultural perceptions.
J.K. Galbraith discusses some of these issues in an article 'The
Artist and the Economist: Why the Twain Must Meet', in which he
writes:

> 'We must cease to suppose that science and the resulting
> technological achievement are the only edge of industrial ad-
> vance. Beyond science lies the talent of the designer. Will-
> ing or unwillingly, he or she is vital for industrial pro-
> gress in the modern world ... and design depends not alone on
> the availability of artists; it invokes the depth and quality
> of the whole artistic tradition. It is on this that industrial
> success comes to depend.'

The idea that we need to look beyond science and the resulting
technological achievement is central to the concept of design
management. Science can discover, discover new materials for example: engineering can improve production processes, but, however
inventive and ingenious the scientist and engineer are, unless
management looks beyond this to identify markets and understand
their needs and plans to invest in a product that will appeal and
sell, the inventiveness of the scientist and ingeniousness of the
engineer are wasted. Galbraith's idea that the artist is vital for
industrial progress needs some refinement. He may mean 'designer'
when he writes 'artist' and is thinking of the application of
visual values and visual thinking. But I believe he means that
the artist contributes in general terms to the building up of
society's cultural values, a theme that he takes up when he writes
of the depth and quality of the whole artistic tradition. Taking
a long span of time, I think he is right to assert that industrial
success comes to depend on the whole artistic tradition, but our
problem today is that we have to find ways quickly to improve the
design of our products so that they penetrate new markets and increase their share of existing markets without waiting for a general improvement of the level of design appreciation in society.

John Blake, of the Design Council in London, tells a story

about the British radiant-heat manufacturer, 99% of whose sales were of glowing coal-effect electric fires, and in it he poses the question that confounds many designers. Popular taste can be a pervasive form of preference and one about which no modern or post-modern movement can do much. What currently does seem to be amiss is that such a large gap exists between the values of many designers and the society to be served. Blake mischievously reminds the design community to keep thinking about it! We can help the design community by helping to improve the process of design management; but this improvement must be about an understanding of the design process and seeing management itself as a design process.

The first requirement in finding solutions to product-manufacturing problems is to have clear company policy on what is to be achieved. Product growth and range, investment policy, etc., are all part of this. Projection of the company's image is also a vitally important requirement. It is unlikely that projecting a false image will stand up to time; if the company's image is seen to be false, market confidence will be lost. I see design management as essentially these two mutually supporting elements: product strategy and company image. It follows that a company needs a policy for product strategy that it is capable of implementing and actually does implement, and that it has an image of itself that is realistic and attainable. This product strategy and company image have to match those that the market is seeking, and this means that they have to be updated and undergo controlled evolution. By having a design policy, one can expect to have a more effective and efficient realization of total company objectives.

If we seek to identify cases of successful product strategy (and this may be either the identification of a new product or the improvement of a product in ways that allow it to capture a market, to give but two examples), we are likely to find that there are two polarities of design-management characteristics. Many successful products have been the result of the 'prima donna' approach; the Olivetti story is an example. The Issigonis Mini is another example of this approach - one man has a vision of a product, has a sufficient allocation of development resources, and finally has executive authority to see the production of his visions through to completion. The other polarity is the team approach, which in these days can be associated with successful Japanese products. There are, of course, Japanese designers who have international reputations, but most often successful Japanese products can be assigned not to one man, but to the team.

The manner of manufacture of anything but a simple inexpensive product with a limited market requires the welding together of a range of management skills: market research, product research, investment, good fiscal policy, personnel management, product engineering, product distribution, after-sales service and maintenance, etc. This suggests that, although it may always be possible for a 'prima donna' or 'impressario' to mastermind the whole process, in most cases it is the informed team approach that is likely to be more successful. Since the result is multi-disciplinary, so the team needs to command a range of skills. The qualities that are now associated with managing design as distinct from 'management' are likely to be present only in a team that

is clear about objectives, clear about company image, and highly
motivated by the 'elegance' of the total process of the chosen
project strategy.

My own company, Sabre International Textiles, has more than a
half-century's experience in designing and manufacturing knitwear,
particularly men's knitwear. In 1986, we launched with great success our first collection of women's high-fashion knitwear. But,
for the preceding two years, management was engaged in conducting
social and market research, briefing and recruiting specialized
designers, developing the final design and production brief, organizing the advertising and marketing, and, above all, integrating design into all of these processes, from social-survey meetings with prospective consumers to final production and market
response.

Managing design, of course, includes knowing how to use designers and also recognizing that the total process of manufacturing
and trading needs to be thought of in design terms. Without attempting to define design clearly, any definition must recognize
a mixture of objective ingredients, such as flair, imagination,
inventiveness, and creativity, or, as Galbraith put it, the depth
and quality of the whole artistic tradition. I am not suggesting
that all managers should be taught to be designers; but I am suggesting that a manager with a feeling for the elegant solution is
less than 100% effective. Management education can at least make
potential managers more aware of this dimension. Conversely, design education must develop far more awareness of the numerate,
production, and other factors on which efficient and effective
industry depends. I do not believe that management education divorced from design education and design education divorced from
computing, engineering, and business education can be successful.

In 1980, I persuaded the British Government to set up a commission, which I subsequently chaired, to consider how to develop design awareness among managers. This was a pioneering initiative to
tackle the virtual absence of the management of design from the
curricula of business and management courses. Though the initial
aim is modest, to promote the communication of design issues to
post-graduate management students, the ultimate target is to fos-
ter a generation of industrial managers who are not merely un-
afraid of using design but also have empathy with the design process and pride in their capacity to put it to good use. It has to
happen, and not only in the United Kingdom!

While researching for the commission's report (1), we did not
find that the education of managers in Britain was particularly
behind that of our competitors, for instance, little teaching on
managing product design and product strategy was found in Japan;
indeed, very little management teaching at all occurs in Japan,
where companies tend to prefer in-house training - but with what
substantial effect!

What we *did* find was that our successful competitors do have
a culture in which designers are highly regarded and in which top
management regards good design as a business priority. This is
not sentimentality but hard financial sense. As our report remarks,
the approach in the U.S.A. to design, for example, is a highly
pragmatic one, in which design, as any other element of business

activity, needs to 'earn its keep' and receives attention on that basis. The experiences of those companies that have made good design a priority supports the view that design can indeed earn its keep.

We need to recognize that fundamental changes are occurring throughout world industry: a shift of emphasis away from systems, especially control and resources, towards product or services; companies are competing with each other, not simply by efficiency and their system of production, accounting, or distribution, but also on the basis of product design and product quality.

What is needed is for top management to recognize this change and to devote time to formulating design policies for the company and to ensuring that the policies are put into practice. In this respect, managing design has two key aspects: the first is that top management must make policy decisions about design standards and the organization of the company's entire design activity. The second is the maintenance at *all levels* of the high quality of management of activities connected with individual design projects.

The target for achieving this change must then be senior management. Managing design is the complete awareness of the significance of design projects by managers and of the techniques through which that awareness is articulated; this will not be achieved unless the most senior levels in companies wish it.

Decisions in the company on adopting design and product strategies are crucial. Top managers obviously must be concerned with formulating strategy across the whole range of activities. However, the importance of design, both as a determinant of corporate strategy and as a significant component of it, are usually inadequately appreciated. The design expertise of a company (or lack of it) has a direct influence on strategic planning: which products to promote, what markets to exploit, what rate of expansion to aim for, and so on. The strategy requires decisions to be taken about where to concentrate design effort and what kind of effort is needed. No effective design work can be expected unless these strategic issues have been tackled.

Determining design policies is, I repeat, a major management responsibility and within it defining and setting corporate design standards are critically important. Aspects of design to be stressed and areas of excellence to be developed must be decided if a recognizable 'distinctive competence' is to be achieved. These standards need to be set out precisely and, where possible, described in quantitative terms. This is relatively easy for technical aspects of design (measures such as working life or failure rates are possible examples) but rather more difficult for aesthetic aspects. Even so, knowledge of styling trends, current use of colours, and reports of consumer tests are just a few of the references that may be used in setting standards for design, which, if not tackled directly, will occur by default.

The success of many businesses depends ultimately upon skill in this one activity. If management is consistently able to achieve high quality and relevant design results, the chances of long-term prosperity are high. The key to such achievement lies in evaluating design results in terms both of the characteristics of the actual design created and of the return on the investment in the designing process. Inevitably, this takes managers into questions such as what is 'good' or 'bad' design, whether a design solution is the optimum given the resources available, and whether the solution is appropriate to the needs of the market and of the company.

Finally, management needs to be reminded constantly that designing is for people. However described and however persuaded by the techniques of commercial promotion, the users of all our products are human beings. Beyond the point-of-sale barrier are men, women, and children, even textile manufacturers, whose changing social needs are waiting to be satisfied. It is with them that products either die or stay profitably alive.

Too few manufacturers in Europe understand or take the trouble to find out what it is that these customers really require. An all-too-common reaction is that 'we already know what they want'. But, of course, it is not true. The most successful companies are those that are fanatical about the need to involve all levels of their management in developing an interface and exchange of ideas with their customers.

There is nothing, absolutely nothing, about the techniques of managing design that is beyond the capability of any one of us to achieve. It is, in fact, very simple, but we need to develop and incorporate these techniques and, above all, cultural attitudes into our everyday thinking and action so that we can gain the confidence and knowledge to create world-beating products.

REFERENCE

(1) 'Managing Design' (Report of the van Praag Commission), CNAA, Department of Trade and Industry, and Design Council, London, 1984.

Sabre International Textiles Ltd,
Sunbury-on-Thames,
Middlesex,
England.

The Representation of Knitted Fabric Structures by Using Microprocessors

J.A. Wilson, W.D. Cooke, and A. Bahadori

Abstract

Many advanced CAD systems are now available to help the knitwear
designer. There are, however, a number of ways in which such systems could be improved. Research undertaken at UMIST has led to
the development of an inexpensive and flexible CAD system that enables the designer rapidly to create a representation of a desired
knitted structure, which gives the same visual impression as the
real knitted structure would. Current programs allow the representation of both jacquard and purl-knitted structures. Work is continuing at UMIST with the aim of producing realistic screen images
and printouts of a wide range of fabrics.

1. NOTATION OF KNITTED-FABRIC DESIGNS

Much time is spent by both 'in-house' and consultant knitwear designers in graphing out knitted-fabric designs by using traditional
systems of notation. Whatever system of notation is used, this is
a tedious business, allowing little room for any alterations that
may become necessary. A designer may have to graph out a design
idea two or three times before being entirely happy with it.

2. CURRENT CAD SYSTEMS FOR THE KNITTED-FABRIC DESIGNER

2.1 What the Current CAD Systems Do

There are now many CAD systems that take much of the tedium out of
the graphing process. Designs can be built up quickly, alterations
can be made easily, and designs can be viewed in repeat. Some systems even allow the design to be viewed as garment pieces, i.e., a
sleeve or a body.

2.2 Disadvantages of the Current Systems

Whereas these systems have made life easier for the designer who
is able to work with them, they do little for the majority of designers. Nearly all have been developed for specific knitting
machines - there are few flexible systems that allow designers to
design for several machine types.

The clever ones are very expensive. Most are not really used as a tool for the creative designer; rather, they are an aid to the technician - to be used to translate the designer's work into a form to enable fabric to be produced.

Despite all the advances made and the undoubted sophistication of many systems, the pattern created on screen and the ultimate printout is still relatively elementary, usually a series of small coloured squares that can be given individual colour values. The end-result is really just a computer-generated version of the traditional designer's graph. The trained designer and mechanic may be able to look at such a representation of a fabric and envisage the actual fabric that will result, but there are problems in trying to explain to the untrained eye what the actual fabric will look like.

3. CURRENT CAD SYSTEMS FOR WEAVE DESIGNERS

There are now CAD systems for weave designers that give images, both on screen and as printouts, that closely resemble the fabric structure. The target of this development was to create such a system.

4. THE PHILOSOPHY BEHIND THE RESEARCH

The philosophy behind the research is to enable the designer to create rapidly, by using a simple desktop computer, a representation of the desired knitted structure, which gives the same visual impression as the real knitted structure would.

5. THE COMPUTER

The work was aimed initially to help domestic-machine knitters and to help in the field of education. The computer chosen for this work was the BBC because it was relatively inexpensive and was widely found in the U.K. in both the home and education circles. For the commercial markets, programs have now been developed for IBM PCs and Macintosh Mac+ computers.

6. THE STITCH CHARACTERS

6.1 Initial Development

The simplest weft-knitted structure of plain fabric, which is knitted on one set of needles, was looked at closely. This structure was considered in fabric form, as loop diagrams, and as magnified photographic images.

The work initially targeted the plain face stitch, and several characters were developed to represent this loop structure.

Two character sets were developed: in the first, individual characters were developed to look like the loop diagram of a face stitch, whereas, in the second set, characters were developed which, when repeated, shoud look like fabric (no consideration was given as to whether or not the characters in this second set looked like loop diagrams or not).

6.2 Comparison of Face Characters

The simplest way of using the characters is to repeat them in isolation from any other character (Figures 1 and 2).

From photographs and printouts of these characters, it is possible to select those characters that produce the most realistic fabric impression on the monitor.

6.3 Randomization of the Face Characters

Although the best of the face characters produce acceptable fabric impressions, there is something missing from their appearance when compared with a real fabric. All give the impression of fairly rigid and stiff fabrics.

A close examination of many fabrics by using an image analyser showed up a variability of loop shape and size that results in an over-all random effect. In order to simulate this effect, a number of different face-loop characters were randomized, and this improved the representation of the fabric (Fig. 3).

This stage of the work was particularly time-consuming, since, for example, four stitch characters can be permutated from 30 in 657 720 ways. In addition, it is possible to give different weightings or priorities to each of the characters that would double or treble this very high number. Naturally, not all the combinations were tried out, and subjective limits were placed on the workable combinations to keep the number within reasonable limits.

It should be noted that the appearance of a particular character is modified by the characters that border on it, both above and below and on either side.

7. BACK-STITCH CHARACTERS

A series of back-stitch characters was developed by using a similar process to that used in the development of the face-stitch characters.

8. PURL FABRICS

Purl fabrics are created by knitting both face and back stitches in the same wale (vertical column of stitches). The appearance of such fabrics can be generated by mixing front and rear characters as required.

Owing to the mixing of face and back stitches, the characters that had been selected as the best face and back stitches to represent the face and reverse sides of plain fabric did not always work in these purl structures. Further work was carried out to arrive at the best characters for such purl fabrics (Figures 4 and 5).

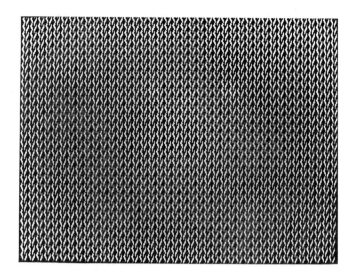

Fig. 1

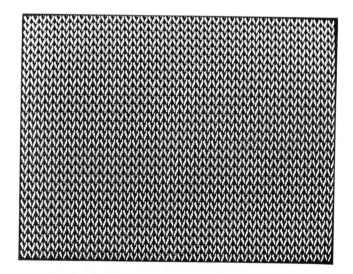

Fig. 2

312

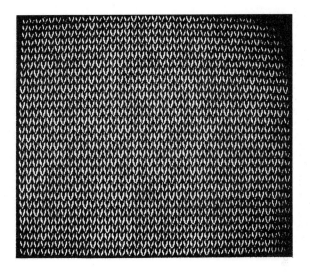

Fig. 3

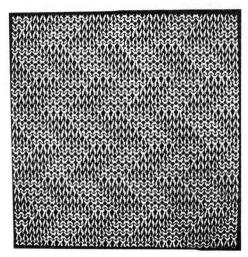

Fig. 4

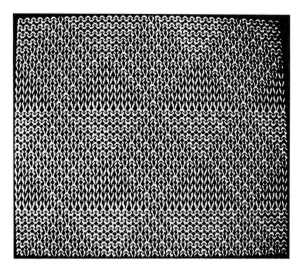

Fig. 5

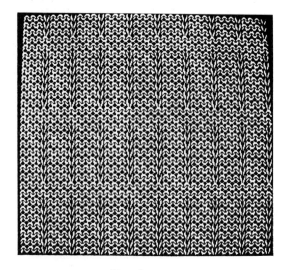

Fig. 6

314

9. RIB FABRICS

Rib fabrics can easily be generated by using any of the selected
face characters with any of the reverse characters (Fig. 6).

10. DEVELOPMENT OF DESIGN PAPERS

As well as photographs, printouts of the random face characters
were used to select the best combinations of face stitches.

Reducing and enlarging these printouts on a photocopier gave
papers that relate to different gauges of machine (i.e., the number of needles per inch).

These papers can be used by a designer in place of conventional
graph paper and give a much better idea of how the design will
eventually look in fabric form.

11. THE AVL LINK-UP

It was at this point that it was felt that the concept had been
developed sufficiently for it to be considered a commercial proposition.

AVL, a company that makes and markets dobby looms with computer
interface, was well known by the research team: the Textile Department at UMIST has one of AVL's looms. Aimed at craft users and, as
a teaching system, at colleges and universities, the AVL weave
program gives a realistic representation of woven fabrics on screen
and as hard copy.

Since the initial knitting program developed by the research
team was aimed at a similar market to AVL's and AVL's hard-copy
output was considered ideal for the knitted structures developed,
it was decided to approach AVL.

This approach was greeted with enthusiasm by AVL and soon, with
the help of a programmer at AVL, the original jacquard and purl
programs were brought together in one improved program. Controlled
by an AMX 'mouse', rather than via the keyboard, the new program
was much more 'user-friendly'. Other improvements included an increase in the design area and the introduction of a scroll facility.

12. THE PROGRAM IN USE

Students on the Textile Design and Design Management BSc Honours-
degree course at UMIST are already using the system and are particularly enthusastic.

13. THE FUTURE

Work is continuing at UMIST with the aim of producing realistic
images of a wide range of fabrics.

University of Manchester Institute of
Science and Technology,
Manchester,
England.